1993 Edition

STUDY GUIDE TO ACCOMPANY

WEST'S FEDERAL TAXATION

INDIVIDUAL INCOME TAXES

William H. Hoffman, Jr.
University of Houston

James E. Smith
College of William and Mary

Eugene Willis
University of Illinois-Urbana

Prepared by
Gerald E. Whittenburg
San Diego State University

WEST PUBLISHING COMPANY
St. Paul   New York   Los Angeles   San Francisco

WEST'S COMMITMENT TO THE ENVIRONMENT

In 1906, West Publishing Company began recycling materials left over from the production of books. This began a tradition of efficient and responsible use of resources. Today, up to 95% of our legal books and 70% of our college texts are printed on recycled, acid-free stock. West also recycles nearly 22 million pounds of scrap paper annually—the equivalent of 181,717 trees. Since the 1960s, West has devised ways to capture and recycle waste inks, solvents, oils, and vapors created in the printing process. We also recycle plastics of all kinds, wood, glass, corrugated cardboard, and batteries, and have eliminated the use of styrofoam book packaging. We at West are proud of the longevity and the scope of our commitment to our environment.

Production, Prepress, Printing and Binding by West Publishing Company.

CONTENTS

PREFACE

This Study Guide has been designed to be used as a supplement to the 1993 Edition of *West's Federal Taxation: Individual Income Taxes*. Its purpose is to help you master the material presented in the text.

The Study Guide contains two features to help you understand individual income taxes.

> *Chapter Highlights* -- This section provides statements about key concepts presented in the text.

> *Tests for Self-Evaluation* -- Over 1,000 questions and problems are presented along with answers so that you may see how well you understand the material in the text. The answers are keyed to the page numbers in the text.

I recommend the following approach as a method to use this Study Guide effectively:

- Study the textbook chapter.

- Review the Chapter Highlights section of the Study Guide. If something is not clear to you, review the chapter in the textbook.

- Mark the Test for Self-Evaluation and resolve your missed answers by referring to the solutions and to the textbook.

It is important that you use this Study Guide as an aid to mastering the material in the textbook, and not as a replacement for it.

Gerald E. Whittenberg, May 1991

CHAPTER

1

AN INTRODUCTION TO TAXATION AND UNDERSTANDING THE FEDERAL TAX LAW

CHAPTER HIGHLIGHTS

A review of the history of the U.S. Federal tax system is helpful for the student to gain an understanding of the principles which have shaped the development of the system. This chapter introduces the student to the structure of the U.S. Federal tax system, the major types of taxes, and the organizational aspects of administering the tax law.

I.   HISTORY OF U.S. TAXATION

A.   There have been several income taxes in the past. The first income tax was enacted in 1634 in the Massachusetts Bay Colony. The first U.S. income tax was passed in 1861 to help finance the Civil War. In 1894, the Supreme Court, in *Pollock v. Farmers' Loan and Trust Co*, held the early individual income taxes were unconstitutional. In response to this Supreme Court decision, a constitutional amendment was passed to authorize the individual income tax. The Sixteenth Amendment, which was ratified in 1913, gave Congress the power to impose and collect an income tax. Before the Sixteenth Amendment, the corporate income tax was held to be an excise tax, and therefore deemed to be constitutional by the Supreme Court.

B.   Various Revenue Acts were passed between 1913 and 1939. In 1939 these Acts were codified into the Internal Revenue Code of 1939, which was later recodified in 1954 and renamed in 1986 as the *Internal Revenue Code of 1986.*

C. Over the years the income tax has become the major source of revenue for the Federal government. During World War II, the tax went from a select tax to a mass tax. The individual and corporate income taxes constitute 54 percent of all Federal budget receipts. Social Security taxes represent 34 percent of Federal receipts.

D. Adam Smith listed certain criteria with which to evaluate a particular tax or tax structure. These "canons of taxation" are *equality, convenience, certainty,* and *economy.*

II.   THE TAX STRUCTURE

A. Tax Rates.

A progressive tax is one in which the tax rates increase as the tax base increases. The Federal income, gift, and estate taxes and most state income taxes are progressive taxes.

A proportional tax is one in which the rate of tax remains constant regardless of the size of the tax base.

III.   MAJOR TYPES OF TAXES

A. Property taxes or ad valorem taxes are taxes that are based on value. The tax is usually imposed on realty or personalty. Realty taxes are a major source of revenue for local government, while personalty taxes generally have low compliance by taxpayers, except for personal property taxes on items such as inventory, automobiles, boats, etc.

B. Transaction taxes impose a tax on transfers of property and are normally computed as a straight percentage of the value of the property involved.

Excise taxes are taxes on products such as gasoline, telephone usage, air travel, alcohol and tobacco. Both the Federal and state government usually impose some form of excise tax.

Sales taxes differ from excise taxes in that sales taxes are applied to many different transactions, while excise taxes are applied to one product or transaction. A use tax is designed to prevent circumvention of the sales tax, such as where a resident of a state with a sales tax buys products in another state in an attempt to avoid the sales tax. Many states allow local sales taxes by cities, counties, etc., in addition to the general sales tax.

Death taxes are taxes imposed either on the right to pass property at death (estate tax) or the right to receive property from a decedent (inheritance tax).

The Federal estate tax is designed to prevent large concentrations of wealth from being kept within the same family. The unified transfer credit eliminates or reduces the estate tax liability for small estates. For deaths after 1986, estate tax on a taxable estate up to $600,000 is eliminated by a credit of $192,800. The Federal government does not impose an inheritance tax.

Most states levy some form of death tax. If the death tax is an inheritance tax, the rates are generally lower for close family members, and get larger the more distant the heir.

The Federal gift tax was enacted into law to complement the estate tax because without it, it would be possible to avoid the estate tax by making lifetime gifts and eliminating the gross estate. Ordinarily, taxable gifts are those gifts that exceed $10,000 per year per donee, reduced by any marital deduction. The Federal gift tax is determined by taking into account prior taxable gifts so that the tax rate is based on cumulative taxable gifts.

C. In the United States income taxes are levied by the Federal government and most state governments and are the most popular form of tax. Income taxes are imposed on individuals, corporations, and certain estates and trusts. The tax formula for individuals is:

       Income (broadly conceived)
-   <u>Exclusions</u>
=   Gross income
-   <u>Certain business deductions</u>
=   Adjusted gross income
-   Greater of itemized deductions or the
     standard deduction
-   <u>Exemptions</u>
=   <u>Taxable income</u>

       Tax on taxable income
-   <u>Credits and withholding</u>
=   <u>Tax due or refund</u>

For individual taxpayers a standard deduction amount is available to taxpayers who do not itemize deductions.

The Federal income tax applies to corporations. The taxable income of a corporation is the difference between gross income and deductions.

Nearly all the states impose a state income tax on individuals and corporations. Most states pattern their income tax after the Federal income tax and use an adjusted Federal taxable income figure as a base on which to apply the tax. Most states have some form of withholding procedures. The state taxing authorities work closely with the IRS and share information about audits and other changes in tax returns.

D. Employment taxes such as FICA (Federal Insurance Contributions Act) are collected by the Federal government. The FICA tax is comprised of the old age, survivors, and disability insurance tax and the hospital insurance tax.

FICA taxes fund the social security system and are levied on both the employee and the employer. For 1992, an employee's FICA tax is equal to the sum of the old age, survivors, and disability insurance tax of 6.2% of the first $55,500 of wages and the Medicare tax of 1.45% of the first $130,200 of wages. The employer must match the employee's contribution. If an employee pays too much FICA tax because he or she worked two or more jobs, a credit for the excess amount may be claimed.

The FUTA tax is levied only on the employer, with the purpose of providing the states with funds to administer the unemployment program. For 1992, the FUTA tax is equal to 6.2% of the first $7,000 of covered wages. A credit is allowed (up to 5.4%) for any FUTA paid to a state government so that the amount paid to the IRS could be as little as 0.8 percent.

IV. TAX ADMINISTRATION

A. The Internal Revenue Service (IRS), which is part of the Treasury Department, has responsibility for administering the Federal tax law. The IRS uses statistical sampling techniques to select tax returns for audit.

B. IRS audits are classified as "office audits" or "field audits." Office audits are restricted in scope and are conducted in the IRS office. A field audit is comprehensive and is conducted on the premises of the taxpayer or the taxpayer's representative.

C. The general statute of limitations for an IRS assessment is three years from the date the return is filed, unless the return is filed early in which case the limitation period runs from the date the return is due. There is no statute of limitations if no return or a fraudulent return is filed.

D. The interest rate used by the federal government is adjusted quarterly. The IRS charges one percent more than it pays to taxpayers. For the first quarter of 1992, the rate of interest is 10 percent for assessments and 9 percent for refunds. Besides interest, various penalties are applied for non-compliance. For "failure to file" a return a penalty of 5 percent per month, or fraction thereof, is charged up to a 25 percent maximum. The penalty for "failure to pay" is one-half percent per month, or fraction thereof, up to a maximum of 25 percent. If both penalties apply to the same return, the failure to file penalty is reduced by the failure to pay penalty. Penalties also apply where the underpayment is due to negligence or fraud.

V. REVENUE NEEDS & ECONOMIC CONSIDERATIONS

A. Raising revenue is a major function of taxation. However, there are several other functions of the U.S. tax law. The tax law is also used to control the economy. Attempts at stimulation or temperance of the national economy have led to many amendments to the Internal Revenue Code.

The tax law contains many provisions to encourage investment and capital formation.

Lowering the tax rates provides taxpayers with more income to spend, and so is another method used to stimulate the economy. An increase in tax rates would have the opposite effect.

B. Another economic consideration of the tax law is to encourage certain activities. The favorable incentives granted research and development expenditures, the rapid amortization of pollution control facilities and the Foreign Sales Corporations (FSC) are an example of these types of provisions in the tax law. IRAs and other pension plans are also an example of using the tax law to help the economic problem of capital formation.

C. The encouragement of certain industries is another economic consideration of the tax law. Agriculture, for example, is an industry that has special tax benefits.

D.   Small businesses are generally considered to be good for the economy as a whole. Therefore, certain provisions of the tax law are designed to help small businesses.   The S Corporation election is an example of the methods Congress uses to assist small businesses through tax law provisions.

VI.   SOCIAL CONSIDERATIONS

A.   The U.S. tax law contains many provisions intended to achieve social objectives. Examples of such social provisions include:

- Nontaxability of employer sponsored accident and health plans

- Nontaxability of employer paid premiums for group-term insurance

- Qualified pension and profit sharing plans

- Deductions for contributions to charitable organizations

- Credit for child care expenditures

- Disallowance of deductions for expenditures that are against public policy (fines, penalties, etc.)

VII.   EQUITY CONSIDERATIONS

A.   The Federal tax law attempts to alleviate the effect of multiple taxation in several areas. Examples include the deduction for state, local, and foreign income tax and the foreign tax credit.

B.   The wherewithal to pay concept recognizes the inequity of taxing a transaction where the taxpayer lacks the means with which to pay the tax. In some cases the Federal tax rules, such as those applicable where a taxpayer reinvests the proceeds from the sale of a personal residence in a new personal residence, allow the taxpayer to defer recognition of gain when his or her economic situation has not changed significantly.

C.   Mitigating the effect of the concept of an annual accounting period is an equity consideration that deals with the inequities which arise from the arbitrary use of the annual accounting period to divide the taxpayer's life into taxable segments. The annual accounting period concept could lead to different treatment of two individuals who are, from a long range standpoint, in the same economic position. Measures to alleviate this inequity include the carryover procedure for net operating losses, excess capital losses and excess charitable contributions, and the installment method of recognizing gain.

D.   One of the major problems in recent years has been bracket creep which was caused by inflation. Taxpayers were pushed into higher tax brackets without a real increase in income. This problem is addressed by indexing. Each year, beginning in 1989, the tax brackets and the standard deduction are indexed upward by the amount of inflation. Beginning in 1990, the personal and dependency exemptions are also indexed based on inflation.

VIII.   POLITICAL CONSIDERATIONS

A.   Special interest legislation includes tax provisions sponsored as a result of the instigation of influential constituents. Such legislation is inevitable in our political system and can sometimes be justified on economic, social or utilitarian grounds.

B.   Political expediency is responsible for the passage of tax provisions which have popular appeal such as measures that insure wealthy taxpayers pay their "fair" share of tax, the lowering of individual income tax rates and increasing the exemption amount.

C.   State and local influences explain the nontaxability of interest received on state and local obligations, and the extension under Federal tax law of community property tax advantages to residents of common law jurisdictions.

IX.   INFLUENCE OF THE IRS

A.   As protector of the revenue, the IRS has a great deal of influence on shaping the tax law. In this role the IRS tries to close what it sees as loopholes in the tax law.

B.   Many provisions of the tax law are for administrative feasibility, and exist because they simplify the work of the IRS in collecting the revenue or administering the tax law. Withholding procedures place taxpayers on a pay-as-you-go basis and so aid the IRS in the collection of revenue. Interest and penalties imposed for noncompliance with tax laws are also of considerable help to the IRS.

X.   INFLUENCE OF THE COURTS

The Federal courts have influenced the tax law. Some court decisions have been of such consequence that Congress has incorporated them into the Internal Revenue Code. The rule that allows tax-free stock dividends is an example of a court decision being codified.

TEST FOR SELF-EVALUATION

True or False

Indicate which of the following statements are true or false by circling the correct answer.

T   F   1.   The first U.S. Federal income tax was enacted to provide revenues for the Civil War.

T   F   2.   The Supreme Court held that the 1894 income tax law was constitutional since it was a direct tax.

T   F   3.   The Sixteenth Amendment was necessary to enact the corporate income tax of 1909.

T   F   4.   The first Internal Revenue Code was the Internal Revenue Code of 1939.

T   F   5.   The current tax law is the Internal Revenue Code of 1986, as amended.

T   F   6.   The corporate income tax provides the largest percentage of Federal tax revenues.

T   F   7.   During World War II, the income tax was converted from being a select tax to being a mass tax.

T   F   8.   The responsibility for administering the Federal tax law rests with the Treasury Department.

T   F   9.   The Internal Revenue Service openly discloses its audit selection techniques.

T   F   10.   The purpose of the gift tax is to prevent widespread avoidance of the estate tax.

T   F   11.   For 1992, the maximum amount of wages to which the old age, survivors, and disability insurance (OASDI) portion of the FICA tax will be applied is $55,500.

T   F   12.   The United States income tax rates are proportional.

T   F   13.   Tax collections from individual taxpayers account for about 37 percent of the Federal government's budget receipts.

T   F   14.   Ad valorem taxes are taxes that are based on income derived from property.

T   F   15.   Property taxes on personalty have a high rate of compliance, while taxes on realty have a low rate of compliance.

T   F   16.   Excise taxes are levied on specific transactions or products, while sales taxes are collected on transactions involving a wide range of products.

T   F   17.   Excise taxes are sometimes used to influence social behavior.

T   F   18.   The Federal government is the only government allowed to impose excise taxes on products.

T   F   19.   The primary purpose of the estate tax is to generate revenue with which to operate the Federal government.

T   F   20.   For deaths after 1986, the unified transfer tax credit is $192,800.

T   F   21.   State inheritance taxes usually tax all heirs at the same rate.

T   F   22.   The annual exclusion for Federal gift tax purposes is $47,000 per year per donee.

T   F   23.   A taxpayer can minimize his Federal gift tax liability by making several small taxable gifts rather than a single large taxable gift.

T   F   24.   All states impose some form of income tax on individuals who reside in that state.

T   F   25.   Some cities impose an income tax along with the Federal and state income taxes.

T   F   26.   In recent years, tariffs have served the nation more as an instrument for carrying out protectionist policies than as a means for generating revenue.

T   F   27.   The interest rates applicable to underpayments and overpayments of federal income taxes used by the Internal Revenue Service are adjusted every quarter.

T   F   28.   The U.S. Federal income tax rate structure for individuals is becoming less progressive.

T   F   29.   Certain provisions of the U.S. income tax law are designed to help small businesses.

T   F   30.   An example of a social consideration in the tax law is the nontaxability of health plan benefits.

T   F   31.   The wherewithal to pay concept states that a taxpayer should pay the tax on all gains, even when his economic position has not changed.

T   F   32.   Many provisions of the tax law can be explained by looking at the influence of pressure groups on Congress.

T   F   33.   One role assumed by the Internal Revenue Service is that of "protector of the revenue."

T   F   34.   Some of the tax law is justified because it complicates the Internal Revenue Service's task of collecting revenue.

T   F   35.   The courts have established the rule that the relief provisions of the Code are to be broadly interpreted.

T   F   36.   Some court decisions have been of such consequence that Congress has written them into the tax laws.

T   F   37.   The tax law attempts to encourage technological progress.

T   F   38.   Economic considerations in the tax law help regulate the economy.

T   F   39.   One equity consideration of the tax law is the alleviation of multiple taxation.

T   F   40.   Carryback and carryover procedures help mitigate the effect of limiting a loss or deduction to the accounting period in which it was realized.

T F 41. The amounts of the standard deduction, exemptions, and tax brackets will be indexed for inflation in the future.

T F 42. In future years, budget deficit problems will probably influence many of the new tax provisions passed by Congress.

T F 43. For purposes of the gift tax, a special election applicable to married persons allows 75 percent of a gift made by a donor spouse to be treated as being made by the nondonor spouse.

T F 44. In addition to the Federal gift tax, several states impose a state gift tax on their residents.

T F 45. A piggyback state tax its a state income tax based on what is done for federal income tax purposes; such as calculating the state income tax on federal adjusted gross income.

Fill-in-the-blanks

Complete the following statements with the appropriate word(s) or amount(s).

1. Adam Smith's "canons of taxation" are _____, _____, _____, and _____.

2. Tax rates applied to a taxpayer's tax base may be _____ or _____

3. Taxes imposed on luxury items such as alcoholic beverages, tobacco products, and highway fuels are called _____ taxes.

4. Property transferred at death is subject to the Federal _____ tax based on the value of the property.

5. The Internal Revenue Service is part of the Department of _____.

6. Audits other than those settled through correspondence between the taxpayer and the Internal Revenue Service, are classified as _____ audits or _____ audits.

7. The usual statute of limitations is _____ years, but if no return is filed the statute of limitations period is _____.

8. The penalty for failure to file a tax return is _____ percent per month, up to a maximum of _____ percent.

Multiple Choice

Choose the best answer for each of the following questions.

_____ 1. Which of the following is an employment tax?
    a. The gift tax
    b. FICA taxes
    c. Custom duties
    d. Excise taxes
    e. None of the above

_____ 2. Which of the following items will not be subject to indexing under the tax law?
    a. The standard deduction
    b. Personal and dependency exemptions
    c. The child care credit
    d. The individual tax brackets
    e. All of the above are indexed

_____ 3. For 1992, the tax rate for the old age, survivors, and disability insurance portion of the Social Security tax imposed on employees' wages up to $55,500 is:
    a. 1.45%
    b. 6.06%
    c. 6.20%
    d. 7.65%
    e. Some other amount

_____ 4. The installment method of reporting gains is justified on the basis of:
    a. Mitigation of the annual accounting period
    b. Wherewithal to pay
    c. Social consideration
    d. Both a and b
    e. None of the above

_____ 5. Jack Todd's gross income for 1992 is $60,000 and he has business deductions of $6,000. His itemized deductions are $7,000 and he has one personal exemption worth $2,300. For 1992 Jack's taxable income is:
    a. $54,000
    b. $50,700

    c. $47,000

    d. $44,700

    e. Some other amount

6. For 1992, Jeanne Emerson earned wages of $61,000. The total amount of FICA tax due from Jeanne and her employer is:

    a. $4,325.50

    b. $8,651.00

    c. $4,245.75

    d. $9,491.50

    e. Some other amount

7. During 1992, Steve Jones earned $4,000 and Lynne Sass earned $12,000 from Bay Inc. The total FUTA tax payable by their employer before any state credits is:

    a. $420

    b. $240

    c. $682

    d. $660

    e. Some other amount

8. Byron Toole files his tax return 45 days late. Along with the return he remits a check for $6,000 which is the balance of the tax owed. Disregarding interest, what is Byron's penalty for failure to file?

    a. -0-

    b. $60

    c. $540

    d. $600

    e. Some other amount

9. The value added tax is:

    a. Used by many countries in Western Europe.

    b. A form of income tax on corporations.

    c. Like a national sales tax on production.

    d. Both a and c are correct.

    e. All the above are correct.

10. John Williams sold his personal residence for $140,000. The house cost John $84,000. John immediately purchased a new personal residence for $140,000. From this sale John should report a taxable gain of:

    a. -0-

    b. $56,000

    c. $140,000

    d. $84,000

    e. Some other amount

_____ 11. For the first three months of 1992, the interest rate charged by the IRS on money due to the government was:

    a. 9%

    b. 10%

    c. 11%

    d. 12%

    e. 13%

_____ 12. Vicky Wall filed her 19X3 individual tax return on January 15, 19X4. The return was properly signed and filed. The statute of limitations for Vicky's 19X3 return expires on:

    a. January 15, 19X7

    b. April 15, 19X7

    c. January 15, 19X0

    d. April 15, 19X0

_____ 13. Mike Shields had two jobs during 1992. He earned $40,000 from his first employer and $20,000 from his second employer. All of the wages were subject to the FICA tax. When Mike files his tax return he can claim a credit for excess FICA of how much?

    a. -0-

    b. $279.00

    c. $4,590.00

    d. $4,311.00

    e. Some other amount

_____ 14. Which of the following is not an economic consideration of the tax law?

    a. Encouragement of small business

    b. Encouragement of certain industries

    c. The wherewithal to pay concept

    d. Encouragement of certain activities

    e. None of the above

_____ 15. The net operating loss provision of the tax law is an example of:

    a. An economic consideration

    b. A social consideration

    c. A political consideration

    d. An equity consideration

    e. None of the above

16. Which of the following is not a social consideration in the tax law?
    a. Qualified pension and profit sharing plan
    b. Expensing soil and water conservation costs
    c. Child care credit
    d. A speeding ticket paid by a truck driver is nondeductible
    e. All of the above are social considerations

17. Which of the following is the best example of a tax law provision designed to aid in controlling the economy?
    a. Depreciation deduction
    b. Child care credit
    c. Personal exemption
    d. Net operating loss carryover
    e. None of the above

18. Smith Corporation pays $2,000 per month rent on a building to Mary Smith, its sole shareholder. The fair market value of the rent determined at "arm's length" would be $900 per month. Smith Corporation will be allowed a monthly rental deduction of:
    a. -0-
    b. $900
    c. $1,000
    d. $2,000
    e. None of the above

19. A father rents property to his daughter for $10,000 a year. If the IRS wants to examine this transaction it will be interested in:
    a. The tax benefit rule
    b. Installment sales rules
    c. The arm's length concept
    d. Public policy limitations
    e. None of the above

20. Several years ago, T entered into an agreement to rent a building to S for 20 years. During the first year of the lease, S made $60,000 in capital improvements to the building. This year the lease is terminated and T takes possession of the building. The fair market value of the capital improvements in the year of termination is $75,000. In the year of the termination of the lease, T must recognize taxable gain of?
    a. $-0-
    b. $15,000
    c. $60,000

      d. $75,000

      e. Some other amount

_____ 21. On a tax return that is filed 45 days late, Christy pays $33,000 in additional taxes. Of this amount $10,000 is attributable to Christy's negligence. What is Christy's negligence penalty?

      a. $-0-

      b. $500

      c. $2,000

      d. $6,600

      e. Some other amount

SOLUTIONS TO CHAPTER 1

True or False

1.   True   (p. 1-2)

2.   False   The income tax was unconstitutional because it was not apportioned. (p. 1-3)

3.   False   The 1909 corporate income tax was held to be constitutional. (p. 1-3)

4.   True   (p. 1-3)

5.   True   (p. 1-3)

6.   False   The individual income tax provides the largest percent. (p. 1-4)

7.   True   (p. 1-3)

8.   True   (p. 1-17)

9.   False   The IRS does not disclose its audit selection techniques. (p. 1-17)

10.   True   (p. 1-11)

11.   True   (p. 1-15)

12.   False   The U.S. income tax rates are progressive. (p. 1-5)

13. True (p. 1-4)

14. False Ad valorem taxes are based on the value of the property. (p.1-5)

15. False The tax on realty has a high compliance rate. (p. 1-6)

16. True (p. 1-8)

17. True (p. 1-8)

18. False State and local governments can also impose excise taxes. (p. 1-8)

19. False The estate tax is intended to prevent concentrations of wealth. (p. 1-10)

20. True (p. 1-10)

21. False Inheritance taxes generally are imposed on distant heirs at a higher rate. (p. 1-11)

22. False The exclusion is $10,000 per year. (p. 1-11)

23. False The gift tax is based on the taxpayer's cumulative taxable gifts. (p. 1-11)

24. False Several states do not have a state income tax. (p. 1-13)

25. True (p. 1-14)

26. True (p. 1-16)

27. True (p. 1-20)

28. True (p. 1-5)

29. True (p. 1-23)

30. True (p. 1-23)

31. False The wherewithal to pay concept recognizes that under some circumstances, even though a gain has been realized by the taxpayer, the taxpayer's economic position may not have changed. (p. 1-25)

32. True (p. 1-26)

33.   True   (p. 1-28)

34.   False   Some of the law is justified because it simplifies the work of the IRS. (p. 1-28)

35.   False   The relief provisions are narrowly interpreted. (p. 1-29)

36.   True   (p. 1-30)

37.   True   (p. 1-22)

38.   True   (p. 1-22)

39.   True   (p. 1-24)

40.   True   (p. 1-26)

41.   True   (p. 1-26)

42.   True   (p. 1-21)

43.   False   The gift is split 50-50. (p. 1-11)

44.   True   (p. 1-12)

45.   True   (p. 1-13)

Fill-in-the-Blanks

1.   equality, convenience, certainty, economy (p. 1-4)

2.   proportional, progressive (p. 1-5)

3.   excise (p. 1-8)

4.   estate (p. 1-9)

5.   the Treasury (p. 1-17)

6.   office, field (p. 1-19)

7.   three, indefinite (p. 1-19)

8.   five, 25 (p. 1-20)

Multiple Choice

1.   B   (p. 1-14)

2.   C   (p. 1-26)

3.   C   (p. 1-15)

4.   D   (p. 1-26)

5.   D $60,000 - 6,000 - 7,000 - 2,300 = $44,700. (p. 1-13)

6.   B   [(6.2% x $55,500) + (1.45% x $61,000)] x 2 = $8,651.00. (p. 1-15)

7.   C   [$4,000 + $7,000 (maximum)] x 6.2% = $682.00. (p. 1-16)

8.   C   5% per month or fraction thereof, or 10% x $6,000 = $600, less failure to pay penalty of .5% per month or fraction thereof, (1% x $6,000 = $60), which equals $540. (p. 1-20)

9.   D   (p. 1-17)

10.   A   (p. 1-25)

11.   B   (p. 1-20)

12.   B   (p. 1-20)

13.   B $3,060.00 =   ($40,000 x 6.2%) + ($40,000 x 1.45%) employer 1
       1,530.00 =   ($20,000 x 6.2%) + ($20,000 x 1.45%) employer 2
      $4,590.00   Amount paid
      -4,311.00 =   ($55,500 x 6.2%) + ($60,000 x 1.45%) maximum FICA due
      $ 279.00   Credit (p. 1-15)

14.   C   This is an equity consideration. (p. 1-25)

15.   D   (p. 1-26)

16.   B   (p. 1-23)

17.   A   (p. 1-22)

18.   B   (p. 1-30)

19.   C   (p. 1-30)

20.   A   (p. 1-30)

21.   C $2,000 = 20% x $10,000. (p. 1-20)

CHAPTER

2

WORKING WITH THE TAX LAW

CHAPTER HIGHLIGHTS

Familiarity with the statutory, administrative, and judicial sources of the tax law is essential in learning to work with tax legislation. This chapter considers the sources of the tax law, the application of research techniques to tax problems, and the effective use of tax planning procedures.

I.   STATUTORY SOURCES OF THE TAX LAW

    A.   The Internal Revenue Code of 1939 was the first codification of all Federal tax provisions into a logical sequence. The 1939 Code was recodified into the 1954 Code, which was renamed the Internal Revenue Code of 1986. New tax laws are integrated into the 1986 Code.

    B.   For a tax bill to become law, it must be passed by both houses of Congress and signed by the President. Tax legislation is first considered in the House by the Ways and Means Committee. Legislation, once approved by the House of Representatives, is then considered by the Senate Finance Committee, and finally the entire Senate. When the House and Senate cannot agree on the tax bill, the differences are worked out by the Joint Conference Committee.

    C.   The Code is arranged by Subtitles, Chapters, Subchapters, Parts, and Sections. However, to identify any part of the Code, it is only necessary to know the Section number because these numbers are not repeated. The normal progression for a citation is Section, Subsection, Paragraph, and Subparagraph.

II. ADMINISTRATIVE SOURCES OF THE TAX LAW

A. There are numerous administrative sources of Federal tax law. These can be grouped as Treasury Department Regulations, Revenue Rulings and Procedures, and other pronouncements. All are issued by the U.S. Treasury Department or one of its instrumentalities such as the Internal Revenue Service or a District Director.

B. Treasury Department Regulations are the Internal Revenue Service's official interpretation of the Code. They are arranged in Code section sequence with a prefix to designate the type of regulation.

C. Revenue Rulings and Procedures are official pronouncements of the National Office of the IRS. They do not, however, carry the same legal force as Regulations. Revenue Rulings are usually concerned with a restrictive problem or area, while Revenue Procedures are concerned with internal management practices of the IRS. Both Revenue Rulings and Procedures are published weekly by the U.S. government in the *Internal Revenue Bulletin*. Every six months the weekly bulletins are published in a bound volume entitled the *Cumulative Bulletin*.

D. The IRS also makes the following administrative communications:

- Treasury Decisions (TDs) are issued by the Treasury Department to promulgate new Regulations, amend or change existing Regulations, or to announce the government's position on selected court decisions.

- Individual Letter Rulings are issued by the National Office of the IRS in response to a taxpayer's request and describe how the IRS will treat a proposed transaction. Individual Letter Rulings are available for public inspection after identifying details are removed.

- Determination Letters are rulings that generally deal with completed transactions, and are issued by District Directors, instead of the National Office of the IRS.

- Technical Advice Memoranda, released by the National Office of the IRS, are private rulings initiated by the IRS during its audit activities.

- Other items such as Announcements, Notices, and Prohibited Transaction Exemptions are published in the *Internal Revenue Bulletin*.

III. JUDICIAL SOURCES OF THE TAX LAW

A. After a taxpayer has exhausted some or all of the remedies available with the IRS, a dispute can be taken to the Federal courts. The dispute is first heard by a trial court (the court of original jurisdiction) with any appeal taken to the appropriate appellate court.

B. The trial courts include the following:

- **District Courts.** The Federal District Courts are organized into geographical regions, and will hear cases involving any Federal matter, both tax and nontax issues. Taxpayers cannot choose a particular District Court but must use the one having jurisdiction over the case. Each District Court has only one judge and it is the only court in which the taxpayer may have a jury trial.

- **U.S. Claims Court.** The U.S. Claims Court has sixteen judges and meets in Washington D.C. The purpose of this court is to hear any case involving a monetary claim against the Federal government.

- **U.S. Tax Court.** The U.S. Tax Court is a national court with nineteen judges. However, only one judge hears a case unless it is unusual. The Tax Court hears only cases involving tax matters. The Tax Court will follow decisions of the Court of Appeals in the jurisdiction in which the case is being heard. The Tax Court is the only court in which the taxpayer need not pay the deficiency before taking the dispute to court. Before 1943, the Tax Court was called the Board of Tax Appeals (BTA).

- **Small Claims Division of U.S. Tax Court.** The small claims division of the U.S. Tax Court will hear matters involving amounts up to $10,000. The decisions of the small claims division are final and cannot be appealed.

C. The appellate courts include the following:

- **U.S. Court of Appeals.** There are eleven numbered Courts of Appeals plus one for the District of Columbia, and one for the Federal District.

Each Court of Appeals has jurisdiction in a specific geographical region of the country, except the Federal District, which hears cases only from the U.S. Claims Court.

- **U.S. Supreme Court.** The Supreme Court, a nine judge panel, has final say in all tax matters. Appeal to the Supreme Court is by Writ of Certiorari, and acceptance is not automatic.

D. Court decisions are reported in a variety of publications. Decisions of the District Court, U.S. Claims Court, Court of Appeals, and Supreme Court that deal with tax matters are reported in both the CCH *U.S. Tax Cases* (USTC) and the P-H *American Federal Tax Reports* (AFTR) series. All District Court decisions are published by West Publishing Company in their *Federal Supplement Series* (F.Supp.). All decisions of the U.S. Claims Court beginning October 1982 are published in the *Claims Court Reporter* (Cl.Ct.), by West Publishing Company. All decisions of the Courts of Appeals, and U.S. Claims Court decisions prior to October 1982, are published by West in a reporter designated as the *Federal Second Series* (F.2d). Supreme Court decisions are published by West in its *Supreme Court Reporter* (S.Ct.), by the U.S. Government Printing Office in the *United States Supreme Court Reports* (U.S.), and by the Lawyer's Co-operative Publishing Company in its *United States Reports, Lawyer's Edition* (L.Ed.).

The Tax Court issues two kinds of decisions, Regular and Memorandum. Generally, Regular decisions deal with a new or unusual point of law, while Memorandum decisions deal with an established point of law. The Regular decisions of the Tax Court are published by the U.S. government printing office (GPO) in a series designated *Tax Court of the United States Reports* (T.C.). Memorandum decisions are published by CCH in *Tax Court Memorandum Decisions* (TCM) and by Prentice Hall in P-H *T.C. Memorandum Decisions*.

Citations of a court decision generally consist of two parts: (1) the name of the case and the abbreviated title of the report volume and (2) the number or page of the report that contains the text of the decision. After each citation, a parenthetical reference identifies the court rendering the decision and the year the decision was reached.

E. If the IRS loses at the trial court level and does not appeal the decision this does not indicate that the IRS agrees with the result or that it will not litigate similar situations in the future.

IV.   TAX RESEARCH

    A.   The first step in tax research is to identify and define the problem. All facts having a bearing on the problem must be gathered since any omission could have a substantial impact on the conclusion reached.

    B.   The second step in tax research involves locating the appropriate sources of tax law. Most tax research begins with the index volume of a tax service. A tax service is a comprehensive set of books on Internal Revenue law. The major tax services are arranged by Code section number or topic. When using any tax service one should always check for current developments. Besides the tax services there are numerous tax periodicals that are indexed in CCH's *Federal Tax Articles*.

    C.   The third step in tax research, once a source of tax information has been located, is to assess the source in relation to the problem at hand. Some of the characteristics of sources that need to be assessed include conflicting Code provisions and the relative importance of Treasury Regulations, Revenue Rulings, and court decisions.

           The language of the Code can be extremely difficult to comprehend, with extremely long sentences and many cross references between interrelated provisions. Also, occasional conflicts between old and new Code provisions arise. For these and other reasons, great care should be exercised when interpreting the Code.

           The Treasury Regulations are not the law, but have the force and effect of law if they are reasonable interpretations of the Code. The burden of proof rests with the taxpayer to show that a Regulation is wrong. Certain "legislative regulations" are virtually impossible to overturn.
Revenue Rulings carry less weight than the Regulations, but are important reflections of the IRS's position on certain tax matters.

           The validity of a court decision depends on the level of the court, the residence of the taxpayer, and the current status of the decision.

    D.   The fourth step of the tax research process is arriving at a solution based on the information gathered. Often a clear cut answer is impossible to obtain, and a guarded judgment is the best solution that can be given.

    E.   Once a conclusion has been reached, it is necessary to communicate the findings to the client. This is normally done by preparing a memo that explains the findings and how the conclusions were reached. The memo should contain the following:

- A clear statement of the issue(s).

- A short review of the factual pattern.

- A review of the tax law.

- Any assumptions.

- The solution recommended and the logic supporting the conclusion.

- References consulted while doing the research.

V. TAX PLANNING

A. In tax planning, it is necessary to take into account many nontax considerations. What may produce the best tax result may not be an acceptable alternative to the taxpayer. As a general rule, tax planning involves producing the smallest tax within the nontax and legal constraints. Tax considerations should not impair the exercise of sound business judgment by the taxpayer.

B. There is a difference between tax avoidance and tax evasion. Tax avoidance is merely minimization through legal means, while evasion is illegal tax planning.

C. Computer tax research is part of the day-to-day tax practice for many tax professionals. The computer on-line data bases provide the tax practitioner instant access to the entire legal data base. The four major tax research data bases are LEXIS, WESTLAW, PHINet, and ACCESS. These data bases are searched by using a system of key words. The document(s) that meet the search criteria are then displayed on the computer screen for the tax researcher.

TEST FOR SELF-EVALUATION

True or False

Indicate which of the following statements are true or false by circling the correct answer.

T   F   1.   Both Revenue Rulings and Revenue Procedures are published weekly by the U.S. Government in the *Internal Revenue Bulletin.*

T   F   2.   There is only one U.S. Claims Court and it meets in Washington, D.C.

T   F   3.   The U.S. Claims Court has seven judges and the Tax Court has nineteen judges.

T   F   4.   Regulation § 1.61 refers to Internal Revenue Code § 61.

T   F   5.   Appeal to the Supreme Court is by Writ of Certiorari.

T   F   6.   Revenue Ruling 87-61 relates to § 61 of the Internal Revenue Code.

T   F   7.   In general, an U.S. Tax Court Regular decision deals with a new or unusual point of law.

T   F   8.   The Internal Revenue Service usually acquiesces or nonacquiesces to all regular Tax Court decisions.

T   F   9.   To go to the Tax Court, a taxpayer must pay the tax and sue for a refund.

T   F   10.   A jury trial may be obtained in the Tax Court.

T   F   11.   *Bradford v. Comm.,* 56-1 USTC ¶9552 (CA-6, 1956) is an example of a citation from Commerce Clearing House's *United States Tax Cases.*

T   F   12.   Prentice-Hall publishes Revenue Rulings in its *American Federal Tax Reports* (AFTR).

T   F   13.   The United States Tax Court is one of the federal trial courts that is a court of original jurisdiction.

T   F   14.   When confronted with a particularly troublesome problem, the taxpayer may always obtain an individual letter ruling.

T   F   15.   *Morris Alexander v. Comm.,* 61 T.C. 278 is an example of a citation from Commerce Clearing House's *Tax Court of the United States Reports.*

T   F   16.   Temporary Regulations are also issued as proposed Regulations and automatically expire within three years after the date of issuance.

T   F   17. In a challenge by the IRS, the burden of proof is on the taxpayer to show that a Regulation is wrong.

T   F   18. Tax avoidance is illegal tax planning while tax evasion is legal tax planning.

T   F   19. A case is appealed from the U.S. Claims Court to the Court of Appeals for the Federal Circuit and then to the Supreme Court.

T   F   20. *John Smith*, T.C. Memo 1980-32 is the 32nd Tax Court Memorandum decision of 1980.

T   F   21. The Tax Court follows the decisions of the Court of Appeals for the appropriate jurisdiction of the case being heard.

T   F   22. The District Courts hear cases involving both tax and nontax litigation.

T   F   23. The appellate courts are the Supreme Court, Courts of Appeals, and the U.S. Claims Court

T   F   24. The *Cumulative Bulletins* normally are published for six-month periods.

T   F   25. The prefix 1 designates an income tax Regulation when referring to a Treasury Department Regulation.

T   F   26. Tax legislation originates in the House of Representatives Ways and Means Committee.

T   F   27. Technical Advice Memoranda are not available for public inspection.

T   F   28. A taxpayer must pay any tax deficiency assessed by the IRS and then sue for a refund in the U.S. Claims Court.

T   F   29. The phrase *Cert. Granted* indicates that the Supreme Court will hear the tax case.

T   F   30. For a taxpayer residing in California, a decision of the Ninth Circuit Court of Appeals has more precedence than one rendered by the Eleventh Circuit Court of Appeals.

T   F   31. If a taxpayer loses in the Tax Court Small Claims Division, he or she may not appeal to the regular U.S. Tax Court.

T   F   32.   Since Letter Rulings apply to only one taxpayer, the IRS is not required to make Letter Rulings public.

T   F   33.   *Technical Advice Memoranda* (TAMs) are only issued on proposed transactions while Letter Rulings are only issued on completed transactions.

T   F   34.   Under the doctrine of *stare decisis*, each case (except in the Small claims Division) has precedential value for future cases with the same set of controlling facts.

Fill-in-the-Blanks

Complete the following statements with the appropriate word(s) or amount(s).

1.   Federal tax legislation generally originates in the House of Representatives where it is first considered by the _____ _____ and _____ Committee.

2.   When the Senate version of a tax bill differs from that passed by the House, the _____ _____ Committee resolves the differences.

3.   To locate a provision in the Code, all that is necessary is the _____ number of that provision.

4.   The Treasury Department Regulations are arranged in Code _____ sequence.

5.   Every six months the *Internal Revenue Bulletins* are published in a bound volume designated as the _____ _____.

6.   The _____ Office of the Internal Revenue Service issues Individual Letter Rulings, while a _____ _____ issues determination letters.

7.   The Tax Court and Claims Court are both _____ courts.

8.   The Tax Court issues two kinds of decisions, _____ and _____ decisions.

Multiple Choice

Choose the best answer for each of the following questions.

_____ 1. Appeal from the Tax Court is to the:
              a. Court of Appeals
              b. District Court
              c. U.S. Claims Court
              d. Supreme Court
              e. None of the above

_____ 2. If taxpayers choose not to pay a tax deficiency, then they must petition which court?
              a. District Court
              b. U.S. Claims Court
              c. Tax Court
              d. Court of Appeals
              e. None of the above

_____ 3. Which of the following court(s) would have jurisdiction if a taxpayer paid a tax deficiency and sued for a refund?
              a. Tax Court
              b. District Court and U.S. Claims Court
              c. Tax Court and District Court
              d. U.S. Claims Court
              e. None of the above

_____ 4. A decision of which of the following courts could not be found in CCH's *U.S. Tax Cases*?
              a. District Court
              b. Court of Appeals
              c. Supreme Court
              d. U.S. Claims Court
              e. None of the above

_____ 5. Which of the following does not publish a tax service?
              a. Commerce Clearing House
              b. Prentice-Hall
              c. Research Institute of America
              d. U.S. Government
              e. None of the above

_____ 6. The *Federal Tax Articles* index is a three-volume service published by:
              a. U.S. Government

b. Prentice-Hall
c. Commerce Clearing House
d. Matthew Bender, Inc.
e. None of the above

_____ 7. Tax evasion is:
a. Legally minimizing taxes
b. Illegally minimizing taxes
c. The same as tax avoidance
d. None of the above

_____ 8. In *Walter H. Johnson*, 34 TCM 1056, 34 stands for:
a. The year of decision
b. The page number
c. The volume number
d. The paragraph number
e. None of the above

_____ 9. Decisions by which court are published by West Publishing Company in its *Federal Supplement Series* (F.Supp.)?
a. District Court
b. Tax Court
c. U.S. Claims Court
d. Court of Appeals
e. None of the above

_____ 10. The largest grouping of material in the Internal Revenue Code is the:
a. Subtitle
b. Chapter
c. Part
d. Subchapter
e. None of the above

_____ 11. The maximum dollar amount that is within the jurisdiction of the Small Claims Division of the United States Tax Court is:
a. $1,500
b. $2,500
c. $5,000
d. $10,000
e. None of the above

_____ 12. Which of the following Federal courts is not a "national" court?

a. Supreme Court
b. District Court
c. U.S. Claims Court
d. United States Tax Court
e. None of the above

_____ 13. The United States Tax Court:
a. Has nineteen judges
b. Will hear any Federal case
c. Is an appeals court
d. Has jurisdiction over the District Courts
e. None of the above

_____ 14. The *Standard Federal Tax Reporter* is published by:
a. Prentice-Hall
b. Commerce Clearing House
c. Research Institute of America
d. Bureau of National Affairs
e. None of the above

_____ 15. According to the text, the primary purpose of effective tax planning is:
a. Eradicating the tax entirely
b. Deferring the receipt of income
c. Converting ordinary income into capital gain
d. Eliminating tax in the current year
e. None of the above

_____ 16. Which of the following best describes WESTLAW, LEXIS, and ACCESS?
a. New computer tax services
b. Computerized legal data bases that can be used (among other things) for tax research
c. Electronic spreadsheets for tax planning
d. Computer programs that can be used for estate planning for wealthy tax payers
e. Tax return preparation computer programs

_____ 17. At the completion of the tax research process the results are generally set forth in which of the following ways?
a. A phone call to the client
b. A note to the IRS
c. Preparing a tax research memo
d. Adding the results to the LEXIS data base

d. Adding the results to the LEXIS data base
e. Nothing is done formally

_____ 18. Which of the following is not a tax periodical?
a. *The Journal of Taxation*
b. *Taxation for Accountants*
c. *TAXES-the Tax Magazine*
d. *The American Tax Journal*
e. *Estate Planning*

_____ 19. Which of the following is a primary source of tax law?
a. Tax treaties
b. Legal journals
c. Technical Advice Memoranda (TAM)
d. Tax textbooks
e. General Counsel Memoranda (GCM)

_____ 20. In Letter Ruling 8515087, the 087 refers to the:
a. Year of the Letter Ruling
b. Issue of the Bulletin in which the Letter Ruling appears
c. Day of the year the Letter Ruling was issued
d. The number of the Letter Ruling issued during the week

_____ 21. Which of the following is a "secondary" source of tax law?
a. A Tax Court case
b. A Revenue Ruling
c. A tax treaty between the U.S. and Mexico
d. An article on partnership tax in the *Tax Advisor*
e. All of the above are secondary sources

_____ 22. According to the textbook, which of the following trial court decisions is sometimes believed to have the "highest" authority?
a. Tax Court Memorandum decisions
b. Tax Court Regular decisions
c. U.S. Claims Court decisions
d. U.S. District Courts decisions
e. Tax Court Small Claims decisions

_____ 23. What statement is true of a Temporary Regulation?
a. It is issued simultaneously as a Revenue Ruling.
b. It may be cited as precedent.
c. It is first found in the *Internal Revenue Bulletin*.

d. It automatically expires after two year from the date of issuance.
e. All of the above are true.

_____ 24. Which of the following has the lowest tax validity?
a. Letter rulings
b. Regulations
c. Revenue Rulings
d. Revenue Procedures
e. Tax treaty

_____ 25. Which of the following courts has the lowest tax validity?
a. Supreme Court
b. Court of Appeals for the 9th Circuit
c. Tax Court
d. Court of Appeals for the Federal Circuit
e. All of the above are of equal validity

_____ 26. Which of the following is a secondary source of tax law?
a. Revenue Ruling
b. Internal Revenue Code
c. Tax treaty
d. Regulations
e. *Taxation for Accountants*

_____ 27. Which of the following would be considered "authority" for purposes of the accuracy-related penalty under § 6662?
a. Legal opinion of an attorney who is a tax specialist
b. *Harvard Law Review*
c. IRS news and press releases
d. *West's Federal Taxation* (a widely used tax textbook)
e. All of the above are authority

SOLUTIONS TO CHAPTER 2

True or False

1. True   (p. 2-8)

2. True   (p. 2-12)

3. False   The U.S. Claims Court has sixteen judges. (p. 2-13)

4.   True   (p. 2-7)

5.   True   (p. 2-16)

6.   False   It is the 61st Revenue Ruling of 1987. (p. 2-9)

7.   True   (p. 2-17)

8.   False   IRS acquiesces or nonacquiesces to decisions it loses. (p. 2-17)

9.   False   The taxpayer generally does not have to pay the tax in order for the Tax Court to have jurisdiction. (p. 2-13)

10.   False   A jury trial is available only in the District Courts. (p. 2-13)

11.   True   (p. 2-19)

12.   False   Court decisions are published in the AFTR. (p. 2-18)

13.   True   (p. 2-11)

14.   False   There are many issues on which the IRS will not rule. (p. 2-9)

15.   False   *Tax Court of the United States Reports* is published by the federal government. (p. 2-17)

16.   True   (p. 2-8)

17.   True   (p. 2-24)

18.   False   Tax planning (avoidance) is legal while tax evasion is illegal. (p. 2-29)

19.   True   (p. 2-13)

20.   True   (p. 2-18)

21.   True   (p. 2-15)

22.   True   (p. 2-13)

23.   False   The U.S. Claims Court is a court of original jurisdiction. (p. 2-11)

24.   True   (p. 2-8)

25.   True   (p. 2-7)

26.   True   (p. 2-3)

27.   False   They are published by CCH, Prentice-Hall, and other publishers. (p. 2-7)

28.   True   (p. 2-13)

29.   True   (p. 2-16)

30.   True   (p. 2-15)

31.   True   (p. 2-11)

32.   False   Letter Rulings are public information. (p. 2-10)

33.   False   TAMs are on completed transactions, while Letter Rulings are on proposed transactions. (p. 2-11)

34.   True   (p. 2-11)

Fill-in-the-Blanks

1.   House Ways, Means (p. 2-3)

2.   Joint Conference (p. 2-3)

3.   Section (p. 2-5)

4.   Section (p. 2-7)

5.   *Cumulative Bulletin* (p. 2-8)

6.   National, District Director (p. 2-10)

7.   national (p. 2-13)

8.   Regular, Memorandum (p. 2-17)

Multiple Choice

1.   A   (p. 2-13)

2.   C   (p. 2-13)

3.   B   (p. 2-13)

4.   E   (p. 2-19)

5.   D   (p. 2-22)

6.   C   (p. 2-23)

7.   B   (p. 2-29)

8.   C   (p. 2-18)

9.   A   (p. 2-18)

10.   A   (p. 2-5)

11.   D   (p. 2-11)

12.   B   (p. 2-13)

13.   A   (p. 2-12)

14.   B   (p. 2-22)

15.   E   (p. 2-28)

16.   B   (p. 2-31)

17.   C   (p. 2-28)

18.   D   (p. 2-23)

19.   A   (p. 2-26)

20.   D   (p. 2-10)

21.   D   (p. 2-26)

22.   B   (p. 2-20)

23.   B   (p. 2-8)

24.   A   (p. 2-9)

25.   C   (p. 2-20)

26.   E   (p. 2-26)

27.   C   (p. 2-26)

CHAPTER

3

TAX DETERMINATION; PERSONAL AND DEPENDENCY EXEMPTIONS; AN OVERVIEW OF PROPERTY TRANSACTIONS

CHAPTER HIGHLIGHTS

This chapter continues to develop the components of the individual income tax formula. To determine Federal tax liability, an amount known as taxable income must be computed. Taxable income includes all realized income less deductions specifically provided in the tax law. The standard deduction and personal exemption are available for most taxpayers. An overview of property transactions is helpful at this point, although the subject will be covered in greater detail in later chapters.

I.   THE TAX FORMULA

    A.   Taxable income is calculated based on the following formula:

Income (broadly conceived)	$xxxx
Less: Exclusions	xxxx
Gross Income	xxxx
Less: Deductions for AGI	xxxx
Adjusted Gross Income (AGI)	$xxxx
Less: the greater of	
Itemized Deductions, or	
the Standard Deduction	xxxx
Exemptions	xxxx
Taxable Income	**$xxxx**

    B.   The components of the tax formula can be broken down as follows:

- Income includes all taxable and nontaxable income of the taxpayer.

- Exclusions are items of income which Congress has chosen to exclude from the tax base due to various social, economic, equity, and other considerations.

- Gross income is defined in the Code as "all income from whatever source derived", but does not include unrealized gains.

- Deductions for adjusted gross income include ordinary and necessary expenses incurred in a trade or business, alimony paid, and deductible IRA contributions, among others.

- Adjusted gross income (AGI) is an important subtotal which serves as a basis for calculating limitations on certain itemized deductions.

- Itemized deductions are expenses, personal in nature, for which Congress has specifically allowed a deduction. Taxpayers are allowed to use a standard deduction in lieu of itemizing deductions. The base standard deduction amounts are:

Filing Status	1991	1992
Single	$3,400	$3,600
Married, filing jointly	5,700	6,000
Surviving spouse	5,700	6,000
Head of household	5,000	5,250
Married, filing separately	2,850	3,000

- Blind and aged (65 years old) taxpayers are given additional standard deduction amounts of either $700 or $900, depending on their filing status.

- Certain taxpayers are not allowed to use the standard deduction. These taxpayers are:

        □   a married taxpayer filing a separate return when either spouse itemizes deductions

        □   a nonresident alien

        □   an individual with a short tax year, resulting from a change in the annual accounting period

- The calculation of taxable income for an individual who can be claimed as a dependent is subject to special provisions. Dependents cannot claim a personal exemption for themselves on their own tax returns. Also, a dependent's standard deduction is limited to the greater of $600 (for 1992) or the individual's earned income for the year. However, if the individual's standard deduction based on earned income exceeds the normal standard deduction amount, then the standard deduction is limited to the normal amount shown in the text.

- Personal and dependency exemptions give some measure of equity in our tax system by providing relief for taxpayers with families. For 1992 the exemption amount is $2,300.

II. PERSONAL AND DEPENDENCY EXEMPTIONS

A.   The law provides for a personal exemption for the taxpayer and an additional exemption for the spouse if a joint return is filed. The determination of marital status is made at the end of the taxable year. If spouses enter into a legal separation agreement before the end of the taxable year, they are considered to be unmarried at the end of the taxable year.

B.   For an individual to qualify as a dependent, five tests must be met. These tests are:

- support
- relationship or member of the household
- gross income
- joint return
- citizenship or residency

See the flowchart on the following page.

Dependency Exemption Tests Flowchart

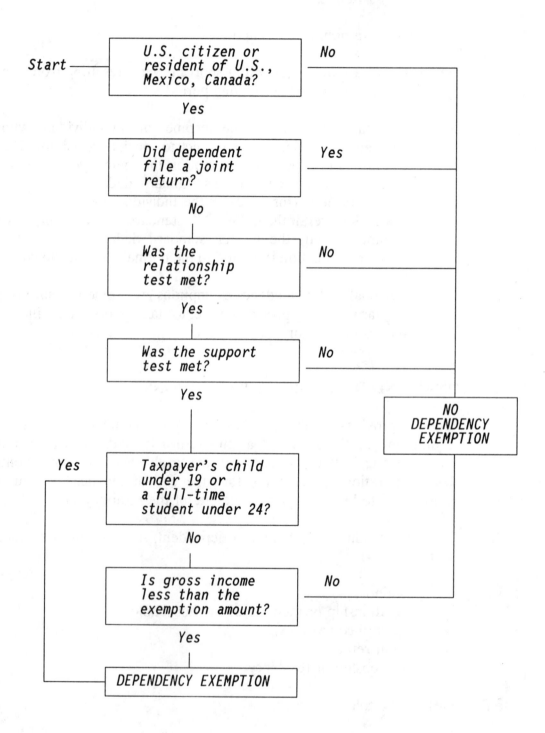

For the support test to be met, over one-half of the dependent's support must be furnished by the taxpayer. The term "support" generally includes expenditures for food, shelter, clothing, medical care, and education.

The relationship test requires that the dependent be a relative specified in the Code or an individual who has a principal place of residence in the taxpayer's household for the entire year.

The dependent's gross income must be less than $2,300 (the 1992 exemption amount) unless the dependent is the taxpayer's child under 19, or the taxpayer's child who is a full-time student under the age of 24.

If the dependent is married, the supporting taxpayer is not permitted a dependency exemption if the person being supported files a joint return with his or her spouse, unless neither the dependent nor the dependent's spouse is required to file a return.

A dependent must be a U.S. citizen or a resident of the U.S. or a country which is contiguous to the U.S.

C.   Under a multiple support agreement, one member of a group of taxpayers who together furnish over one-half of the support of a dependent can claim a dependency exemption even when no one person provides more than 50 percent of the support. Any person who contributed more than 10 percent of the support is entitled to claim the exemption if each person in the group who contributed more than 10 percent files a written consent.

D.   For divorced parents, the Code has established rules to help settle disputes as to who is eligible to claim the children as dependents. For divorce decrees after 1984, the parent with custody is allowed to claim the exemption except where the parents agree in writing that the non-custodial parent can claim the exemption (providing the other conditions for dependency are met).

E.   Starting in 1991, the personal and dependency exemptions are phased out when adjusted gross income reaches a certain level. The exemptions are phased out at the rate of two percent for each $2,500 ($1,250 for married filing separately), or fraction thereof, of adjusted gross income above the threshold amount. The threshold amount varies based the taxpayer's filing status (see the text for the current years amounts).

III.   TAX DETERMINATION

A.   In calculating their tax liability taxpayers use a tax table or a tax rate schedule.

B.   Taxpayers who cannot use the tax tables include estates and trusts, individuals filing a short period return, and individuals with taxable income larger than the maximum amounts in the tables.

C.   For 1992, a taxpayer's income may be subject to tax at rates of 15 percent, 28 percent, and 31 percent. "Net capital gains" are subject to a maximum tax rate of 28 percent.

D.   The "unearned income" of minor children is taxed at their parent's marginal rate. The provision applies to any child if the child:

- has not reached age 14 by the close of the tax year, and

- has at least one living parent, and

- has net unearned income for the tax year.

Net unearned income is unearned income less $600 and less the greater of a $600 standard deduction or the amount of allowable itemized deductions directly connected with the production of the unearned income.

For a child under age 14 the parents may elect to report the child's unearned income on the parent's tax return if the following conditions are met:

- gross income is from dividends and interest only

- gross income is over $600 and less than $5,000

- no estimated tax has been paid by the child

- there is no backup withholding on the child

IV.   FILING CONSIDERATIONS

A.   Filing Requirements.

An individual taxpayer must file a tax return if certain minimum amounts of gross income have been received. (See text for the current dollar amounts).

A self-employed individual with net earnings from self-employment of $400 or more must file a tax return regardless of the dollar amount of gross income.

Special filing requirements apply to individuals who can be claimed as dependents on another taxpayer's return.

Individual taxpayers file either a Form 1040 (long form), Form 1040A (short form), or 1040EZ (certain single taxpayers).

B.   There are five different statuses under which a taxpayer can file. These are single, married filing jointly, married filing separately, head of household, and qualifying widow(er). The amount of tax liability will vary with the filing status.

Single (Schedule X). Taxpayers who are unmarried on December 31, are single unless they qualify as head of household.

Married (Schedule Y). Taxpayers who are married on December 31, are married and must use married filing jointly or married filing separately tax rates.

Head of Household (Schedule Z). Taxpayers may file as head of household if the following conditions are met:

- They are unmarried on December 31,

- They provide over one-half the cost of a household, and

- They have a dependent relative as defined in the Code living in the household (certain unmarried relatives such as a child need not qualify as a dependent and a dependent parent of the taxpayer need not live in the taxpayer's home).

Surviving spouse (Schedule Y). A taxpayer who maintains a household for a dependent child may file as a surviving spouse (joint return rates apply) for the two years immediately following the death of one spouse.

V.   GAINS AND LOSSES FROM PROPERTY TRANSACTIONS -- IN GENERAL

A.   The sale or other disposition of property may result in gain or loss. Realized gain or loss is the amount realized less the adjusted basis of the property. In general, the adjusted basis is the cost of the property plus capital additions, less depreciation (if any).

B.   All realized gains are recognized for tax purposes unless some provision of the tax law provides otherwise. Realized losses may or may not be recognized as a deduction for tax purposes. Losses on personal use property are generally not recognized.

VI.   GAINS & LOSSES FROM PROPERTY TRANSACTIONS -- CAPITAL GAINS

A.   Gains and losses from the sale or exchange of capital assets receive special treatment under the tax law.

B.   The Code defines a capital asset as property owned by the taxpayer other than items such as inventory, accounts receivable, depreciable property, or real estate used in a business.

The principal capital assets held by individuals for personal (nonbusiness) use include automobiles, a personal residence, and assets held for investment (such as stocks, bonds, and land).

C.   For 1992, "net capital gain" is taxed at a maximum rate of 28 percent.

D.   Gains and losses from capital assets must be classified as long-term or short-term. After such classification, long-term gains and losses are netted against one another, and short-term gains and losses are likewise netted against one another. The resulting net short-term capital gain (NSTCG) or net short-term capital loss (NSTCL) and the net long-term capital gain (NLTCG) or net long-term capital loss (NLTCL) are then netted against one another, if possible. If the NSTCG is greater than the NLTCL the net gain is ordinary income; if the NLTCG is greater than the NSTCL, a "net capital gain" results (see C. above).

E.   Capital losses are first offset against capital gains. For individuals, net capital losses are deductible against other income up to a maximum of $3,000 per year. Any loss in excess of $3,000 annually carries forward for an unlimited period. Corporations may not use capital losses as deductions against ordinary income.

TEST FOR SELF-EVALUATION

True or False

Indicate which of the following statements are true or false by circling the correct answer.

T   F   1.   For divorce decrees after 1984, the mother is always eligible to claim the dependency exemption for any child of divorced parents.

T   F   2.   The standard deduction amount for 1992 is $3,600 for single taxpayers, $6,000 for married individuals filing jointly, and $3,000 for married individuals filing separately.

T   F   3.   Itemized deductions are deductible even if they do not exceed the standard deduction amount.

T   F   4.   If married individuals file separate returns and one spouse itemizes, both must itemize.

T   F   5.   For 1992, the personal and dependency exemption amount is $2,300.

T   F   6.   Taxpayers are allowed additional standard deduction amounts for old age and blindness.

T   F   7.   If taxpayers are married at the end of the taxable year, they are considered married for the entire year.

T   F   8.   The additional standard deduction amount for old age or blindness can apply to a dependent of the taxpayer.

T   F   9.   For the support test to be met, a taxpayer must furnish over one-half of the support of the dependent.

T   F   10.   Amounts received by a taxpayer, but not spent, are not considered in determining whether or not the support test for the dependency exemption has been met.

T   F   11.   An adopted child qualifies as the taxpayer's child for purposes of determining an exemption allowance.

T   F   12.   For 1992, all individuals whose gross income is $2,300 or more cannot be a dependent of another taxpayer.

T F 13. If an individual is married and files a joint return with her spouse, she generally cannot qualify as a dependent of another taxpayer.

T F 14. A person who lives in Mexico or Canada could qualify as a dependent of a taxpayer.

T F 15. To qualify for a multiple support agreement, a group of taxpayers must supply over 50 percent of the support of an individual.

T F 16. In order for a taxpayer's dependent parents to qualify him or her for head of household filing status, the parents must live in the taxpayer's home.

T F 17. All realized gains are recognized for tax purposes unless some specific provision of the tax law provides otherwise.

T F 18. For individual taxpayers, net long-term capital losses carry forward for five years and carry back for three years.

T F 19. For 1992, net capital gains of an individual taxpayer are taxed at a maximum rate of 28 percent.

T F 20. Capital assets must be held for over one year in order for realized gains to be considered long-term capital gains.

T F 21. Parents may elect to include their 10-year-old child's interest income of $7,300 on their tax return to prevent the child from having to file a tax return.

T F 22. For the tax year 1992, the additional standard deduction amount for a single taxpayer is $700.

T F 23. A nonresident alien taxpayer is allowed a standard deduction of $3,600 if he or she is single.

T F 24. When filing his or her own tax return, a dependent's basic standard deduction is limited to the greater of $600 or the individual's earned income for the year.

T F 25. A father-in-law and a mother-in-law meet the relationship test for claiming a dependency exemption.

Fill-in-the-Blanks

Complete the following statements with the appropriate word(s) or amount(s).

1. A parent who provides over one-half of the support of a _____ who is under 19 or who is a full-time student under 24 may claim a dependency exemption, without regard to the gross income test.

2. A dependent must be a U.S. citizen or a resident of the United States, _____, or _____.

3. The tax rate schedules are mainly used by _____ income taxpayers while the tax tables are used by low and middle income taxpayers.

4. In calculating their tax liability, taxpayers with income over the ceiling amount will be required to use the tax _____ schedule method in calculating their tax liability.

5. The determination of marital status is generally made at the _____ of the tax year, except where a spouse dies during the year.

6. Form 1040A, 1040EZ, or 1040 is due on or before the 15th day of the _____ month following the close of the tax year.

7. The joint return rate schedule was originally enacted to establish equity for married taxpayers in common law states, because married taxpayers in _____ property states could split their income.

8. Unmarried individuals who maintain a household for dependents are entitled to use the _____ _____ _____ tax rate schedule.

9. Net capital losses may not be used to reduce ordinary income of a _____.

Multiple Choice

Choose the best answer for each of the following questions.

_____ 1. For 1992, the standard deduction amount for a single taxpayer is:
      a. -0-
      b. $3,000
      c. $3,600
      d. $6,000

e. None of the above

2. During 1992, T, a single taxpayer with no dependents, has adjusted gross income of $20,000. She has itemized deductions of $6,500. What is T's taxable income?
   a. $20,000
   b. $11,450
   c. $11,350
   d. $15,850
   e. None of the above

3. Jimmy is 10 years old and during 1992 has interest earnings of $1,700 from a savings account at a local bank. If Jimmy is claimed as a dependent on his parent's tax return, what is Jimmy's "net unearned income?"
   a. -0-
   b. $1,600
   c. $1,100
   d. $500
   e. None of the above

4. For 1992, the maximum tax rate applicable to net capital gains of individual taxpayers is:
   a. 40%
   b. 33%
   c. 31%
   d. 28%
   e. None of the above

5. A head of household taxpayer uses which of the following tax rate schedules?
   a. Schedule X
   b. Schedule Y
   c. Schedule Z
   d. Schedule G
   e. None of the above

6. A taxpayer's child who is under 19 or who is a full-time student under 24 does not have to meet which of the following dependency tests?
   a. Support test
   b. Relationship test
   c. Joint return test
   d. Gross income test
   e. Citizenship test

_____ 7. Walter Kuhn is a divorced individual. He has a dependent son, age 6, who is in the custody of his ex-wife. In addition, Walter supports his dependent mother who does not live in Walter's home. Walter's filing status would be:
   a. Head of household
   b. Married filing jointly
   c. Married filing separately
   d. Single

_____ 8. Which of the following is subtracted from the original basis to obtain the adjusted basis of an asset?
   a. Capital improvements
   b. The gain realized
   c. The gain recognized
   d. Depreciation
   e. None of the above

_____ 9. During the current year, T sells his car for $8,000 (adjusted basis of $7,000) and Exxon stock for $20,000 (adjusted basis of $10,000). What is T's recognized gain?
   a. $11,000
   b. $10,000
   c. $8,000
   d. $1,000
   e. None of the above

_____ 10. Dee Walsh is 66 years old and files as a single taxpayer. For 1992 her standard deduction amount is:
   a. $3,600
   b. $4,000
   c. $4,300
   d. $4,400

_____ 11. Which of the following is a capital asset?
   a. Inventory
   b. Accounts receivable
   c. Stock held as an investment by an individual taxpayer
   d. Real estate used in a business
   e. None of the above

_____ 12. The maximum deduction for capital losses against an individual taxpayer's ordinary income in 1992 is:
   a. $6,000

    b. $5,000
    c. $4,000
    d. $3,000
    e. None of the above

_____ 13. Which of the following is not a deduction for adjusted gross income?
    a. Deductible IRA contributions
    b. Trade or business expenses
    c. Alimony
    d. Moving expenses
    e. None of the above

_____ 14. For individual taxpayers, unused capital losses can be carried forward:
    a. 3 years
    b. 4 years
    c. 5 years
    d. 7 years
    e. None of the above

_____ 15. During 1992 T had a long-term capital gain of $8,000 and a short-term capital loss of $2,000. What is the net amount included in income for T?
    a. $8,000
    b. $6,000
    c. $5,000
    d. -0-
    e. None of the above

_____ 16. Mike Karp owns machinery, with an adjusted basis of $50,000, for use in his car-washing business. In addition, Karp owns his personal residence and furniture, which together cost him $100,000. The capital assets amount to:
    a. $-0-
    b. $50,000
    c. $100,000
    d. $150,000
    e. Some other amount

_____ 17. The highest individual tax rate in the United States for 1992 is:
    a. 15 percent
    b. 33 percent
    c. 31 percent
    d. 28 percent

18. In 1992, for single taxpayers the 31 percent tax bracket starts at taxable income levels over:
    a. $11,744
    b. $21,450
    c. $51,900
    d. $100,000

19. F, age 20 is a full-time student at Big State University (BSU) and is claimed as a dependent on his parents' tax return. During the summer of 1992, F earned $1,800 from a part-time job. His only other income was $1,200 interest on his savings account. What is F's taxable income?
    a. $1,800
    b. $1,200
    c. $3,000
    d. $2,500
    e. Some other amount.

20. Mr. and Mrs. G, both age 48, file a joint tax return for 1992. They provide all the support for their son who is 20 years old and has no visible income. Their daughter, age 22, is a full-time student at a local college. She had $5,300 of income and provided 60% of her own support. How many exemptions should Mr. and Mrs. G claim on their 1992 joint tax return?
    a. 2
    b. 3
    c. 4
    d. 5
    e. None of the above

21. Mr. H, by himself, maintains a home in which he and his unmarried daughter reside. His daughter does not qualify as H's dependent. Mr. H's wife died in 1989. What is Mr. H's filing status for 1992?
    a. Head of household
    b. Surviving spouse
    c. Married filing jointly
    d. Single
    e. None of the above

22. For 1992, K's adjusted gross income is $90,000, and his taxable income is $80,000. K is single. What is K's income tax liability before any credits for 1992?
    a. $19,754.50
    b. $20,009.00

c. $20,454.50
d. $23,775.50
e. Some other amount

23. For 1992, exemptions are phased-out as adjusted gross income exceeds specified amounts. For taxpayers who are married filing jointly, the phase-out starts at?
a. $157,900
b. $131,500
c. $105,250
d. $78,950
e. Some other amount

24. F is retired and lives with his son A. F's total support is provided as follows:

Son A	$4,000
Son B	2,000
Daughter C	1,000
Social Security	4,300

Which of F's children can file a multiple support agreement and claim F as a dependent?
a. A, B, or C
b. A or C
c. A or B
d. B or C
None of the above

25. For 1992, S, a single taxpayer, had adjusted gross income of $190,000. She has one exemption. What is S's allowable exemption for 1992?
a. $-0-
b. $602
c. $1,548
d. $2,150
e. Some other amount

26. W is 66 years old and is single. For 1992, what is the minimum amount of gross income required for W to be required to file a tax return?
a. $-0-
b. $400
c. $5,900
d. $6,800

e. Some other amount

Problems

1.   In each of the independent cases below, indicate the total number of exemptions for the taxpayer, T. Assume any test not mentioned has been met.

____   a.   T is age 70, his wife is age 64, and they file a joint return.

____   b.   T is age 73, blind, and has adjusted gross income of $10,000. His wife is 66 and they file a joint return.

____   c.   T is age 66 and his wife is age 34. During the year, Mrs. T gave birth to a son.

____   d.   T is unmarried and supports her 10-year-old sister who does not live with her. The sister had income of $3,865 from interest on a savings account.

____   e.   T and his wife, W, have a foster child who lived with them the entire year. They provide over one-half the support of the foster child.

____   f.   T and his wife furnish all the support of F, T's father. F is 80 years old and blind. T and W file a joint return claiming F as a dependent.

2.   Cathy West is a secretary, and for 1992 her salary was $18,630. Cathy is single, lives in an apartment and cannot itemize deductions. During the year her employer withheld $3,510 of Federal income taxes from her salary. River Bank paid Cathy $750 of interest on her savings account. Determine the following amounts for Cathy for 1992.

Adjusted Gross Income	19 380
Standard Deduction	(3 600)
Exemption	(2 300)
Taxable Income	13 480
Tax Liability	2021

Withholding   _____

Tax Due or (Refund)   _____

Code Section Recognition

Indicate, by number, the appropriate Code section where the following items are found.

_____   1.   The standard deduction.

_____   2.   Tax rates for individual taxpayers.

_____   3.   Personal exemptions.

_____   4.   The definition of a dependent.

_____   5.   Definition of a capital asset.

_____   6.   Definition of a net capital gain.

SOLUTIONS TO CHAPTER 3

True or False

1.   False   Exemptions are generally based on which parent has custody. (p. 3-11)

2.   True   (p. 3-6)

3.   False   If itemized deductions do not exceed the standard deduction, the taxpayer will compute taxable income using the standard deduction amount. (p. 3-7)

4.   True   (p. 3-8)

5.   True   (p. 3-7)

6.   True   (p. 3-6)

7.   True   (p. 3-23)

8. False The additional standard deduction amounts are not available for dependents. (p. 3-6)

9. True (p. 3-10)

10. True (p. 3-10)

11. True (p. 3-12)

12. False Certain children of the taxpayer do not have to meet the gross income test. (p. 3-12)

13. True (p. 3-12)

14. True (p. 3-13)

15. True (p. 3-10)

16. False Dependent parents do not have to live in the taxpayer's home. (p. 3-24)

17. True (p. 3-25)

18. False Net capital losses of individual taxpayers carry forward indefinitely. (p. 3-27)

19. True (p. 3-26)

20. True (p. 3-26)

21. False The child's gross income must be less than $5,000. (p. 3-19)

22. False The amount is $900. (p. 3-7)

23. False Nonresident aliens are not allowed any standard deduction (p. 3-8)

24 True (p. 3-8)

25. True (p-3-12)

Fill-in-the-Blanks

1.   child (p. 3-12)

2.   Mexico, Canada (p. 3-13)

3.   upper (p. 3-14)

4.   rate (p. 3-15)

5.   end (p. 3-9)

6.   fourth (p. 3-22)

7.   community (p. 3-23)

8.   head of household (p. 3-24)

9.   corporation (p. 3-27)

Multiple Choice

1.   C   (p. 3-6)

2.   C $20,000 - 6,500 - 2,300 = $11,200. (p. 3-7)

3.   D $1,700 - 1,200 = $500. (p. 3-18)

4.   D   (p. 3-26)

5.   C   (Appendix)

6.   D   (p. 3-12)

7.   A   (p. 3-27)

8.   D   (p. 3-24)

9.   A   (p. 3-25)

10.   D $3,600 + 900 = $4,400. (p. 3-7)

11.   C   (p. 3-26)

12. D (p. 3-27)

13. D (p. 3-3)

14. E There is no time limit on the carryforward period. (p. 3-27)

15. B $8,000 - 2,000 = $6,000. (p. 3-26)

16. C (p. 3-26)

17. C (p. 3-15)

18. C (p. 3-15)

19. B ($1,800 + 1,200) - $1,800 (max standard deduction) = $1,200. (p. 3-8)

20. B The daughter does not meet the support test. (p. 3-10)

21. A To be a surviving spouse the daughter must be a dependent. (p. 3-24)

22. C [$11,743.50 + 31% ($80,000 - 51,900)] = $20,454.50. (p. 3-15)

23. A (p. 3-13)

24. C Daughter C does not supply at least 10% of the total support, therefore she is
        not eligible to claim the exemption. (p. 3-10)

25. B 1. $190,000 - 105,250 = $84,750 excess amount
        2. $84,750/$2,500 = 34 x 2 = 68% (phase-out percentage)
        3. 68% x $2,300 = $1,564 amount of exemption phased out
        4. $2,300 - 1,564 = $736 allowable exemption deduction (p. 3-13)

26. D See Figure 3-8 in the text. (p. 3-21)

Problems

1. a. 2; 2 personal (p. 3-9)

    b. 2; 2 personal (p. 3-9)

    c. 3; 2 personal, 1 dependency (p. 3-9)

d. 1; 1 personal, sister fails the gross income test (p. 3-12)

e. 3; 2 personal, 1 dependency (p. 3-12)

f. 3; 2 personal, 1 dependency (p. 3-9)

2.	Adjusted Gross Income:	$19,380	($18,630 + $750)
	Standard deduction:	-3,600	
	Exemption:	-2,300	
	Taxable Income:	$13,480	
	Tax Liability:	$2,022	(15% of taxable income)
	Withholding:	-3,510	
	Refund:	-$1,488	

Tax formula on page 3-2.

Code Section Recognition

1. § 63

2. § 1

3. § 151

4. § 152

5. § 1221

6. §1222

CHAPTER

┌─────────┐
│   │
│   4   │
│   │
└─────────┘

GROSS INCOME:
CONCEPTS AND EXCLUSIONS

CHAPTER HIGHLIGHTS

The calculation of gross income is the first computation needed in the formula for taxable income. This chapter defines gross income and describes certain sources of gross income. The effect of the cash and accrual methods of accounting on the calculation of gross income is also discussed.

I.   GROSS INCOME

    A.   § 61(a) of the tax law defines gross income as "all income from whatever source derived." However, this definition is rather broad so the courts have established the principle that for income to be recognized for tax purposes, it must be realized. Therefore, increases in value (economic income) would not be taxed as income until the property is sold or exchanged.

    B.   Although financial accounting and tax accounting measurement concepts are frequently parallel, they have different purposes. The primary goal of financial accounting is to provide useful information to management, shareholders, creditors, and other interested parties, while the goal of tax accounting is the equitable collection of revenue.

    C.   Gross income is not limited to cash received. Income can be realized in the form of money, property, or services received by the taxpayer.

    D.   Under the "recovery of capital doctrine" the proceeds from the sale or disposition of property are reduced by the basis of the property sold to determine gross income. This is to ensure that income is not taxed until the capital initially invested is recovered.

II.   YEAR OF INCLUSION

A.   As a general rule, taxpayers are required to use a calendar year to report income. However, taxpayers who keep adequate books and records (and meet certain other tests) may use a fiscal year.

B.   The three major methods of accounting used in computing taxable income are the cash method, the accrual method, and the hybrid method.

The cash method of accounting is used by most individuals and many small businesses. Under the cash method, property or services are included in the taxpayer's gross income in the "year of actual or constructive receipt."

The accrual method of accounting is used by many corporations. Under this method, income is recognized "in the year it is earned," regardless of when it is collected. Income is considered earned when (1) all events have occurred which fix the right to receive such income, and (2) the amount of the income can be determined with reasonable accuracy.

The hybrid method is a combination of cash and accrual accounting concepts.

Chapter 18 discusses the limitations applicable to accounting periods and methods.

C.   Exceptions applicable to the cash method include the following:

- The "doctrine of constructive receipt" limits an individual's ability to shift income arbitrarily to a later taxable year. If a taxpayer is entitled to receive income and the income is made available to him, it must be included in gross income.

- Income set apart or made available is not constructively received if it is subject to substantial restrictions. For example, the increase in cash surrender value on ordinary life insurance is not taxed as the policy increases in value.

- When a lender makes a loan with an original issue discount, the accrued interest must be reported each year, regardless of the taxpayer's accounting method. Interest on long-term bonds issued at a discount must also be accrued. Interest on U.S. Series E or EE Savings Bonds is usually deferred until the bonds mature; however, a taxpayer may make an election to use the accrual method which requires that the annual increase in the bond's redemption value be included in gross income. By making the accrual election, the taxpayer prevents the bunching of income in a future year.

- No income is realized when money is borrowed. Receipt of funds under an obligation to repay is not a taxable event.

D. Exceptions to the accrual method include the following:

- "Prepaid income" is generally taxed in the year of receipt. Many court cases have been brought against the IRS by taxpayers arguing that the proper matching of revenue and expenses requires that income is recognized only when it is earned (e.g. the accrual method). The IRS has modified its position in several areas.

- Generally, a taxpayer can elect to defer "advance payments for goods" if the taxpayer's method of accounting for the sale is the same for tax and financial reporting purposes.

- A taxpayer can defer "advance payments for services" to be performed by the end of the tax year following the year of receipt. Such "services" do not include prepaid interest, amounts received under guarantee or warranty contracts, or prepaid rent.

III. INCOME SOURCES

A. Income from personal services must be included in the gross income of the person who "performs the services." A mere assignment of income will not shift the tax liability.

B. Income from property (e.g. interest, dividends, rent) must be included in the gross income of the "owner of the property."

When property is sold with accrued interest, a portion of the selling price is treated as interest and taxed to the seller in the year of sale. Under IRS rules interest accrues daily.

Dividends, unlike interest, do not accrue on a daily basis. Dividends are normally taxed to the taxpayer who is entitled to receive them, the holder of the stock on the corporation's record date.

C.   A partner in a partnership or a shareholder in an S Corporation must "include his or her share of income" from these entities on his or her individual tax return. The income must be included in the partner's or shareholder's return for the year with or within which the entity's tax year ends. Beneficiaries of estates and trusts are generally taxed on income earned by the estate or trust that is actually distributed or required to be distributed to them. Any excess income is taxed to the estate or trust.

D.   In nine states -- Louisiana, Texas, New Mexico, Arizona, California, Washington, Idaho, Nevada, and Wisconsin -- marital rights to the ownership of property are controlled by community property laws. Income from personal services (e.g. salaries and wages) is treated as being earned equally by both spouses. Income from community property is taxable as community income, one-half to each spouse. Income from separate property is taxable to the person who owns the property, except in Texas, Louisiana, and Idaho, where the income from separate property is community income.

E.   Under § 66, spouses living apart in community property states will be taxed only on their separate earnings from personal services if the following conditions occur:

- The individuals live apart for the entire year.

- They do not file a joint return with each other.

- No portion of the income is transferred between the individuals.

IV.   ITEMS SPECIFICALLY INCLUDED IN GROSS INCOME

A.   Post-1984 Alimony and Separate Maintenance Payments. For divorces after 1984, alimony is defined as cash payments meeting the following three conditions:

- The decree does not specify the cash payments are not alimony.

- The payor and payee are not members of the same household.

- There is no liability for payments after the death of the payee.

If the payment meets the definition of alimony, the amount is deductible by the payor and included in the gross income of the payee.

If the divorce decree is executed after 1986, special recapture rules apply if the payments exceed $15,000 in the first or second year. In the third year, the payor must include the excess alimony payments for the first and second years in gross income and the payee is allowed a deduction for the excess alimony payments. The recaptured amount is computed as follows:

$$R = D + E$$
$$D = B - (C + \$15,000)$$
$$E = A - [(B - D + C)/2 + \$15,000]$$

Where,

R = amount of recapture in Year 3.
D = recapture from Year 2.
E = recapture from Year 1.
A, B, C are the alimony payments in Years 1, 2, and 3, respectively.

For 1985 and 1986 agreements, special recapture rules may apply in the 2nd and 3rd years if alimony payments decrease by more than $10,000.

For post-1984 decrees, if cash payments would be reduced by a "contingency related to a child," then the amount of the potential reduction in the payments is considered child support. The amount of the payment which is considered child support under this provision is not deductible by the payor or income to the payee.

Under post-1984 rules, transfers of appreciated property to a former spouse under a divorce decree are not taxable events.

B. Pre-1985 Alimony Rules. Alimony payments are taxable to the recipient and deductible by the payor if such payments are:

- made under a legal obligation such as a decree of divorce or separate maintenance.

- for a period of more than 10 years or contingent.

- in discharge of a legal obligation arising from the marital or family relationship.

The Regulations define marital or family obligation as an obligation for support. Since the obligation for support must arise under state law, the alimony treatment varies with the state in which the taxpayer is domiciled.

C. Imputed Interest on Below-Market Loans. If a taxpayer makes a "below-market interest rate" loan to a related party, there can be imputed interest. The imputed interest is income to the lender and deductible to the borrower. The rate of imputed interest is the rate the Federal government pays on new borrowings, compounded semiannually. This rate is adjusted monthly and published by the IRS. These rules apply to the following types of loans:

- Gift loans

- Compensation-related loans

- Corporation-shareholder loans

- Tax avoidance loans

The below-market rules do not normally apply to gift loans between individuals where the total loans between the related parties are $10,000 or less, unless income producing property is purchased. On loans between individuals of $100,000 or less, the imputed interest cannot be greater than the net investment income earned by the borrower in that year, unless there is evidence of tax avoidance. Interest is not imputed on loans of $100,000 or less if the borrower's net investment income is $1,000 or less, unless there is evidence of tax avoidance.

D. Income From Annuities. Amounts received as annuity payments are included in gross income subject to the following rules:

- For collections on or after the annuity starting date, the recipient may exclude a portion of the payment that represents a recovery of his or her investment. The formula is as follows:

$$\text{Percent Excluded} = \frac{\text{Investment in the contract}}{\text{Total expected return}}$$

- The exclusion ratio applies until the annuitant has recovered his or her investment in the contract. Once the investment is recovered, all subsequent payments are fully taxable. If the annuitant dies before recovering his or her investment, the unrecovered cost is deductible in the year the payments cease.

E. Prizes and Awards. Under § 74, the fair market value of "prizes and awards" (other than qualified scholarships) is included in gross income. If the award is for recognition of religious, charitable, scientific, educational, artistic, literary, or civic achievement, the recipient transfers the prize to a qualified governmental unit or nonprofit organization, the recipient is selected with no action on his or her part, and if no substantial future services are required, then the award may be excluded from gross income. Certain employee achievement awards can be excluded from gross income. The maximum amount of such an employee award is $400 ($1,600 for qualified plan awards).

F. Group Term Life Insurance. There is an exclusion for premiums on up to $50,000 of "group-term" life insurance provided to employees. An amount, based on a Uniform Premium table supplied by the Internal Revenue Service, must be included in the employee's gross income for each $1,000 of coverage over $50,000. If the group-term insurance plan discriminates in favor of certain key employees, the § 79 exclusion does not apply and special rules apply in determining the amount to be included in the employee's gross income.

G. Unemployment Compensation. All unemployment compensation benefits are included in gross income.

H. Social Security Benefits. Part of a taxpayer's Social Security benefits may be included in gross income. The amount included is the lesser of:

- 50% of Social Security benefits, or

- 50% of [Modified AGI + 50% (Social Security benefits) - base amount]

Modified AGI is the taxpayer's AGI from all sources except Social Security, plus any tax exempt interest income. The base amount is:

- $32,000 for married taxpayers filing jointly

- $0 for married taxpayers filing separately

- $25,000 for all other taxpayers

TEST FOR SELF-EVALUATION

True or False

Indicate which of the following statements are true or false by circling the correct answer.

T F 1. The general definition of gross income is found in § 161(a).

T F 2. The term "income" is used in the Code but is not separately defined.

T F 3. Economic income is the sum of the taxpayer's change in net worth and the actual consumption of goods and services during the tax period.

T F 4. An accountant's concept of income is based on the recognition principle.

T F 5. For any individual taxpayer, financial income and taxable income are always the same amount.

T F 6. For post-1984 divorce decrees, payments must be made in cash to qualify as deductible alimony.

T F 7. Amounts received for damages to property or to goodwill of a business are income only to the extent the amount received exceeds the adjusted basis of the assets.

T F 8. Corporate taxpayers must always use the cash method of accounting.

T F 9. A cash basis taxpayer has some degree of control over the timing of the recognition of income and expenses.

T F 10. The benefits of the group-term life insurance premium exclusion are not available to proprietors and partners.

T F 11. The interest on U.S. "Series EE" savings bonds must always be reported using the cash method of accounting.

T   F   12.   Prepaid income is always income in the year payment is received.

T   F   13.   Taxable income from personal services can be shifted to other taxpayers such as family members.

T   F   14.   In all community property states (Texas, California, etc.), income derived from separate property is separate income.

T   F   15.   On the sale of stock, dividends are generally taxed to the person who is entitled to receive the dividends.

T   F   16.   Income from property must be included in the gross income of the owner of the property.

T   F   17.   If a taxpayer is entitled to receive income, which is made available to him, he cannot "turn his back" on it and refuse the income.

T   F   18.   Most individual taxpayers use the cash method of accounting.

T   F   19.   The recovery of capital doctrine means that the amount received from a sale of property is reduced by the adjusted basis in arriving at the taxable gain on the property sold.

T   F   20.   For pre-1985 divorce decrees, alimony and separate maintenance payments are not included in gross income.

T   F   21.   For pre-1985 divorce decrees, payments paid for over 10 years will generally be treated as alimony.

T   F   22.   For divorce decrees dated in 1985 and 1986, if the alimony payments decrease by more than $5,000 between years, then the excess over $5,000 will be recaptured.

T   F   23.   The premiums on the first $50,000 worth of non-discriminatory group-term life insurance provided to an employee can generally be excluded from gross income.

T   F   24.   If the interest charged on a loan is less than the Federal rate, the imputed interest is the difference between the amount that would have been charged at the Federal rate and the amount actually charged.

T   F   25. If a group-term life insurance plan discriminates in favor of key employees, the key employees must include in gross income the lesser of the actual premiums paid by the employer or the amount calculated from the Uniform Premiums table.

T   F   26. A cash basis taxpayer must recognize income when a check is received, even if the check is received after banking hours.

T   F   27. A taxpayer includes funds received from an agent (such as an auctioneer) in the year the funds are received from the agent, not in the year the agent collected the funds.

Fill-in-the-Blanks

Complete the following statements with the appropriate word(s).

1. Income from property belongs to the _____ of the property.

2. Every partner in a partnership must report his or her _____ share of partnership income.

3. Income from personal services is treated as being earned equally by both spouses in a _____ property state.

4. The Supreme Court in *Eisner v. Macomber* added the _____ requirement to the judicial definition of income.

5. The primary goal of _____ accounting is to provide useful information to interested parties, while the goal of _____ accounting is the equitable collection of revenue.

6. The _____ accounting period is a basic component of the U.S. tax system.

7. The Regulations require that the _____ method be used for determining purchases and sales when a taxpayer maintains an inventory.

8. Dividends are generally taxed to the person who owns the stock as of the corporation's _____ date.

9. Property may be held as _____ property in a community property state if it is acquired before marriage or by gift or inheritance following marriage.

Multiple Choice

Choose the best answer for each of the following questions.

_____ 1. A bank deposits $500 in interest in a savings account on December 31, 1992. The depositor withdraws $2,000 on January 3, 1993. How much income must be recognized for 1992?
   a. $2,000
   b. $500
   c. $1,500
   d. None of the above

_____ 2. On December 1, 1992, T receives $3,000 for three months rent (December, January, and February) of an office building. T is an accrual basis taxpayer. How much income must be recognized for 1992?
   a. $-0-
   b. $1,000
   c. $2,000
   d. $3,000
   e. None of the above

_____ 3. Revenue Procedure 71-21 applies to which of the following?
   a. Prepaid rent
   b. Services
   c. Prepaid interest
   d. Amounts under warranty contracts
   e. None of the above

_____ 4. T and his wife live in Texas. During the year, T earned a salary of $20,000 and his wife earned a salary of $10,000. If they file separate income tax returns, T would report how much income?
   a. $-0-
   b. $10,000
   c. $15,000
   d. $20,000
   e. None of the above

_____ 5. Which of the following is not a community property state?
   a. Texas
   b. New York
   c. California

    d. New Mexico
    e. Washington

_____ 6. Dave Jones, a calendar year taxpayer, owns 30% of Z Corporation, an S Corporation. For the year ended December 31, 1992, Z Corporation had taxable income of $100,000. During the year the corporation made distributions of $20,000. Dave's dividend income from other corporations was $25,000. What is Dave's taxable income from the corporations for 1992?
    a. $25,000
    b. $45,000
    c. $55,000
    d. $125,000
    e. None of the above

_____ 7. For 1992, Jill Adams, a single taxpayer, received $10,000 in Social Security benefits. Her adjusted gross income was $40,000 and she had no tax-free interest income. How much of the Social Security benefits should Jill include in her income?
    a. $-0-
    b. $5,000
    c. $10,000
    d. $7,500
    e. Some other amount.

_____ 8. Judy Davis has savings bonds (Series EE) which increase in redemption value by $600 during 1992. In addition, Judy has $1,000 in interest on her savings account at Big Town Savings & Loan. If Judy has not made any elections and she is a cash basis taxpayer, she should report taxable interest income of:
    a. $-0-
    b. $600
    c. $1,000
    d. $1,600
    e. None of the above

_____ 9. A lawyer drafts a will for a dentist in exchange for dental work. The dentist would normally have charged $400 for this work. Since the attorney normally charges $300 for drafting a will, he paid the dentist $100 in cash. Based on this transaction, how much should the dentist include in his gross income?
    a. $-0-
    b. $100
    c. $300
    d. $400

e. None of the above

_____ 10. Lisa Smith owned stock in X Corporation, which originally cost $100,000. She sold the stock for $75,000 plus 10% of X's income in the year of sale plus 10% of five additional years of income. The value of the future income cannot be determined in the year of sale. Collections in the first year are $84,000. What is Lisa's taxable gain in the first year?

   a. $-0-
   b. $9,000
   c. $25,000
   d. $16,000
   e. None of the above

_____ 11. In November 1992, John Lewis entered into a contract to deliver goods to a customer in March 1993 for $12,000. John uses the accrual method of accounting for both financial and tax purposes. He collected $8,000 in 1992 and the balance in 1993. John did not have the goods in stock on December 31, 1992. The cost of the goods to him is $9,000. How much net income must John report in 1992?

   a. $-0-
   b. $1,000
   c. $5,000
   d. $8,000
   e. None of the above

_____ 12. Sky Corporation sells service contracts for 12 and 24 month periods. In September 1992, the company sold $8,000 of the 12-month contracts and $10,000 of the 24-month contracts. If the company services each customer each month (October, November, and December 1992), how much income should be reported for 1992 if Sky Corporation follows Rev. Proc. 71-21?

   a. $2,000
   b. $6,000
   c. $8,000
   d. $12,000
   e. None of the above

_____ 13. Vicki Cohen owns 25 percent of K&A Partnership. For the 1992 tax year the partnership had net income of $200,000. During the year Vicki withdrew $35,000 from her capital account. What is Vicki's reported share of net income from K&A?

   a. $-0-
   b. $35,000

c. $50,000
d. $200,000
e. None of the above

_____ 14. On July 15 the Board of Directors of R Corporation declared a $1 per share dividend payable July 30 to shareholders of record on July 25. As of July 15 Norman Beatty owned 1,000 shares. On July 16 he sold 700 shares to Sam Wise for the fair market value, and he gave 300 shares to his son. How much dividend income must Norman report?
a. $-0-
b. $300
c. $700
d. $1,000
e. None of the above

_____ 15. Dave Berg, an employee of P.K. Inc., is covered by a group-term life insurance policy that has a face amount of $60,000. The company pays all the policy premiums which amount to $500 per year. According to Reg. Sec. 1.79-3, the cost of a policy for a man Dave's age is 48 cents per $1,000 per month. How much income should Dave report on his tax return?
a. $-0-
b. $57.60
c. $500.00
d. $345.60
e. Some other amount

_____ 16. Robert Bowen is divorced in the current year. He makes cash payments to his ex-wife of $1,000 per month. When their son, who is in the wife's custody, turns 18 years old the payments are reduced to $600 per month. How much can Robert deduct as alimony each month?
a. $-0-
b. $400
c. $600
d. $1,000
e. Some other amount

_____ 17. Nicky Smith goes on the T.V. game show, Wheel of a Deal. She wins cash of $15,000 and a new car with a fair market value of $20,000. How much income must Nicky report from these winnings?
a. $-0-
b. $15,000
c. $20,000

d. $35,000

e. Some other amount

18. In the current year Dave Smith receives stock from his employer worth $25,000. The stock cannot be sold by Dave for seven years. Dave estimates that the stock will be worth $60,000 after the seven years. In the current year how much income must Dave recognize?

a. $-0-

b. $25,000

c. $35,000

d. $60,000

e. Some other amount

19. T retired last year after investing $100,000 in an annuity which pays $12,000 per year. T had a life expectancy of 10 years at the annuity starting date. What is T's income for the current year assuming T receives $12,000 during the current year?

a. $-0-

b. $2,000

c. $10,000

d. $12,000

e. None of the above

20. Larry Boxer, a cash basis taxpayer, paid $42,000 for an 18-month certificate-of-deposit with a maturity value of $50,000. The effective interest rate on the certificate was 12 percent. If Larry bought the certificate on June 30 of the current year, how much interest income should he report?

a. $2,520

b. $3,000

c. $5,040

d. $6,000

e. Some other amount

21. Under a current year's divorce decree, Oliver Whittington has to pay his ex-wife alimony. The cash payments are as follows:

Year 1	32,000
Year 2	25,000
Year 3	-0-

What is Oliver's alimony deduction for Year 1?

a. $-0-

   b. $32,000
   c. $22,000
   d. $12,000
   e. Some other amount

_____ 22. Assume the same facts as question 21. What is the amount of alimony that Oliver will have to recapture in Year 3?
   a. $-0-
   b. $10,000
   c. $19,500
   d. $9,500
   e. Some other amount

_____ 23. Under a current year's divorce decree, Van Ballew transfers appreciated property to his ex-wife. The property has a fair market value of $150,000 and an adjusted basis to Van of $60,000. From the transaction Van should report a taxable gain of:
   a. $-0-
   b. $60,000
   c. $90,000
   d. $150,000
   e. Some other amount

_____ 24. If Van Ballew's wife in question 23 above were to sell the property 3 years later for $160,000, how much gain should she report?
   a. $-0-
   b. $90,000
   c. $100,000
   d. $10,000
   e. Some other amount.

_____ 25. During the first six months of the current year the Federal imputed interest rate is 9 percent and during the second six months it is 10 percent. On January 1, a father gives his son an interest-free loan of $50,000. For the current year, what is the amount of interest income that the father must recognize and what amount of interest expense is the son treated as incurring?
   a. $-0-
   b. $4,863
   c. $4,750
   d. $5,000
   e. Some other amount

_____ 26. Assume the same facts as in question 25. How much of a "gift" has the father made to his son?
a. $-0-
b. $4,863
c. $4,750
d. $5,000
e. Some other amount

_____ 27. Z, a cash basis taxpayer, gave Y bonds with a face amount of $10,000. The bonds have a stated annual interest rate of 9%. The gift was made on February 10, 1992 and interest was paid December 31, 1992. How much interest income must Z recognize in 1992?
a. $-0-
b. $101
c. $799
d. $900
e. Some other amount

_____ 28. M owned the following stock on January 1, 1992:

	Basis	FMV
ABC Corp.	$200	$220
DEF Corp.	$175	$170

During the year M sold the ABC stock for $215 and the DEF stock for $180. M's income under the *economic* concept of income is:
a. $-0-
b. $5
c. $20
d. $35
e. Some other amount

_____ 29. On June 30, 1992, Q purchased for $7,500 a 30-month, $10,000 certificate of deposit from Shakie Bank & Trust. The yield to maturity on the certificate was 12%, interest compounded semi-annually. What is Q's interest income for the six months ended on December 31, 1992.
a. $-0-
b. $600
c. $500
d. $450
e. Some other amount

_____ 30. S Corporation purchased a group-term life insurance plan which covered only management and officers of the company. Mr. S received $250,000 of life insurance under this plan. The cost to S Corporation for the premiums of Mr. S's insurance was $3,100. The Uniform Premium amount for each $1,000 of insurance for a man S's age is $9 annually. Mr. S must include in gross income:
   a. $-0-
   b. $2,250
   c. $2,575
   d. $3,100
   e. Some other amount

_____ 31. P owns a life insurance policy with a face amount of $100,000. On January 1, 1992 the policy had a cash surrender value of $15,000 and on December 31, 1992 the cash surrender value was $16,500. During the year, P paid premiums on the policy of $2,500. What amount of income must P report from this insurance policy for 1992?
   a. $-0-
   b. $1,000
   c. $1,500
   d. $2,500
   e. None of the above

Code Section Recognition

Indicate, by number, the appropriate Code Section where the following items are found.

_____ 1. The definition of gross income.

_____ 2. Provision allowing the IRS to determine accounting methods.

_____ 3. Treatment of community property income of spouses living apart.

_____ 4. Alimony and separate maintenance payments.

_____ 5. The taxation of income from annuities.

_____ 6. Prizes and awards.

_____ 7. Group-term life insurance.

_____ 8. Unemployment compensation payments.

_____ 9. Taxation of Social Security benefits.

SOLUTIONS TO CHAPTER 4

True or False

1. False The definition of gross income is found in § 61. (p. 4-2)

2. True (p. 4-2)

3. True (p. 4-3)

4. False The accountant's concept is based on the realization principle. (p. 4-3)

5. False Financial income concepts may differ from those used in determining taxable income. (p. 4-4)

6. True (p. 4-20)

7. True (p. 4-5)

8. False Most corporations use the accrual method. (p. 4-7)

9. True (p. 4-7)

10. True (p. 4-32)

11. False Taxpayers may elect the accrual method. (p. 4-11)

12. False In some cases an accrual basis taxpayer may be able to defer recognition of the income under Rev. Proc. 71-21. (p. 4-13)

13. False The assignment of income does not shift the tax liability. (p. 4-14)

14. False In Texas, Louisiana, and Idaho income derived from separate property is community income. (p. 4-17)

15. True (p. 4-15)

16.   True   (p. 4-14)

17.   True   (p. 4-9)

18.   True   (p. 4-7)

19.   True   (p. 4-15)

20.   False   They are included in the gross income of the recipient. (p. 4-19)

21.   True   (p. 4-22)

22.   False   The decrease must be over $10,000. (p. 4-21)

23.   True   (p. 4-32)

24.   True   (p. 4-24)

25.   False   The *greater* of the actual premiums paid by the employer or the amount calculated from the Uniform Premiums table must be included in the employee's gross income. (p. 4-33)

26.   True   (p. 4-8)

27.   False   It is taxable in the year collected by the agent. (p. 4-16)

Fill-in-the-Blanks

1.   owner (p. 4-14)

2.   distributive (p. 4-16)

3.   community (p. 4-18)

4.   realization (p. 4-3)

5.   financial, tax (p. 4-4)

6.   annual (p. 4-6)

7.   accrual (p. 4-7)

8. record (p. 4-15)

9. separate (p. 4-17)

Multiple Choice

1. **B** (p. 4-7)

2. **D** The entire $3,000 is taxable when received. (p. 4-12)

3. **B** (p. 4-13)

4. **C** 50% ($20,000 + 10,000) = $15,000. (p. 4-17)

5. **B** (p. 4-17)

6. **C** 30% ($100,000) + $25,000 = $55,000. (p. 4-17)

7. **B** Lesser of:

   (1) 50% x $10,000 = $5,000, or
   (2) 50% x [$40,000 + 50%($10,000) - $25,000] = $10,000. (p.4-33)

8. **C** (p. 4-11)

9. **D** $300 + 100 = $400. (p. 4-4)

10. **A** The $84,000 is a recovery of capital. (p. 4-5)

11. **A** The income is reported in 1993. (p. 4-13)

12. **D** 3/12 ($8,000) + $10,000 = $12,000. (p. 4-13)

13. **C** 25% ($200,000) = $50,000. (p. 4-16)

14. **B** Norman is taxed on the dividends related to 300 shares because the gift was made after the declaration date. (p. 4-15)

15. **B** $.48 x [($60,000 - 50,000)/$1,000] x 12 months = $57.60. (p. 4-33)

16. **C** The contingent amount is disguised child support. (p. 4-23)

17.   D   (p. 4-30)

18.   A   (p. 4-10)

19.   B $100,000/($12,000 x 10 years) x $12,000 = $10,000 excluded
           $12,000 - 10,000 = $2,000 included. (p. 4-29)

20.   A   (.12 x $42,000) x 1/2 year = $2,520. (p. 4-10)

21.   B   (p. 4-20)

22.   C   D = $25,000 - ($0 + 15,000) = $10,000
           E = $32,000 - [($25,000 - 10,000 + 0)/2 + $15,000] = $9,500
           R = $10,000 + 9,500 = $19,500. (p. 4-21)

23.   A   (p. 4-20)

24.   C $160,000 - 60,000 = $100,000. (p. 4-20)

25.   B   Jan. 1 to June 30:   9% x $50,000 x 1/2 year $2,250
           July 1 to Dec. 31:   10% x $52,250 x 1/2 year 2,613
                                             $4,863   (p.4-24)

26.   B   (p. 4-24)

27.   B   9% x $10,000 x (41 days/365 days) = $101. (p. 4-16)

28.   B   Economic income is the change in the FMV of the taxpayer's assets. ($215 - $220) + $180 - $170) = $5 (p. 4-3)

29.   D   Q must use the current interest method, $7,500 x .12 x (6/12) = $450. (p. 4-10)

30.   D   The plan is discriminatory, therefore the greater of the actual premiums paid or the Uniform Premium amount is included in income. (p. 4-33)

31.   A   The increase in value is not taxed because of "substantial restrictions" on the life insurance policy. (p. 4-10)

Code Section Recognition

1.   § 61

2.   § 446

3.   § 66

4.   § 71

5.   § 72

6.   § 74

7.   § 79

8.   § 85

9.   § 86

CHAPTER

$$\boxed{5}$$

GROSS INCOME: EXCLUSIONS

CHAPTER HIGHLIGHTS

This chapter focuses on those items which are specifically excluded from gross income by Congress.

I. **EXCLUSIONS FROM GROSS INCOME--STATUTORY AUTHORITY**

  A. As a general rule, everything received by a taxpayer is income unless a "specific statutory exclusion" can be found. Congress has chosen to exclude certain items from gross income for various social, economic, and equity purposes.

  B. The courts also influence the enactment of provisions providing for the exclusion of certain items from gross income. For example, in a District Court case the court held that insurance reimbursement proceeds for the cost of temporary living quarters after a fire were income. However, Congress was not satisfied with this decision and enacted a provision to exclude such insurance proceeds from income.

II. **GIFTS AND INHERITANCES**

  A. The value of property received by gift or inheritance is excluded from gross income under § 102. A gift is "a voluntary transfer of property by one taxpayer to another without any valuable consideration or compensation there from." The payment must be made "out of affection, respect, admiration, charity, or like impulses."

B.   Gifts made in a business setting often represent compensation for past, present, or future services and are not gifts. In most cases, transfers from employers to employees may not be treated as gifts.

III.   LIFE INSURANCE PROCEEDS

A.   In general, the proceeds of life insurance are excluded from the income of the beneficiary of the policy. However, if the policy is transferred for valuable consideration or is an amount due from the decedent, the net proceeds of the policy will be included in income. The net proceeds will not be included if the policy is transferred to the following:

- a partner of the insured

- a partnership in which the insured is a partner

- a corporation in which the insured is an officer or a shareholder

- a transferee whose basis in the policy is determined by reference to the transferor's basis

The first three exceptions facilitate the use of life insurance to fund buy-sell agreements.

B.   Interest that is earned on the reinvestment of life insurance proceeds is subject to the income tax.

IV.   EMPLOYEE DEATH BENEFITS

A.   Payments made by an employer to a deceased employee's spouse, children, or other beneficiaries will generally be excluded from gross income. The maximum exclusion allowed to the employee's beneficiaries is a total of $5,000. The exclusion does not pertain to payments made out of legal obligation such as the decedent's accrued salary. The $5,000 exclusion must be split among the beneficiaries proportionally based on the total death benefits received.

B. Amounts in excess of $5,000 may be excluded as a gift if they were made as an act of "affection or charity" by the employer. Generally, however the IRS considers employee death benefits to be compensation for prior services and not gifts.

V. SCHOLARSHIPS

A. A scholarship is "an amount paid or allowed to, or for the benefit of, an individual, . . ., to aid such individual in the pursuit of study or research." The recipient must be a candidate for a degree at an educational institution.

B. Scholarship grants for tuition and related expenses are excluded from income under § 117 of the Code. Other scholarship amounts received (e.g. room and board) are included in the taxable income of the recipient.

C. Employees of nonprofit educational institutions are allowed to exclude a tuition waiver from gross income. Generally the exclusion is limited to undergraduate tuition waivers.

VI. COMPENSATION FOR INJURIES AND SICKNESS

A. A person who suffers harm caused by another is often paid damages. Generally, the reimbursement for loss of income is taxed in the same manner as the income being replaced by the damages. If the damages represent a recovery of a previously deducted expense, income may arise under the tax benefit rule. Payments for personal injury are specifically excluded from the gross income of the person receiving the payment.

Punitive damages arising from a claim of physical injury or physical sickness are excluded from gross income, while all other punitive damages are fully taxable.

B. Workers' compensation payments and benefits from accident and health insurance policies purchased by the taxpayer are specifically excluded from gross income under § 104.

VII. EMPLOYER SPONSORED ACCIDENT AND HEALTH PLANS

A. When persons suffer damages by another they are often entitled to damages.

The receipt of damages are generally taxed the same as the income replaced.

B. Premiums paid on "employer sponsored" accident and health plans are excluded from the income of the employee and are deductible by the employer. When the employee collects the insurance benefits, such benefits are considered taxable income with the following exceptions:

- Payments received for the medical care of the employee, spouse, and dependents are excluded except to the extent the payments are reimbursements for medical expenses which were deducted in the previous year or the payments are reimbursements of expenses that do not meet the test for deduction as a medical expense under the Code.

- Payments for the permanent loss or the loss of the use of a member or function of the body or the permanent disfigurement of the employee, spouse, or dependent are also excluded.

C. Amounts received under employer medical reimbursement plans are excluded from gross income unless the plan discriminates in favor of certain groups of employees (e.g. management level). Benefits which are paid only to a particular group of employees must be included in income.

VIII.   MEALS AND LODGING

A. The value of meals and lodging provided to an employee, the employee's spouse, and the employee's dependents is excluded from gross income if certain conditions are met. To qualify for the exclusion, meals must be furnished by the employer on the business premises of the employer and be for the convenience of the employer. In addition to these tests, lodging must be a condition of employment for an employee to be able to exclude it.

B. Under certain conditions, an employee of an educational institution can exclude the value of campus housing provided by the employer. Generally, the employee does not recognize income if he or she makes annual rent payments equal to or greater than 5 percent of the value of the facility; however, if the rent payments are less than 5% of the value of the facility, the difference must be included in gross income. A "minister of the gospel" can exclude the rental value of a home furnished as compensation. Military personnel are allowed exclusions under various circumstances.

IX.   OTHER EMPLOYEE FRINGE BENEFITS

    A.   The following employee benefits are excluded from the gross income of an employee by special provisions in the tax law:

- The value of child care services paid by an employer, enabling the employee to work, limited to the lesser of $5,000 annually ($2,250 if married, filing separately), or the taxpayer's earned income. For married taxpayers, the earned income of the spouse with the lesser amount of earned income is used for the limitation.

- The value of the benefits under a qualified group legal services plan, limited to $70 annual premium value per employee.

- The value of gymnasium and athletic facilities.

- Qualified employer provided educational assistance, limited to $5,250 annual amount.

- Undergraduate tuition reductions granted to family members of an employee of a nonprofit educational institution.

    B.   A cafeteria plan is an employee plan that offers employee a choice between cash and some other form of compensation (benefit). If a plan meets the requirements under the tax law, then the employee can choose between nontaxable benefits (e.g. health insurance) or taxable income in the form of a cash payment.

    C.   The tax law establishes four broad classes of nontaxable employee benefits. These benefits are:

- No-additional cost services. An employee of an airline can fly for free if the seat would otherwise be empty.

- Qualified employee discounts. In the case of services, employees do not have to report as income employee discounts up to 20 percent. In the case of property, employees do not have to report as income employee discounts provided the discount does not exceed the employer's gross profit margin. The exclusion is not available for real property.

- Working condition fringes. Employees can exclude those items from gross income that would be deductible if the employees had paid them. In addition, certain nondeductible items such as free parking do not have to be included as income.

- *De minimis* fringes. Small benefits, such as using the company copy machine, do not have to be reported as income.

X.   FOREIGN EARNED INCOME

   A.   A U.S. citizen is generally subject to U.S. tax on total worldwide income. However, qualified U.S. citizens working abroad can exclude up to $70,000 per year of earned income. In addition, an exclusion is allowed for a reasonable amount of housing costs in the foreign country in excess of a base amount. The base amount of "housing allowance " is 16 percent of the pay for a GS-14 (Step 1) Federal employee.

   B.   To qualify for the exclusion the taxpayer must either be a resident of the foreign country, or present in the country for 330 days during any 12 consecutive months.

   C.   The taxpayer may include the foreign income in gross income and elect to claim a credit for foreign taxes paid as an alternative to (A) above.

XI.   INTEREST ON CERTAIN STATE AND LOCAL GOVERNMENT OBLIGATIONS

   A.   Taxpayers can exclude interest on the "obligations of state and local governments" from their gross income. However, the interest on certain types of state and local government bonds is taxable.

XII.   DIVIDENDS

   A.   A dividend payment to a shareholder with respect to the ownership of stock is normally included in income to the extent of the corporation's earnings and profits. Distributions in excess of earnings and profits are a nontaxable recovery of capital to the extent of the taxpayer's basis in the corporation's stock and any distributions in excess of basis are taxed as capital gains.

   B.   The following items are not considered regular dividends for tax purposes:

- payments received on savings and loan association deposits,

- patronage dividends from cooperatives,

- mutual life insurance dividends, and

- capital gain distributions from mutual funds.

C. Generally, no income is recognized on the receipt of stock dividends on stock.

XIII. EDUCATIONAL SAVINGS BONDS

A. For certain savings bonds issued after 1989, an exclusion is available with respect to bonds redeemed to provide funding for higher education. Taxpayers may exclude interest on Series EE savings bonds that are redeemed to pay for qualified higher education expenses. To qualify the following requirements must be met:

- The bonds must be issued after December 31, 1989, and

- The bonds must be issued to an individual who is at least 24 years old at the time of issuance.

B. Once modified adjusted gross income exceeds $40,000 ($60,000 on a joint return) the exclusion begins to be phased out. The exclusion is phased out entirely when modified adjusted gross income reaches $55,000 ($90,000 on a joint return). See text for the exclusion calculation.

XIV. TAX BENEFIT RULE

A. Under the tax benefit rule, if a taxpayer obtains a deduction for an item in one tax year and in a later year recovers a portion of the prior deduction, the recovery is included in taxable income in the year it is received. Examples of items subject to this rule include bad debts, prior taxes, and delinquency amounts.

B. The recovery of a deduction which did not yield a tax benefit in a prior year is not included in gross income under the tax benefit rule.

XV.   INCOME FROM DISCHARGE OF INDEBTEDNESS

A.   The transfer of appreciated property in satisfaction of a debt is treated first as a sale of the property and then as payment of the debt. Any gain on the sale of the property must be recognized as income.

B.   Under the Bankruptcy Act, the discharge of indebtedness is not recognized as income to the taxpayer whose debt is forgiven. The realized gain from the discharge of the debt is applied against the taxpayer's basis in the assets, effectively deferring the gain until the assets are sold.

TEST FOR SELF-EVALUATION

True or False

Indicate which of the following statements are true or false by circling the correct answer.

T   F   1.   Public assistance payments (welfare) are generally nontaxable.

T   F   2.   Gifts in a business setting are always excluded from gross income.

T   F   3.   A $5,000 employee death benefit exclusion is allowed to the beneficiaries of the employee.

T   F   4.   Life insurance proceeds are always excluded from the gross income of the recipient.

T   F   5.   The interest element received by a beneficiary on life insurance proceeds taken in installments is excluded from income.

T   F   6.   A transfer of appreciated property in satisfaction of a debt is a realizable event for income tax purposes.

T   F   7.   The maximum exclusion for employee child care fringe benefits is $5,000 per year.

T   F   8.   Under the tax benefit rule if a taxpayer obtains a deduction in one year and later recovers a portion of the prior deduction, the recovery produces taxable income.

T   F   9.   There are limits on the use of tax-exempt bonds to finance private business activities.

T   F   10. A United States citizen is generally subject to U.S. tax on his total income regardless of the geographic origin of the income.

T   F   11. To be excluded from gross income, meals furnished by an employer to an employee must be on the business premises and be for the convenience of the employer.

T   F   12. Workers' compensation benefits are included in the gross income of the taxpayer receiving the benefits.

T   F   13. The maximum foreign earned income exclusion is $70,000, plus a limited exclusion for foreign housing costs.

T   F   14. To qualify for the foreign earned income exclusion, the taxpayer must be either a bona fide resident of the foreign country or present in the country for 250 days during any 12 consecutive months.

T   F   15. Dividends on a mutual life insurance policy are taxable to the owner of the policy only if the policy has a cash surrender value of $5,000 or more.

T   F   16. "Cafeteria" plans allow employees to choose nontaxable benefits rather than cash compensation and have the benefits remain nontaxable to the employee.

T   F   17. Ministers can exclude from gross income the rental value of a home furnished as compensation or a rental allowance used to provide a home.

T   F   18. Professor Gomez's son is enrolled as an undergraduate student at the nonprofit university where he teaches. The university waived the tuition of $6,000 for the son. Professor Gomez must include the $6,000 in his income because his son went to school for free.

T   F   19. Scholarship income used for expenses of room and board is treated as earned income for purposes of calculating the standard deduction for one who is claimed as a dependent of another taxpayer.

T   F   20. If the amount of a scholarship eligible for exclusion is not known at year end the transaction is held open until the education expenses are paid.

T   F   21. Generally, punitive damages are not taxed to the recipient because they represent a penalty to the person causing the damages.

T   F   22.   Generally, if an employee has an option of taking cash instead of employer-provided housing then the amount is taxable.

T   F   23.   Employer-paid parking for company officers qualifies as a working condition fringe benefit and would not be income to the officers.

T   F   24.   The annuity rules are used to apportion an installment payment of life insurance proceeds between the principal and interest on earnings from reinvestment of the life insurance proceeds.

T   F   25.   Under a Cafeteria plan, an employee is permitted to choose between cash and nontaxble benefits (e.g. child care).

Fill-in-the-Blanks

Complete the following statements with the appropriate word(s) or amount(s).

1.   Amounts received as qualified scholarships to cover the cost of tuition and related expenses are _____ from gross income.

2.   To be excluded from gross income, meals must be on the _____ _____ of the employer and be furnished for the _____ of the employer.

3.   U.S. taxpayers are allowed a _____ against U.S. tax for foreign income taxes paid.

4.   The interest on _____ and _____ government bonds is usually exempt from the Federal income tax.

5.   If a taxpayer obtains a deduction for an item in one year and later recovers a portion of that deduction, the recovery produces income under the tax _____ rule.

Multiple Choice

In each of the following independent situations, Questions 1 through 7, indicate the amount "included" in 1992 gross income for T. (Note: Unless otherwise stated, assume T is a cash basis calendar year individual taxpayer and the year involved is 1992).

_____ 1. T, a single taxpayer, received $1,100 in dividends on his Texaco Inc. stock and
$600 on Harrod stock (a U.K. Corporation).
a. $-0-
b. $1,100
c. $1,700
d. $1,600
e. Some other amount

_____ 2. T received gifts of $7,000 in cash and an automobile with a fair market value
of $2,000 (cost $12,000).
a. $-0-
b. $2,000
c. $7,000
d. $9,000
e. Some other amount

_____ 3. T Corporation sues Z Corporation and recovers $500,000 lost income damages
and $300,000 in punitive damages for loss of income.
a. $-0-
b. $300,000
c. $500,000
d. $800,000
e. Some other amount.

_____ 4. T recovered $10,000 of $18,000 that was deducted for tax purposes in 1990.
a. $-0-
b. $10,000
c. $15,000
d. $5,000
e. Some other amount

_____ 5. On the death of his father, T received $50,000 (cash value of the policy is
$24,000) as the beneficiary of his father's life insurance policy.
a. $-0-
b. $50,000
c. $24,000
d. $26,000
e. Some other amount

_____ 6. T inherited several AT&T bonds. The bonds had a fair market value of
$70,000 at the date of death. After receiving the bonds, he was also paid
$2,000 in interest.

a. $-0-
b. $72,000
c. $70,000
d. $2,000
e. Some other amount

_____ 7. As the result of an accident on the job T is disabled. Under workers' compensation insurance, he received $7,200.
a. $-0-
b. $2,000
c. $7,200
d. Some other amount

_____ 8. Pat Brown (a single taxpayer) received the following income for 1992.

Salary	$30,000
Dividends from G.M. stock	1,000
Interest on City of Houston bonds	2,000
Life insurance proceeds	10,000
Dividends on Mexican stock	1,600

What is Pat's gross income for 1992?
a. $42,600
b. $31,000
c. $32,600
d. $30,000
e. Some other amount

_____ 9. Sam Houston died in the current year. His employer paid $8,000 to his widow and $4,000 each to his two children as a qualified death benefit. Of the $8,000 she received, how much may his widow exclude from her gross income?
a. $-0-
b. $2,500
c. $5,000
d. $8,000
e. Some other amount

_____ 10. T works for a hospital which provides employees free meals in a lunch room. During 1992 the value of the meals received by T are $2,300. If T had eaten all the meals available at the hospital, he would have eaten $4,800 worth of meals. The reason the hospital provides the meals is so that employees will be available for emergencies. How much will T have to include in his income

from the free meals?
a. $-0-
b. $2,300
c. $4,800
d. $2,500
e. Some other amount.

_____ 11. In the current year Armadillo Airlines covers an employee with a qualified dental plan at a cost of $200. In addition, its employees are allowed to fly for free on a standby basis, and this same employee takes free flights valued at $3,000. The employee is also provided with free parking at the airport worth $400 per year. Of these amounts, how much must the employee include in his gross income for the current year?
a. $-0-
b. $200
c. $3,200
d. $3,600
e. Some other amount

_____ 12. Chris Audette had adjusted gross income of $5,000 after deducting a bad debt of $2,000. Her itemized deductions and personal exemptions were $6,600. The next year, much to her surprise, Chris collected the bad debt. How much must she include in income for the year of recovery?
a. $-0-
b. $200
c. $400
d. $1,000
e. Some other amount

_____ 13. Janis Rasmussen owed Friendly Bank and Trust $50,000 on an unsecured note. She paid off the note with stock worth $50,000 (basis of $40,000). How much gain must Janis recognize on the transfer of the stock to the bank?
a. -0-
b. $10,000
c. $40,000
d. $50,000
e. Some other amount

_____ 14. Mike Fontaine is an employee of Mega Corporation. As an employee, Mike received the following fringe benefits.

Benefit	Value
Free use of company gym	$200
10% discount on $250 TV (employer's standard gross profit margin, 25%)	25
Free company parking	400
Personal use of copy machine	8

If the plan does not discriminate, what amount of these fringe benefits must Mike report as income on his tax return?

a. $-0-
b. $1,233
c. $600
d. $400
e. Some other amount

_____ 15. During the current year Alfred Allen sustained a serious injury while on the job. As a result of his injury, Allen received the following amounts during the same year:

Workers' compensation payments	$2,400
Reimbursement from employer's accident and health plan for medical expenses paid by Allen	1,800
Damages for personal injuries	8,000

How much of the above amounts should Allen include in his gross income for the current year?
a. $12,200
b. $8,000
c. $1,800
d. $-0-
e. Some other amount

Use the following information for Questions 16 through 19.

Laura Lewis has been legally separated from her husband, Herman, since 1990. Their three-year old son, Ronald, lived with Laura for the entire year of 1992. Under the written separation agreement between Laura and Herman, Herman is obligated to pay Laura $300 per month for alimony and $200 per month for child support, or a total of $6,000 annually. However Laura received a total of only $300 from Herman during 1992. Laura's other income in 1992 was from the following sources:

Salary	$20,000
Interest on savings account	100
Interest on federal income tax refund	60

In addition, Laura's father, Albert, gave Laura a gift of 500 shares of Liba Corporation common stock in 1992. Albert's basis for the stock was $4,000. At the date of the gift, the fair market value of the Liba stock was $3,000.

_____ 16. What is Laura's filing status for 1992?
   a. Single
   b. Married filing separate return
   c. Unmarried head of household
   d. Married head of household
   e. None of the above

_____ 17. How much alimony is included in Laura's 1992 taxable income?
   a. $-0-
   b. $300
   c. $3,600
   d. $6,000
   e. Some other amount

_____ 18. How much interest is included in Laura's 1992 taxable income?
   a. $-0-
   b. $60
   c. $100
   d. $160
   e. Some other amount

_____ 19. How much is included in Laura's 1992 taxable income for the 500 shares of Liba stock?
   a. $-0-
   b. $3,000
   c. $3,500
   d. $4,000
   e. Some other amount

Use the following information for Questions 20 through 22.

John Budd, who was 58 at the time of his death on July 1, 1992, received

$1,000 of interest in 1992 on municipal bonds. John's wife Emma, age 57, received a $300 television set in 1992 as a "gift" for opening a long-term savings account at a bank. On John's death, Emma received life insurance proceeds of $60,000 under a group policy paid for by John's employer. In addition, an employee death benefit of $7,500 was paid to Emma by John's employer. Emma did not remarry in 1992. Emma is the executrix of John's estate.

_____ 20. How much taxable interest was received by John and Emma in 1992?
    a. $-0-
    b. $300
    c. $1,000
    d. $1,300
    e. Some other amount

_____ 21. How much of the group-term life insurance proceeds should be excluded from 1992 taxable income?
    a. $-0-
    b. $5,000
    c. $50,000
    d. $60,000
    e. Some other amount

_____ 22. How much of the employee death benefit should be excluded from 1992 taxable income?
    a. $-0-
    b. $4,500
    c. $5,000
    d. $7,500
    e. Some other amount

_____ 23. In 1991, Claire Gracies' proceeds from the redemption of qualified educational savings bonds during the taxable year were $10,000 (principal of $6,000 and interest of $4,000). Her qualified higher education expenses were $8,000. How much of the interest is excludible (before any phase out)?
    a. $-0-
    b. $4,000
    c. $3,200
    d. $2,400
    e. Some other amount

_____ 24. Assume the same facts as in question 23, except Claire's modified adjusted gross income is $49,000 and she files as a single taxpayer. How much interest is excludible after the phase out?

a. $-0-
b. $3,200
c. $1,504
d. $1,696
e. Some other amount

_____ 25. A, age 20, is a full-time student at Small State University and is studying for his bachelor's degree. During 1992 he received the following cash payments:

Scholarship		
Books and tuition	$5,000	
Meals and lodging	2,000	$7,000
Interest income		600
Cash support from a rich uncle		2,000
Loan from financial aid office		$4,000

What is A's adjusted gross income for 1992?

a. $-0-
b. $2,600
c. $7,600
d. $11,600
e. Some other amount

_____ 26. P purchased an insurance policy on his life with his son as the beneficiary. P paid $28,000 in premiums. The policy had a cash surrender value of $34,000 when P died and his son collected the face amount of $150,000. How much income must the son report as beneficiary of the policy?

a. $-0-
b. $28,000
c. $34,000
d. $150,000
e. Some other amount

_____ 27. In 1992, Z was required to pay $200 of interest and $100 of penalties because her tax return was filed late. The return was late because her CPA was overworked and did not get a chance to finish the return. The CPA reimbursed Z $300 for the interest and penalties due the IRS. How much of the reimbursement is income to Z?

a. $-0-
b. $100

c. $200
d. $300
e. Some other amount

_____ 28. During 1992, F was reimbursed by his employer sponsored health insurance plan for the following medical expenses:

Doctor visits	$2,000
Hospital stay for son's illness	5,000
Cost of hair transplant	3,000
Prescription drugs	2,000

How much income (if any) must F report from these reimbursements?
a. $-0-
b. $2,000
c. $3,000
d. $12,000
e. Some other amount

_____ 29. BAD Corporation's management is allowed to purchase goods from the company for a 20% discount and all other employees are allowed a 10% discount. The employer's usual gross profit margin is 25%. B, president of the company, purchased from BAD Corporation goods for $1,600 when the price charged to customers was $2,000. How much income must B report from the purchase of the goods?
a. $-0-
b. $400
c. $1,600
d. $200
e. Some other amount

_____ 30. Big Private University (BPU) allows the children of employees the attend for a special tuition rate that is 30% of the regular tuition. T is an employee of BPU and her child attends the school on a full time basis (paying the special tuition rate). Regular tuition at BPU is $10,000 per year. How much does T have to include in income from the tuition reduction?
a. $-0-
b. $3,000
c. $7,000
d. $10,000
e. Some other amount

_____ 31. T qualifies for the foreign earned income credit. He was present in Ecuador for all of 19x2, except for 21 days when she was in the U.S. T's salary for 19x2 was $80,000. What is T's earned income exclusion?
   a. $-0-
   b. $65,973
   c. $70,000
   d. $80,000
   e. Some other amount

Code Section Recognition

Indicate, by number, the appropriate Code Section where the following items are found.

_____ 1. Gifts and inheritances.

_____ 2. Life insurance proceeds.

_____ 3. Scholarships.

_____ 4. Workers' compensation.

_____ 5. Exclusion for meals and lodging.

_____ 6. Interest on state and local obligations.

_____ 7. Tax benefit rule.

_____ 8. Exclusion for higher education savings bonds interest

SOLUTIONS TO CHAPTER 5

True or False

1. True (p. 5-3)

2. False Gifts in a business setting may be included in gross income. (p. 5-4)

3. True (p. 5-7)

4.   False   Proceeds may be included in gross income if the policy was transferred for valuable consideration. (p. 5-5)

5.   False   The interest portion of the installment payment received is generally included in income. (p. 5-6)

6.   True   (p. 5-26)

7.   True   (p. 5-15)

8.   True   (p. 5-25)

9.   True   (p. 5-23)

10. True   (p. 5-13)

11. True   (p. 5-13)

12. False   Workers' compensation is excluded from gross income. (p. 5-11)

13. True   (p. 5-22)

14. False   330 days, not 250 days. (p. 5-21)

15. False   The dividends are not dividends. (p.5-24)

16. True   (p. 5-16)

17. True   (p. 5-15)

18. False   The tuition reduction is not income to Professor Gomez. (p. 5-9)

19. True   (p. 5-8)

20. True   (p. 5-8)

21. False   Punitive damages are included in gross income unless they are considered compensation for physical injuries or physical sickness. (p. 5-11)

22. True   (p. 5-14)

23. True   (pp. 5-19)

24.　True　(p. 5-6)

25.　True　(p. 5-16)

Fill-in-the-Blanks

1.　excluded (p. 5-8)

2.　business premises, convenience (p. 5-13)

3.　credit (p. 5-21)

4.　state, local (p. 5-22)

5.　benefit (p. 5-25)

Multiple Choice

1.　C　$1,100 + 600 = $1,700. (p. 5-23)

2.　A　(p. 5-2)

3.　D　$300,000 + 500,000 = $800,000 (p. 5-9, 11)

4.　B　(p. 5-25)

5.　A　(p. 5-4)

6.　D　(p. 5-2)

7.　A　(p. 5-11)

8.　C　$30,000 + 1,000 + 1,600 = $32,600. (pp. 5-4, 5-22, 5-23)

9.　B　($8,000/$16,000) x $5,000 = $2,500 excluded. (p. 5-7)

10.　A　(p. 5-13)

11.　A　(pp. 5-12, 17, 19)

12.   C $7,000 - 6,600 = $400 tax benefit from deduction. (p. 5-27)

13.   B $50,000 - 40,000 = $10,000 (p. 5-26)

14.   A · (pp. 5-17-19)

15.   D   (pp. 5-10-12)

16.   C   Chapter 3

17.   A   Chapter 4

18.   D   Chapter 4

19.   A   (p. 5-2)

20.   B   The value of the T.V. set "gift" is interest. (p. 5-4)

21.   D   (p. 5-4)

22   C   (p. 5-7)

23.   C   ($8,000/$10,000) x $4,000 = $3,200. (p. 5-25)

24.   D $3,200 - [(($49,000 - 41,950)/$15,000) x $3,200] = $1,696. (p. 5-25)

25.   B $2,000 + 600 = $2,600. (p. 5-8)

26.   A   (p. 5-4)

27.   A   Since the reimbursement is for amounts that are not deductible (personal interest and penalties), none of the reimbursement is included in income. (p. 5-25)

28.   C   Cosmetic surgery is not allowed as a medical deduction; therefore the reimbursement is included in gross income. (p. 5-12)

29.   B   The plan discriminated therefore the discount is income. (p. 5-19)

30.   A   (p. 5-9)

31.   B   (344 days/365 days) x $70,000 = $65,973. (p. 5-22)

Code Section Recognition

1. § 102

2. § 101

3. § 117

4. § 104

5. § 119

6. § 103

7. § 111

8. § 135

CHAPTER

6

DEDUCTIONS AND LOSSES: IN GENERAL

CHAPTER HIGHLIGHTS

All deductions are a matter of legislative grace. For an expenditure to be deductible, it must be specifically authorized by Congress. This chapter introduces and classifies deductions *for* adjusted gross income and deductions *from* adjusted gross income. Specific provisions in the tax law which disallow or limit certain deductions are discussed in detail.

I.   CLASSIFICATION OF DEDUCTIONS

A.   Deductions of individual taxpayers fall into one of two classifications, deductions *for* adjusted gross income, or deductions *from* adjusted gross income.

Section 62 specifies the expenses which are deductible for adjusted gross income. The common deductions *for* AGI include:

- trade or business deductions

- certain reimbursed employee business expenses

- losses on the sale of property other than personal use property

- rent and royalty expenses

- alimony payments (Section 215)

- contributions to self-employed retirement plans

- deductions for retirement savings (Section 219)

- a portion of certain lump-sum pension distributions

The more common deductions *from* AGI include:

- expenses for the production or collection of income

- expenses for the management, conservation, or maintenance of property held for the production of income

- expenses for the determination, collection, or refund of any tax

- charitable contributions

- medical expenses in excess of 7.5 percent of adjusted gross income

- certain state and local taxes (e.g. real estate, state and local income taxes)

- personal casualty losses

- certain personal interest

- certain miscellaneous deductions (in excess of 2% of AGI).

Deductions related to the production of rent and royalty income are deductions *for* adjusted gross income.

B.   Trade or business expenses are deductible *for* AGI. For any business expenditure to be deductible, it must be "ordinary and necessary." An ordinary expense is one that is normal, usual, or customary in the type of business being conducted by the taxpayer. A necessary expense is one that is appropriate and helpful in furthering the taxpayer's trade or business. Certain payments such as charitable contributions, illegal bribes and kickbacks, and fines and penalties are excluded as trade or business deductions.

C.   Reasonableness Requirement. Besides being ordinary and necessary, the Code specifies that salaries must be "reasonable." The courts have expanded this requirement to cover all business expenses.

II.   TIMING OF EXPENSE RECOGNITION

A.   Timing of Expense Recognition. In general, the taxpayer's method of accounting (cash or accrual) will determine the period in which a deduction can be taken. There are limitations on the use of the cash method of accounting by certain taxpayers.

B.   The expenses of cash basis taxpayers must be paid in cash before they can be deducted. The issuance of a note or other promise to pay does not qualify as a cash payment. Cash basis taxpayers, as well as accrual basis taxpayers, cannot deduct capital expenditures.

C.   Accrual basis taxpayers can deduct an expense by meeting the "economic performance test." This test is met only when the service, property, or use of property giving rise to the liability is actually performed for, provided to, or used by the taxpayer.

II.   DISALLOWANCE POSSIBILITIES

A.   Public Policy Limitation. The Code denies a deduction for an expenditure that is against public policy. Expenses that are against public policy include bribes, kickbacks, fines, and penalties. In general, legal expenses are deductible if incurred in the taxpayer's trade or business.

The usual expenses relating to the operation of illegal business, other than those contrary to public policy, are deductible. However, under the tax law illegal drug traffickers are not allowed a deduction for the ordinary and necessary expenses incurred in their business. They are only allowed a deduction for cost of goods sold.

B.   Political Contributions and Lobbying Activities. Generally, no business deduction is allowed for political contributions. A taxpayer may deduct certain lobbying expenditures if he has a direct interest in the proposed legislation. Dues or expenses paid to an organization of individuals with a common direct interest in proposed legislation are also deductible. Expenses which are incurred to influence the public on political matters may not be deducted.

C.   Investigation expenses for determining the feasibility of entering a new business or expanding an existing business are deductible if the taxpayer is already engaged in a similar business. If the taxpayer is not engaged in a similar business, and a new business is acquired, such expenses are capitalized and may be amortized over 60 months or more. In the event the new business is not acquired, investigation expenses are usually nondeductible.

D. Hobby Losses. Under § 183, if a taxpayer can show that an activity was entered into with the intent of making a profit, and not for personal pleasure, then any losses are fully deductible.

The hobby loss rules apply when the taxpayer cannot show that the activity was engaged in for profit. Hobby expenses are only deductible up to the amount of hobby income. The expenses are deductible in the following order:

- amounts deductible under other Code sections (e.g. property taxes)

- amounts deductible as if the activity is engaged in for profit, but only if those amounts do not affect the basis of property (e.g. maintenance).

- amounts deductible as if the activity is engaged in for profit which affect the basis of property (e.g. depreciation).

The tax law states that if a profit is made for "three of five consecutive years" (two of seven years for activities involving horses) then the activity is presumed to be engaged in for profit, and the hobby loss rules do not apply.

If the above presumption is not met, the activity may still qualify as a business if the taxpayer can show a profit-making intent. The Regulations stipulate nine relevant factors in distinguishing between profit seeking activities and hobbies. The relevant factors are:

- whether the activity is conducted in a business like manner

- the expertise of the taxpayers

- time and effort expended

- expectation that the assets will appreciate

- the previous success of the taxpayer in similar activities

- the history of income and loss from the activity

- the relationship of profits to losses

- the financial status of the taxpayer

- elements of personal pleasure in the activity

E.   Vacation homes have loss rules similar to the hobby loss provisions. If the home is rented for 15 days or more and is used for personal purposes for more than the greater of 14 days or 10 percent of the days actually rented, then the deductions for depreciation, maintenance, etc., will be limited to the revenue generated. If the home is rented for 15 days or more, but personal use is not more than the greater of 14 days or 10 percent of the days rented, the home is considered rental property. Finally, if the vacation home is rented for less than 15 days, all rental income is excluded and all rental expenses, other than mortgage interest and property taxes, are disallowed.

Expenses must be allocated between personal and rental days. Expenses, other than property taxes and interest, are allocated on the basis of the total days of use. The IRS and the courts disagree on the allocation of taxes and interest. According to the courts, taxes and interest are to be allocated on the basis of 365 days; however, according to the IRS taxes and interest should be allocated in the same manner as other expenses, on the basis of total days of use.

F.   Expenditures Incurred for the Taxpayer's Benefit or Obligation. For an expenditure to be deductible, it must be incurred for the taxpayer's "benefit or be the taxpayer's obligation." Thus a taxpayer cannot claim a deduction for paying the expenses of another individual.

G.   Disallowance of Personal Expenditures.

No deduction is allowed for personal, living, or family expenses unless specifically provided in the Code. Exceptions provided in the Code include:

- charitable expenses

- medical expenses

- expenses for the determination, collection, or refund of tax

- tax advice in divorce proceedings

H. Disallowance of Unrealized Losses. For a loss to be deductible, a loss must in fact be realized by the taxpayer. "Losses in value" will not cause a tax deduction. Any loss deducted is limited to the taxpayer's adjusted basis in the asset.

I. Disallowance of Deductions for Capital Expenditures. Capital expenditures related to depreciable or amortizable property are added to the basis of the property and may be written off over the life of the property. Often it is difficult to distinguish repairs and maintenance from capital expenditures. The Code defines a capital expenditure as "any amount paid out for new buildings or for permanent improvements or betterments made to increase the value of any property or estate." Other expenditures are considered repairs and maintenance.

In some cases, taxpayers are permitted an election to capitalize certain expenditures, such as property taxes, which would otherwise be currently expensed.

Exceptions in the Code regarding the deductibility of capital expenditures include the election to expense certain mineral development costs, intangible drilling costs, qualified farm land clearing expenditures, and research expenditures.

J. Transactions Between Related Parties. The tax law places restrictions on transactions between certain related parties due to the potential for "sham" transactions and tax avoidance schemes. Losses and unpaid expenses and interest are "not deductible" if incurred between related parties. However, any disallowed loss may be used to reduce a future gain on the property.

Related parties (as defined in § 267) include:

- siblings, spouses, ancestors, and lineal descendants of the taxpayer

- a corporation owned more than 50 percent (directly or indirectly) by the taxpayer

- two corporations that are members of a controlled group

- a series of other complex relationships between trusts, corporations, estates, and individual taxpayers

Under the constructive ownership rules, stock owned by certain related parties is deemed to be owned by the taxpayer for the disallowance provisions.

K.   Substantiation Requirements. To be deductible, expenses must be substantiated by the taxpayer.   Travel, entertainment, and business gifts must satisfy more stringent substantiation requirements.

L.   Expenses Related to Tax-Exempt Income.   No deduction is allowed for expenses (including interest expense incurred to purchase or carry tax-exempt obligations) related to the production of tax-exempt income.

TEST FOR SELF-EVALUATION

True or False

Indicate which of the following statements are true or false by circling the correct answers.

T   F   1.   The courts have established the doctrine that an item is not deductible unless a specific Code provision allows the deduction.

T   F   2.   To be deductible under § 162 or § 212, an item must be ordinary and necessary.

T   F   3.   Alimony, medical expenses, and state and local taxes are deductions from adjusted gross income.

T   F   4.   The term "trade or business" is clearly defined by statute in the Code.

T   F   5.   Expenses incurred in the determination, collection, or refund of any tax are deductible under § 212.

T   F   6.   To be deductible, salaries must be reasonable.

T   F   7.   As a general rule, taxable income shall be computed under the method of accounting that the taxpayer regularly uses to compute income and keep his or her books.

T   F   8.   Accrual basis taxpayers cannot take a current deduction for capital expenditures except through amortiation or depreciation over the life of the asset.

T   F   9.   Legal expenses are never deductible as ordinary and necessary business expenses if incurred in a trade or business activity.

T   F   10.   In order for an accrual basis taxpayer to deduct an expense, it must pass the "economic performance test."

T   F   11.   Investigation expenses are always deductible by a taxpayer entering a new trade or business.

T   F   12.   If an activity shows a profit for three of five years (two of seven years for activities involving horses), then the Code presumes it is not a hobby.

T   F   13.   If a residence is rented for 15 days or more, § 280A limits the deductions related to the home if the taxpayer uses the home for personal purposes for more than the greater of 14 days or 10 percent of the days actually rented.

T   F   14.   A taxpayer can claim a deduction for interest he paid on his son's mortgage. (The son is not the taxpayer's dependent).

T   F   15.   In general, § 262 disallows deductions for personal, living, and family expenses.

T   F   16.   The tax law disallows a deduction for expenses incurred in producing tax-exempt income.

T   F   17.   Due to the voluntary nature of the tax law, upon audit the IRS bears the burden of determining the validity of the expenses deducted on the taxpayer's return.

T   F   18.   § 267 disallows losses and certain deductions between related parties.

T   F   19.   Goodwill is a depreciable asset for tax purposes.

T   F   20.   Personal legal fees are generally deductible by individual taxpayers.

T   F   21.   Expenses associated with a taxpayer's vacation home are deductible in full.

T   F   22.   To be deductible, an expense must be incurred for the taxpayer's benefit or arise from the taxpayer's obligation.

T   F   23.   Most expenses of hobbies (to the extent of income from the hobby) are deductible from AGI subject to the 2 percent of AGI limitation.

(T)   F   24.   The courts have held that taxes and interest on a vacation home should be allocated over 365 days a year, while the IRS has determined that taxes and interest should be allocated on the basis of total days of use.

(T)   F   25.   T rented her condo in Utah for 180 days. If T used the condo for 20 days of personal use, it would be classified as a "personal/rental" asset.

Fill-in-the-Blanks

Complete the following statements with the appropriate word(s) or amount(s).

1.   The items that are disallowed under the related party rules are _losses_ ~~personal~~, unpaid interest and unpaid expenses.

2.   The expenses of a residence which is rented for 15 days or more and is used for personal purposes for more than the greater of (1) _14 15_ days or (2) _10 %_ percent of the total days rented, must be limited to the rental income generated by the property.

3.   On December 1, 19X1, a taxpayer is required to pay three months rent, $3,000, on a building used in her business. If she is a cash basis taxpayer, her rent deduction for 19X1 is _3,000_.

4.   The nondeductibility of bribes, kickbacks, fines, and penalties is justified by being against _public_ _policy_.

5.   If an activity is deemed to be a hobby, the trade or business expenses are deductible only to the extent of the _income_ from the hobby.

6.   One basic concept in the tax law is that a deduction cannot be taken until a loss is _incurred (realized)_.

7.   § 212 allows a deduction for expenses due to the production or _collection_ of income.

8.   Expenses under the accrual method of accounting are deductible when _incurred_ and under the cash method when _~~expended~~ paid_.

9.   Lobbying expenditures are deductible provided the proposed legislation is of

direct
_____ _personal_ interest to the taxpayer.

Multiple Choice

Choose the best answer for each of the following questions.

_____ 1. Which of the following is not a deduction for adjusted gross income?
        a. Alimony
        b. State income tax
        c. Trade or business expenses
        d. IRA contributions
        e. None of the above

_____ 2. § 212 covers expenses for the production or collection of income and tax
        return preparation fees. Which of the following is not a § 212 deduction?
        a. Repair expense on a rental house
        b. A fee paid to a CPA for preparing a tax return
        c. Interest expense on a personal residence
        d. Safe deposit box rental used to store stock certificates
        e. None of the above

_____ 3. Elizabeth Kirk is a physician. In her spare time she wants to become a famous
        stock car racer. In the current year Elizabeth incurs the following costs:

Stock car purchases	$40,000
Entry fees	5,000
Driving lessons	10,000
Travel expenses to races	15,000
	$70,000

        Of the races entered by Elizabeth this year, her total earnings are $250. In all
        probability, the IRS will allow Elizabeth to deduct what amount of the above
        expenditures (before any 2% limit)?
        a. -0-
        b. $250
        c. $30,000
        d. $70,000
        e. None of the above

_____ 4. Under § 183, if an activity is not engaged in for profit, deductions related to
        the activity will be limited. Which of the following is likely to be deemed a

hobby by the IRS?

a. A CPA in private practice

b. A ranch owned by an executive that has shown a profit for four of the last five years

c. An individual borrowing money to open a gift shop

d. A physician who operates a photography studio at a loss for five consecutive years

e. None of the above

_____ 5. Several years ago, Mary Smith purchased a house on a hillside in California for $150,000 to be used as her personal residence. During the current year there is a recession in the local area. As a result, her house is now worth only $80,000 (which can be substantiated by Mary). Mary's deductible tax loss for the current year is:

a. -0-

b. $70,000

c. $80,000

d. $150,000

e. Some other amount

_____ 6. During the current year, Lee Marvin pays $5,000 to an attorney to obtain a divorce. Of this amount, $2,000 is for tax advice about the divorce settlement. How much, if any, of the $5,000 is deductible before considering any limitation based on AGI?

a. -0-

b. $2,000

c. $3,000

d. $5,000

e. None of the above

_____ 7. David La Rue made illegal business kickbacks of $10,000 and paid fines of $8,000 during the current year. How much of the expenses can be deducted on his tax return before considering any limitation based on AGI?

a. -0-

b. $8,000

c. $10,000

d. $18,000

e. None of the above

_____ 8. If a taxpayer paid $5,000 interest on a note, the proceeds of which were used to purchase Texas state bonds, and the bonds produced interest income of $4,000, how much of an interest deduction would be allowed?

a. -0-
b. $1,000
c. $4,000
d. $5,000
e. None of the above

9. T owns 33 percent of the stock in T Corporation, 33 percent is owned by T's mother, and 33 percent by T's father. On January 1, 19X1, T loans T Corporation $100,000 at 9 percent interest annually. T Corporation is an "accrual" basis taxpayer while T is a cash basis taxpayer. T Corporation pays the current interest on December 29, 19X1. How much interest is deductible by T Corporation for 19X1?
    a. -0-
    b. $4,500
    c. $9,000
    d. None of the above

10. T pays $5,000 interest on his home mortgage, and pays $3,000 on his son's mortgage. The son does not qualify as T's dependent. How much of an interest deduction will T be allowed (before considering any limitations)?
    a. -0-
    b. $3,000
    c. $5,000
    d. $8,000
    e. None of the above

11. T rents her vacation home for 30 days and lives in it for 10 days during the current year. Her gross income from rent payments was $4,000 and she incurred the following expenses:

Taxes and interest	$3,000
Utilities and maintenance	800
Depreciation	4,000
Total	$7,800

Using the IRS approach, what amount of income or loss must T report from this rental?
    a. -0-
    b. $200 income
    c. $3,800 loss
    d. $1,850 loss
    e. None of the above

_____ 12. Robert Lee owns a chain of motels in California. He flies to Arizona to investigate the possibility of buying an automobile dealership. All of the expenses for the trip are deductible in the current year if:
    a. The automobile dealership is purchased
    b. The auto dealership is not purchased
    c. Would never be deductible
    d. Robert already owns an auto dealership and does not purchase the Arizona dealership
    e. None of the above

_____ 13. During the current year, Mary Burnette purchased a lot with an old house on it for $100,000. She immediately had the house demolished at a cost of $15,000. Four months later the lot is sold for $160,000. How much gain should be recognized by Mary?
    a. -0-
    b. $15,000
    c. $45,000
    d. $60,000
    e. None of the above

_____ 14. Under § 267(c), the disallowance between related parties provision, which of the following is not a related family member?
    a. Spouse
    b. Son or daughter
    c. Grandchild
    d. Grandparent
    e. All of the above are related

_____ 15. Which of the following expenses are not deductible under § 212?
    a. Trade or business expenses
    b. Expenses for the production of income
    c. Expenses for the management, conservation, or maintenance of property held for the production of income
    d. Expenses for the determination, collection, or refund of any tax
    e. None of the above

_____ 16. Pancho Suggs is in the business of importing certain illegal substances. In this business, Pancho incurs the following expenses:

Cost of goods sold	$200,000
Payoffs to customs agents	100,000
Cost of installing false bottom in trunk of car	10,000
Distribution expenses	50,000
Packaging (baggies)	5,000
Kickbacks to narcotic agents	75,000
	$440,000

Of the total, what amount would be deductible by Pancho?
a. -0-
b. $440,000
c. $340,000
d. $200,000
e. None of the above

_____ 17. During 1992 X, a single taxpayer, had a salary of $28,000 and incurred the following expenses:

Alimony paid	$5,000
Charitable contributions	1,000
Interest on home mortgage	6,000
Deductible contribution to an IRA	2,000
Moving expense	2,000
Real estate taxes	1,500

What is X's adjusted gross income for 1992?
a. $28,000
b. $26,000
c. $21,000
d. $19,000
e. Some other amount

_____ 18. Using the information from question 17, what is X's taxable income for 1992?
a. $8,350
b. $10,500
c. $11,500
d. $13,500
e. Some other amount

_____ 19. G, is self-employed. He hires his 19 year-old daughter (who has just passed introductory accounting with a D+) as an accountant for the summer at a rate of $25.00 per hour. G has a full-time bookkeeper who has worked for G for many years and he pays her $10.00 per hour. G, most likely, has a deductible business expenses as a result of the payments to his daughter of

a. $10.00 per hour
b. $15.00 per hour
c. $25.00 per hour
d. None of the above

_____ 20. B incurred the following expenses during the current year:

Interest on son's home mortgage	$6,000
Payment of son's property taxes	2,000
Payment of son's state income tax	1,000
Payment of son's gambling debts	3,000

What amount of the above can B consider in calculating her itemized deductions for the current year?

a. $-0-
b. $1,000
c. $3,000
d. $8,000
e. Some other amount

Code Section Recognition

Indicate by number the appropriate Code Section where the following items are found.

_____ 1. Deduction for trade or business expenses.

_____ 2. Deduction for expenses in producing income.

_____ 3. Loss deductions.

_____ 4. Deductions for adjusted gross income (AGI).

_____ 5. Hobby losses.

_____ 6. Vacation home rentals.

_____ 7. Losses between related parties.

_____ 8. Capital expenditures.

_____ 9. Expenses relating to tax-exempt income.

_____ 10. Casualty losses.

SOLUTIONS TO CHAPTER 6

True or False

1.   True   (p. 6-2)

2.   True   (p. 6-3)

3.   False   Alimony is a deduction for AGI. (p. 6-3)

4.   False   The term is not defined in the Code. (p. 6-4)

5.   True   (p. 6-3)

6.   True   (p. 6-5)

7.   True   (p. 6-7)

8.   True   (p. 6-8)

9.   False   Legal expenses which are incurred in connection with a trade or business are deductible. (p. 6-11)

10. True   (p. 6-9)

11. False   The expenses are not deductible. (p. 6-13)

12. True   (p. 6-14)

13. True   (p. 6-17)

14. False   The mortgage is not the taxpayer's obligation. (p. 6-19)

15. True   (p. 6-19)

16.   True   (p. 6-246)

17.   False   The burden of proof for substantiating expenses deducted is on the taxpayer. (p. 6-24)

18.   True   (p. 6-22)

19.   False   Goodwill is not amortizable for tax purposes. (p. 6-21)

20.   False   Personal legal fees, other than those related to tax advice, are not deductible. (p. 6-11)

21.   False   Vacation home expenses are limited to the income generated. (p. 6-16)

22.   True   (p. 6-19)

23.   True   (p. 6-14)

24.   True   (p. 6-17)

25.   True   (p. 6-17)

Fill-in-the-Blanks

1.   losses (p. 6-22)

2.   14, 10 (p. 6-17)

3. $3,000 (p. 6-8)

4.   public policy (p. 6-10)

5.   income (p. 6-14)

6.   realized (p. 6-21)

7.   collection (p. 6-3)

8.   incurred, paid (p. 6-8)

9.   direct (p. 6-12)

Multiple Choice

1. B (p. 6-2)

2. C (p. 6-3)

3. B (p. 6-14)

4. D (p. 6-14)

5. A Deductions are allowed only for losses that have been realized. (p. 6-21)

6. B (p. 6-11)

7. A (p. 6-11)

8. A (p. 6-24)

9. C 9% ($100,000) = $9,000; the interest is paid. (p. 6-23)

10. C (p. 6-19)

11. D Note: this is "rental" property because it is only used 10 days for personal purposes.

Gross income	$4,000	
Less: rental expenses		
Taxes & interest (75%)	-2,250	
Utilities and maintenance (75%)	-600	
Depreciation (75%)	-3,000	
Loss	-$1,850	(p. 6-16)

12. D (p. 6-13)

13. C $160,000 - 100,000 - 15,000 = $45,000. (p. 6-21)

14. E (p. 6-22)

15. A (p. 6-3)

16. D $200,000. Drug dealers are allowed cost of goods sold only. (p. 6-11)

17.   C   Salary $28,000
          IRA   -2,000
          Alimony   -5,000
          AGI $21,000   (p. 6-2)

18.   A   AGI $21,000
          Mortgage interest   -6,000
          Charitable contributions   -1,000
          Taxes   -1,500
          Moving expense   -2,000
          Exemption   -2,150
          Taxable income $ 8,350   (p. 6-3, prior chapter)

19.   A   Wage payments must be reasonable to be deductible. (p. 6-5)

20.   A   The payment must be for B's benefit or B's obligation. (p. 6-19)

Code Section Recognition

1.   § 162

2.   § 212

3.   § 165

4.   § 62

5.   § 183

6.   § 280A

7.   § 267

8.   § 263

9.   § 265

10.   § 165

CHAPTER

7

PASSIVE ACTIVITY LOSSES

CHAPTER HIGHLIGHTS

The treatment of at-risk amounts and passive losses is one of the areas of concern for many taxpayers. The purpose of these rules is to limit the use of tax shelters to reduce a taxpayer's tax liability. The rules for application of the at-risk rules and the passive loss limitation are very complex, but must be understood in order to have a working knowledge of the U.S. income tax system.

I.   THE TAX SHELTER PROBLEM

For many years tax shelters represented a popular way for taxpayers to avoid taxes. The ability of taxpayers to avoid or reduce tax through the use of tax shelters has been limited by the at-risk rules and the passive loss rules. These two provisions have made the tax shelter investments of the past nearly obsolete. If they make investments in many activities, especially real estate, taxpayers must have a working knowledge of these provisions because of their impact on tax liability.

II.   AT-RISK LIMITS

A.   The tax laws provide an at-risk limitation on losses from business and income-producing activities. A loss deduction is limited to the amount the taxpayer has at risk. The amount at risk is generally the sum of the following:

•   The adjusted basis of property and amount of cash contributed to the activity,

- Any amount borrowed for use in the activity for which the taxpayer has personal liability

- The taxpayer's share of the net earnings, decreased by the taxpayer's share of losses and withdrawals from the activity.

A taxpayer is not considered at risk with respect to borrowed amounts if either one of the following is true:

- The taxpayer is not personally liable for repayment of the debt (nonrecourse loans).

- The lender has an interest (other than as a creditor) in the activity (except to the extent provided by the Regulations).

Recapture of previously allowed losses occurs to the extent the at-risk amount is reduced below zero. This occurs when the amount at-risk is reduced by distributions to the taxpayer, changes in the status of debt from recourse to nonrecourse, or by any arrangement that affects the taxpayer's risk of loss.

Generally a taxpayer's amount at risk is determined separately with respect to separate activities. However, activities are treated as one activity if the activities constitute a trade or business and either of the following is true:

- The taxpayer actively participates in the management of the trade or business

- In the case of a partnership or S corporation, at least 65 percent of the entity's losses is allocable to persons who actively participate in the management of the trade or business.

III.   PASSIVE LOSS LIMITS

A.   Classification of Income and Losses.

For tax years after 1986, income and losses are classified into three categories:

- Active (salary, trade or business, etc.)

- Passive (rental income, etc.)

- Portfolio (interest, dividends, etc.)

Passive losses cannot be used to offset income from the other two categories. Any unused passive losses may be carried over to offset future passive income or used when the taxpayer disposes of his investment in the passive activity.

B. Taxpayers Subject to the Passive Loss Rules. The passive loss rules apply to individuals, estates, trusts, closely held C corporations, and personal service corporations. The reason that the passive loss rules apply to personal service corporations is to prevent taxpayers from sheltering personal service income by acquiring passive activities at the corporate level. A personal service corporation is a corporation which meets the following conditions:

- the principal activity is the performance of personal services, and

- services are substantially performed by owner-employees.

There is one important exception to the above rules for corporations. A "closely held" C corporation can deduct passive losses against active income but not portfolio income.

C. Disallowed Passive Losses.

Losses from passive activities acquired after October 22, 1986 are disallowed in full. The disallowance of passive losses for activities acquired before October 23, 1986 was phased in over a five-year period as follows:

1987	65% allowed
1988	40% allowed
1989	20% allowed
1990	10% allowed
1991 on	none

Although the phase-in rules do not apply in 1991 and future years, the rules are important to understand.

D. Passive Activities Defined.

A passive activity is defined under § 469 as:

- Any trade or business in which the taxpayer does not "materially participate."

- Any rental activity (regardless of the taxpayer's level of participation).

E.   Material Participation.

If a taxpayer materially participates in a nonrental activity, any loss from that activity will be treated as an active loss that can offset other active income. The Code provides that material participation requires the taxpayer to be involved in the operation of the activity on a regular, continuous and substantial basis. The Temporary Regulations provide the following specific tests.

- The individual participates in the activity for more than 500 hours during the year.

- The individual's participation in the activity for the year constitutes substantially all the participation in the activity of all individuals (including nonowner employees) for the year.

- The individual participates in the activity for more than 100 hours during the year, and the individual's participation in the activity for the year is not less than the participation of any other individual (including nonowner employees) for the year.

- The activity is a significant participation activity for the taxable year, and the individual's aggregate participation in all significant participation activities during the year exceeds 500 hours. A significant participation activity is one in which the individual's participation exceeds 100 hours during the year.

- The individual materially participated in the activity for any five taxable years (whether or not consecutive) during the ten taxable years that immediately precede the taxable year.

- The activity is a *personal service activity* and the individual materially participated in the activity for any three preceding taxable years (whether or not consecutive).

- Based on the facts and circumstances, the individual participates in the activity on a regular, continuous, and substantial basis during the year.

F.   Rental Activities.

According to the tax law, any rental activity is to be treated as a passive activity. A rental activity is defined as any activity where payments are principally for the use of tangible property.

There are six exceptions to the automatic treatment of an activity as a rental activity for purposes of the passive loss definition. These exceptions allow the activity to be excluded from automatic classification as a passive activity, but the activity is subject to the material participation test in order to avoid classification as a passive activity under the general rule. The six exceptions are as follows:

- The average period of customer use for such property is seven days or less.

- The average period of customer use for such property is 30 days or less, and significant personal services are provided by the owner of the property.

- Extraordinary personal services are provided by the owner of the property without regard to the average period of customer use.

- The rental of such property is treated as incidental to a non-rental activity of the taxpayer.

- The taxpayer customarily makes the property available during defined business hours for nonexclusive use by various customers.

- The property is provided for use in an activity conducted by a partnership, S corporation, or joint venture in which the taxpayer owns an interest.

G.   Calculation of Passive Losses.

Passive activity loss should be computed by performing the following two procedures:

- Compute the passive loss or income for each separate passive activity.

- Offset net passive income from profitable activities against net passive losses from unprofitable activities.

H. Identification of Passive Activity.

The Regulations provide guidance as to what constitutes an activity for passive activity purposes. The first step in determining what constitutes an activity is to identify a taxpayer's undertakings. Each undertaking is a separate activity. An undertaking may include diverse business and rental operations. The primary factors in identifying an undertaking are location and ownership. Generally, the rule provides that business and rental operations that are conducted at the same location and are owned by the same taxpayer are part of the same undertaking. Business and rental operations that are conducted at different locations or are not owned by the same person constitute separate undertakings.

The basic undertaking rule is modified if the undertaking includes both rental and nonrental operations. In this situation, the rental and nonrental operations must generally be treated as separate activities. Under a special rule, rental and nonrental activities may be treated as a single operation if either the rental or nonrental gross income is less than 20 percent of the gross income from the undertaking.

I. Income Not Treated as Passive. In calculating the passive income or loss from an activity, portfolio income is not considered unless the portfolio income arises in the ordinary course of business. A single activity may have both a passive loss and portfolio income.

J. Deductions Not Treated as Passive. In order for a deduction to be included in the calculation of a taxpayer's passive income or loss, the item must arise in connection with the conduct of a passive activity. Passive activity deductions do not include deductions or losses which are directly related to portfolio income or certain other expenses which are specified in the Regulations, for example, the deductions for qualified residence interest and charitable contributions.

K. Suspended Losses. If a passive loss is disallowed because of insufficient passive income to offset it, it becomes suspended. The at-risk limitations are applied first, as well as other provisions which influence the determination of taxable income, before a taxpayer's suspended loss under the passive loss provisions can be determined. A taxpayer's basis in the investment is reduced by deductions even if the deductions are not allowed in the current year because of the passive loss rules. Suspended losses are carried over indefinitely and are applied against future years' passive income. If the passive activity is disposed of, the suspended losses can be offset against active and portfolio income. Suspended losses for each passive activity must be determined separately on a prorata basis.

L. Passive Credits. Credits arising from passive activities can only be used against regular tax attributable to passive income. Any excess passive credits are carried over indefinitely into future years. If a taxpayer has a passive loss for a tax year, then no passive credits can be used. If the taxpayer's tax is calculated using the alternative minimum tax (see Chapter 12), then no passive credits can be used. The passive credit is lost if there is no regular tax generated when the activity is disposed of.

M. Real Estate Rental Activities. There is a limited exception for rental real estate activity losses. Under this special provision, up to $25,000 of losses on rental real estate activities of an individual may be deducted against active and portfolio income. This annual $25,000 deduction is reduced by 50 percent of the taxpayer's AGI in excess of $100,000. Thus, the entire deduction is phased out when AGI reaches $150,000. If a married taxpayer files separately, then the $25,000 deduction is normally reduced to zero. Adjusted gross income is calculated without regard to the IRA deduction, social security benefits, and net losses from passive activities. To qualify for the $25,000 deduction, the taxpayer must meet the following two requirements:

- Actively participate in the rental activity.

- Own 10 percent or more of all interests in the activity.

The $25,000 allowance is considered only after all qualifying rental real estate losses and gains are netted against other passive income. Losses in excess of the $25,000 allowance are passive losses.

N. Dispositions of Passive Interests.

When a taxpayer disposes of his or her entire interest in a passive activity, any disallowed suspended losses are deductible. In general, if the current and suspended losses of passive activities exceed the gain realized or if the sale results in a realized loss, the sum of the following is treated as a loss which is not from a passive activity:

- Any loss from the activity for the tax year (including suspended losses of the activity disposed of), plus

- Any loss realized on the disposition in excess of net income or gain for the tax year from all passive activities (without regard to the activity disposed of).

TEST FOR SELF-EVALUATION

True or False

Indicate which of the following statements are true or false by circling the correct answer.

(T) F   1.   In general, the passive loss rules apply to real estate rental activities for tax years after 1986.

T   **(F)**   2.   All debt on property qualifies as an amount at risk.

T   **(F)**   3.   In general, the deduction of passive losses against active and portfolio income is not allowed.

T   **(F)**   4.   The $25,000 exception for rental real estate losses applies only to corporations and partnerships.

(T) F   5.   In general, the special $25,000 allowance for rental real estate losses is reduced by 50% of a taxpayer's modified AGI over $100,000.

(T) F   6.   An investment as a limited partner is a passive activity for purposes of the tax law.

T   **(F)**   7.   Credits from passive activities can be used to offset a taxpayer's regular tax liability arising from passive income or a taxpayer's alternative minimum tax liability arising from passive income.

T   **(F)**   8.   Passive credits are carried back three years and then forward for ten years, and if not used in that time period they are lost forever.

T   **(F)**   9.   The amount at-risk is decreased each year by the taxpayer's share of income and by the taxpayer's share of losses and withdrawals from the activity.

T   **(F)**   10.   Recapture of previously allowed losses occurs to the extent the at-risk amount is reduced below zero.

(T) F   11.   Generally, a taxpayer's amount at-risk is separately determined with respect to separate activities.

T F   12. Passive loss rules apply to individuals, estates, trusts, closely held C corporations, and personal service corporations.

T **F**   13. Individual taxpayers are allowed to offset passive losses against portfolio income but not against active income.

T F   14. In general, personal service corporations are subject to the passive loss rules.

T **F**   15. If a taxpayer participates in an activity for more than 300 hours during the year, then he is considered to have materially participated in that activity.

T F   16. If a taxpayer's participation in an activity for the taxable year constitutes substantially all the participation in the activity of all individuals for the year, then the taxpayer materially participates in the activity.

T F   17. If a taxpayer materially participated in an activity for any five of the ten preceding tax years, then the taxpayer materially participates in the activity for the current year.

T **F**   18. If the average period of customer use of rental property is seven days or less, then the activity is considered a nonrental activity subject to the material participation standards.

T **F**   19. The owner of a public golf course that sells weekly and monthly passes would automatically be subject to the passive loss rules.

T F   20. When a passive activity is sold in a taxable transaction, the suspended loss can be used to offset any realized gain.

T F   21. Investments in oil partnerships are subject to the at-risk limitations, but are not subject to the passive loss limitations.

Fill-in-the-Blanks

Complete the following statements with the appropriate word(s) or amount(s).

1. Tax credits attributable to passive activities can be carried forward ___indefinitely___ or

until the activity is disposed of in a taxable transaction.

2.   A transfer at death of a taxpayer's interest in an activity results in the suspended losses being allowed to the extent they exceed the ___*step up*___ in basis allowed.

3.   In a disposition of a taxpayer's interest in a passive activity by gift, the suspended losses are added to the ___*basis*___ of the property.

4.   Any passive activity losses disallowed for a taxable year may be carried ___*forward*___.

5.   To qualify for the $25,000 rental real estate loss deduction under the passive loss limitation rules, the taxpayer must ___*actively*___ ___*participate*___ in the activity.

Multiple Choice

Choose the best answer for each of the following questions.

_____   1.   Colm O'Broin invests $20,000 in a limited partnership which financed the rest of its operations by the use of nonrecourse loans. If Colm's share of the loss this year is $25,000, how much may he deduct on his tax return in the current year without regard to the limitations on the deduction of losses from passive activities?
         a. $-0-
         b. $5,000
         c. $20,000
         d. $25,000
         e.   Some other amount

_____   2.   T's AGI this year is $120,000 without deducting IRA contributions or passive losses. What is the maximum amount that T can deduct if he has real estate losses of $18,000 from a rental house acquired in 1988 (T actively participates in the activity)?
         a. $-0-
         b. $15,000
         c. $18,000
         d. $10,000
         e.   Some other amount

_____   3.   Leonie Huddie's adjusted basis in a passive activity was $20,000 at the beginning of the year. Her loss from the activity during the year was $4,000 and she had no other passive activity income for the year. Her passive activity credits for the year were $1,000. At the end of the year her adjusted basis in the passive activity would be:

    a. $20,000
    b. $19,000
    c. $16,000
    d. $15,000
    e. Some other amount

_____ 4. Carol Smith owes $40,000 of tax, disregarding net passive income, and $55,000 of tax considering both net passive income and other taxable income (before any credits). The maximum amount of passive credits that can be used by Carol for this year is:

    a. $-0-
    b. $15,000   ✓ 7-25
    c. $40,000
    d. $55,000
    e. Some other amount

_____ 5. In 1991, T invests $25,000 in a limited partnership. T's share of the partnership's 1991 loss was $5,000. For 1992, T's share of the partnership's income is $10,000. What is T's amount at-risk at the end of 1992?

    a. -0-
    b. $25,000
    c. $30,000
    d. $15,000
    e. Some other amount

_____ 6. The passive loss rules are applied at the owner level for which of the following entities?

    a. S corporations
    b. Partnerships
    c. C corporations
    d. a. and b.
    e. a. and c.

_____ 7. For 1992, Megan Inc., a closely held C corporation (not a personal service corporation), has $600,000 of passive losses from rental activities, $500,000 of active business income, and $200,000 of portfolio income. How much of the passive loss may offset other income?

    a. -0-
    b. $200,000
    c. $300,000

d. $500,000

e. Some other amount

8. Same as number 7, except Megan is an individual. How much of the passive loss may offset other income?
   a. -0-
   b. $200,000
   c. $300,000
   d. $500,000
   e. $600,000

9. Which of the following items is not portfolio income?
   a. Interest on a savings account
   b. Dividends on stock of a U.S. Corporation
   c. Interest on U.S. Savings Bonds
   d. Dividends on stock of a Foreign Corporation
   e. All of the above are portfolio income

10. If an activity is a personal service activity, how many prior years must an individual participate in the activity to be considered a material participant in the activity after withdrawal from the activity?
    a. One
    b. Two
    c. Three
    d. Five
    e. Seven

11. Rachel Fletcher owns an apartment building (acquired in 1989) and a gift shop in the same location. She materially participates in the gift shop business and is an active participant in the apartment rental business. The apartment building shows a $15,000 loss for the current year while the gift shop has a $25,000 profit. Assuming Rachel has no other income, she should report net income (loss) from these two ventures of?
    a. ($15,000)
    b. $25,000
    c. $10,000
    d. $40,000
    e. Some other amount

12. Under a special exception, rental and nonrental operations may be treated as a single operation if gross income from the rental or nonrental operation is less than what percentage?

a. 10%
b. 20%
c. 50%
d. 80%

_____ 13. L owns a business that is a passive activity. The business had a loss for 1992 determined as follows:

Operating income	$70,000
Dividends (on investments)	15,000
Total income	$85,000
Operating expenses	-$80,000
Investment interest	-8,000
Loss on sale of stock	-3,000
Net loss	-$6,000

What is L's passive loss from this business in 1992?
a. $-0-
b. ($6,000)
c. ($10,000)
d. ($3,000)
e. Some other amount

_____ 14. J sold an apartment building with an adjusted basis of $200,000 for $250,000. In addition, J has current and suspended losses associated with that specific apartment building of $60,000. How much of the $60,000 loss can J use to offset ordinary and portfolio income?
a. $-0-
b. $10,000
c. $50,000
d. $60,000
e. Some other amount

_____ 15. F, a physician, earned $300,000 from her medical practice in 1992. She received $55,000 in dividends and interest during the year. In addition, she incurred a loss of $60,000 from an investment in a passive activity. What is F's income for 1992 after considering the loss from the passive investment?
a. $300,000
b. $305,000
c. $355,000
d. $295,000

e. Some other amount

16. Which of the following would be a passive rental activity?
    a. T rents "go-carts" to customers.
    b. T owns a motel and rents rooms by the day to guests.
    c. T rents tuxedos to customers for parties etc.
    d. T owns and rents 2,500 apartments which he manages full time.
    e. None of the above

17. Y spends 20 hours a week, for 50 weeks a year operating a clothing store. He also owns a restaurant in another state which is managed by a full-time employee. Which of the activities (if any) are a passive activity?
    a. The clothing store
    b. The restaurant
    c. Both are passive activities
    d. Neither is a passive activity
    e. None of the above

18. U dies owning a passive activity with an adjusted basis of $50,000. Its fair market value at that date was $85,000. There are suspended losses relating to the property of $10,000. What is the passive loss deduction allowed on U's final tax return?
    a. $-0-
    b. $5,000
    c. $10,000
    d. $15,000
    e. Some other amount

19. In 1992, Y invests $50,000 in the Big Tex Oil Partnership by the use of nonrecourse loans. Big Tex spends $70,000 on intangible drilling cost applicable to Y interest during the year. What is Y's amount at-risk at the beginning of the next year?
    a. $-0-
    b. $20,000
    c. $50,000
    d. $70,000
    e. Some other amount

20. Same a question 19. What is Y's amount subject to the passive loss limitations?
    a. $-0-
    b. $20,000

    c. $50,000
    d. $70,000
    e. Some other amount

Code Section Recognition

Indicate, by number, the appropriate Code Section where the following items are found.

_____   1.   Passive loss limitations.

_____   2.   The at-risk rules.

SOLUTIONS TO CHAPTER 7

True or False

1.   True   (p. 7-6)

2.   False   The debt cannot be nonrecourse debt. (p. 7-3)

3.   True   (p. 7-2)

4.   False   It applies to individuals. (p. 7-27)

5.   True   (p. 7-27)

6.   True   (p. 7-15)

7.   False   Passive credits can only be used against regular tax attributable to passive income. (p. 7-25)

8.   False   Passive activity credits carry forward for an indefinite period until the activity is disposed of. (p. 7-25)

9.   False   The taxpayer's share of income increases the amount at-risk. (p. 7-3)

10.   True   (p. 7-4)

11.   True   (p. 7-4)

12.   True   (p. 7-6)

13.   False   Passive losses cannot offset portfolio income or active income. (p. 7-6)

14.   True   (p. 7-6)

15.   False   The test is more than 500 hours per year. (p. 7-11)

16.   True   (p. 7-12)

17.   True   (p. 7-13)

18.   True   (p. 7-15)

19.   False   Exception 5 to general rental rule. (p. 7-17)

20.   True   (p. 7-29)

21.   True   (p. 7-3)

Fill-in-the-Blanks

1.   indefinitely (p. 7-25)

2.   step-up (p. 7-30)

3.   basis (p. 7-30)

4.   forward (p. 7-24)

5.   actively participate (p. 7-27)

Multiple Choice

1.   C   Limited to his amount at risk in the activity. (p. 7-3)

2.   B $25,000 - (50% of AGI ($120,000) over $100,000) = $15,000 maximum. (p. 7-27)

3.   C   (p. 7-23)

4. B (p. 7-25)

5. C $25,000 - 5,000 + 10,000 = $30,000. (p. 7-3)

6. D (p. 7-6)

7. D Under an exception, closely held corporations can offset passive losses against active income. (p. 7-6)

8. A Individuals cannot offset passive losses against portfolio income or active income. (p. 7-6)

9. E (p. 7-6)

10. C (p. 7-13)

11. C $25,000 - 15,000 = $10,000. (p. 7-20)

12. B (p. 7-20)

13. C $70,000 - 80,000 = ($10,000). (p. 7-21)

14. B $50,000 - 60,000 = ($10,000). (p. 7-28)

15. C $300,000 + 55,000 = $355,000. (p. 7-6)

16. D No matter how large, rental activities are generally passive. (p. 7-9)

17. B There is no material participation in the restaurant. (p. 7-9)

18. A The suspended loss is deductible only to the extent it exceeds the step-up in basis. (p. 7-30)

19. A There would be a $20,000 unused loss for 1993. (p. 7-3)

20. A The passive loss limitations do not apply to oil & gas partnerships. (p. 7-3)

Code Section Recognition

1. § 469

2.   § 465

CHAPTER

8

DEDUCTIONS AND LOSSES: CERTAIN BUSINESS EXPENSES AND LOSSES

CHAPTER HIGHLIGHTS

This chapter discusses certain business expenses and losses which are deducted from gross income to arrive at the taxpayer's adjusted gross income. Casualty losses are also discussed, although personal casualty losses are considered itemized deductions rather than deductions for adjusted gross income.

I.   BAD DEBTS

    A.   When a taxpayer sells goods or services on credit and the account receivable subsequently becomes worthless, a bad debt deduction is allowed provided the income arising upon the creation of the receivable was previously recognized. Cash basis taxpayers are not allowed a deduction for bad debts since income is not reported until the cash is collected.

    B.   Allowable methods. For tax years after 1986, all taxpayers, except for certain financial institutions, must use the specific charge-off method for deducting bad debts. The specific charge-off method allows a deduction when a specific debt becomes partially (business only) or totally worthless (business or nonbusiness).

    C.   As a result of the repeal of the use of the reserve method, the balance in any bad debt reserve is includible in income ratably over a period of four years, starting with tax years beginning in 1987.

D. Business Versus Nonbusiness Bad Debts. Bad debts fall into one of two classifications: business bad debts or nonbusiness bad debts. Debts that arise from a taxpayer's trade or business are business bad debts while all other debts are nonbusiness bad debts. The primary difference in the tax treatment is that business bad debts are ordinary deductions while nonbusiness bad debts are treated as short-term capital losses.

E. Under the tax law, qualified individuals can elect to deduct losses on deposits in qualified financial institutions as personal casualty losses in the year in which the loss can be reasonably estimated.

F. Loans Between Related Parties. Loans between related parties create problems in determining whether the loan was bona fide, or a gift. If there is no debtor-creditor relationship established, the debt to a related party may be a gift. If the debt is not repaid, the bad debt deduction will be lost and a gift tax may be incurred.

II. WORTHLESS SECURITIES

A. Losses arising from worthless securities, such as stocks and bonds, are generally treated as capital losses deemed to have occurred on the last day of the tax year.

B. Securities in Affiliated Corporations. If stock is from an affiliated company, in which the corporate holder owns 80 percent of the voting power of all classes of stock and at least 80 percent of each class of nonvoting stock of the affiliated company, then ordinary loss treatment is allowed.

C. Small Business Stock. Another exception to the capital loss rule on worthless securities is for qualified "small business" or "§ 1244 stock." Individual taxpayers are allowed ordinary loss treatment limited to $50,000 ($100,000 for a joint return) per year for losses on stock that qualifies as small business stock. Any losses over the above limits are capital losses.

III. LOSSES OF INDIVIDUALS

A. Casualty Losses. An individual taxpayer may deduct losses under § 165(c) in each of the following circumstances:

• the loss was incurred in a trade or business,

- the loss was incurred in a transaction entered into for profit, or

- the loss was caused by casualty or theft.

A casualty loss is "the complete or partial destruction of property resulting from an identifiable event of a sudden, unexpected, or unusual nature." Thus, casualties would include such items as hurricanes, tornadoes, floods, storms, shipwrecks, fires, auto accidents, and mine cave-ins.

B.   Events that are not casualties are those due to "progressive deterioration," such as termite damage, rust, and erosion. Such events are not considered casualty losses since they are not "sudden and unexpected."

C.   Theft Losses. A theft loss includes larceny, embezzlement, and robbery. It does not include misplaced items. Theft losses are deductible in the year the loss is "discovered," not the year of theft. A partial deduction is allowed if a settlement is arrived at which is less than the property's adjusted basis.

D.   When to Deduct Casualty Losses. As a general rule, casualty losses are deducted in the year of the casualty. However, if the casualty is in an area designated as a disaster area by the President of the United States, then the taxpayer may elect to treat the loss as having occurred in the previous taxable year. When a "reasonable prospect of full recovery" exists, no deduction for a casualty loss may be taken.

E.   A taxpayer must include in gross income the reimbursement for a casualty loss sustained and deducted in a previous year, to the extent the previous deduction resulted in a tax benefit.

F.   Measuring the Amount of the Loss.

In computing the amount of a casualty loss, it is necessary to divide the property into that held for personal use and that held for business use. Property held for "personal use" is subject to a $100 statutory reduction in the otherwise allowable deduction. This $100 reduction does not apply to business use property. Personal casualty losses are deductible only to the extent they exceed 10 percent of AGI after reduction by the $100 floor.

The amount of the gross casualty loss deduction, before the $100 floor amount and before the 10 percent of adjusted gross income limitation applicable to personal casualty losses, is the lesser of (1) the adjusted basis of the property, or (2) the decrease in fair market value of the property.

The only exception to this rule is the complete destruction of business property, in which case, the adjusted basis is used to measure the loss.

To determine the dollar amount of a casualty loss, an appraisal before and after the casualty is needed. An estimate of the amount of the loss may also be made through the cost of repairs to the damaged property.

G.   Casualty Gains and Losses. If a taxpayer's personal casualty gains exceed personal casualty losses, the gains and losses will be treated as capital gains and losses. If the personal casualty losses exceed the personal casualty gains, then the gains and losses are netted. In determining whether personal casualty gains exceed personal casualty losses, the casualty losses must first be reduced by the $100 statutory floor. Personal casualty losses in excess of personal casualty gains are deductible subject to the 10 percent of AGI limitation. Casualty gains and losses from business properties are not netted with personal casualty gains and losses.

IV.   RESEARCH AND EXPERIMENTAL EXPENDITURES

A.   § 174 of the Code controls the tax treatment of research and experimental expenditures. A taxpayer may elect to expense all such costs in the current year. If the election is made for the first year in which the expenses are incurred, the taxpayer does not need the consent of the IRS.

B.   A taxpayer may also elect to defer and amortize research and experimental expenditures over a period of not less than 60 months. If the election to expense or defer is not made, the taxpayer must capitalize such expenses.

V.   NET OPERATING LOSSES

A.   To remove inequities that may be caused by the requirement that annual tax returns be filed, taxpayers are allowed a deduction for net operating losses (NOL). An NOL deduction is allowed in a given period for a business related loss incurred in another period. In computing an NOL, several adjustments have to be made to reflect a true economic loss.

B.   Carryback and Carryover Periods. Once the NOL is calculated, the amount can be carried back or forward. For loss years, the loss is carried "back three years and forward fifteen years." Alternatively, the taxpayer may elect to carry the loss forward only.

C. Computation of the NOL.

Adjustments must be made to an individual's taxable loss so that it reflects only losses related to the operation of a trade or business since the NOL is intended as a relief provision only for business income and losses. All casualty and theft losses, including personal casualty and theft losses, are also allowed in computing the NOL.

The following items must be added to the taxpayer's taxable income to arrive at the NOL deduction:

- the deductions for personal and dependency exemptions,

- the NOL carryovers and carrybacks from other years,

- the excess of nonbusiness capital losses over nonbusiness capital gains,

- the excess of business capital losses over the sum of business capital gains plus the excess of net nonbusiness capital gains and nonbusiness income over nonbusiness deductions, and

- the excess of nonbusiness deductions over the sum of nonbusiness income plus the amount of nonbusiness capital gains over nonbusiness capital losses.

A taxpayer who does not itemize deductions adds the excess of nonbusiness deductions over nonbusiness income by substituting the standard deduction amount for itemized deductions.

D. When an NOL is carried back to a prior year, the taxable income and tax liability for the year to which the loss is being carried must be recomputed. Deductions based on the amount of adjusted gross income, other than charitable contributions, must be recomputed based on the new adjusted gross income after the NOL. Any tax credits limited by tax liability must also be recomputed based on the reduced amount of tax due. After computing the refund claim for a carryback year it is necessary to determine the amount of the net operating loss that is left to carry into other years.

TEST FOR SELF-EVALUATION

True or False

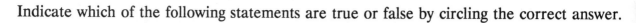

Indicate which of the following statements are true or false by circling the correct answer.

(T) F   1.   To be written off as a bad debt, accounts receivable must have been previously included in income.

(T) F   2.   Nonfinancial institutions must use the specific charge-off method for bad debts.

T (F)   3.   Nonbusiness bad debts are deductible in the year of partial or total worthlessness.

(T) F   4.   Qualified insolvent financial institution losses may be deducted by certain individuals as personal casualty losses.

8-15 (T) F   5.   Amounts spent for consumer surveys, advertising, or promotion qualify under § 174 as research and experimental expenditures.

(T) F   6.   In certain situations, loans between related parties may be classified as gifts.

T (F)   7.   Worthless securities always generate an ordinary loss.

(T) F   8.   Worthless securities are treated as having become worthless on the last day of the taxable year.

(T) F   9.   Within certain dollar limits, individual taxpayers may recognize an ordinary loss as opposed to a capital loss on the disposition of "§ 1244 stock".

(T) F   10.   Losses recognized by a corporation as a result of ~~the~~ *ordinary* the worthlessness of stock in an affiliated company are long-term capital losses.

(T) F   11.   All casualty and theft loss deductions are subject to a $100 statutory floor.

T (F)   12.   A loss caused by rust will be deductible as a casualty loss under § 165.

(T) F   13.   To be deductible, casualty damage must be to the taxpayer's property.

T (F)   14.   Disaster area casualty losses must be deducted in the year of the casualty.

T (F)   15.   The gross amount of a personal casualty loss is the larger of (1) the adjusted basis of the property, or (2) the decrease in fair market value.

T (F)   16.   The general rule for NOL carrybacks and carryovers is three years back and seven years forward.

(T) F   17.   Personal and dependency exemptions are ~~allowed~~ *not* allowed as deductions in arriving at an individual taxpayer's NOL.

(T) F   18.   A taxpayer may elect to expense research and experimental expenditures.

T (F)   19.   The maximum loss on § 1244 stock that may be treated as an ordinary loss is $50,000 for a joint return.

T (F)   20.   "Small business stock" under § 1244 can only be common stock.

(T) F   21.   Prior year net operating losses are ~~subtracted from~~ *added back to* taxable income in arriving at the current year net operating loss.

(T) F   22.   In determining the amount of an NOL remaining to be carried to another tax year, modified taxable income for a year into which an NOL is carried must be determined without the deduction for personal and dependency exemptions.

(T) F   23.   A taxpayer's loss on property used in a trade or business is not limited to loss caused by fire, storm, shipwreck, or other casualty, or by theft.

Fill-in-the-Blanks

Complete the following statements with the appropriate word(s) or amount(s).

1.   A taxpayer may use the ___specific___ ___charge off___ method in taking a deduction for bad debts.

2.   A business bad debt is an ___ordinary___ loss while a non-business bad debt is a short-term capital loss.

3.   A theft loss is taken in the year of ___discovery___ not in the year of occurrence.

4.   The three tax treatments for research and experimental expenditures include capitalization, ___expense___ , and deferment.

5.   If the deferral method is chosen for research and experimental costs, they must be written off over a period of not less than ___60___ months.

6. As a general rule, net operating losses are carried back _____3_____ years and carried forward _____15_____ years.

7. In computing an individual taxpayer's net operating loss, adjustments are required to bring the tax loss to a true ____economic____ loss.

8. When a net operating loss is carried into a nonloss year, the ____taxable net____ income and income tax must be recomputed.

Multiple Choice

Choose the best answer for each of the following questions.

_____ 1. Simple Simon, a calendar year taxpayer, owns stock (not § 1244 stock) in Big Corporation (a publicly-held company). The stock was acquired on November 1st of last year. The cost of the stock was $10,000. On March 1st of the current year the stock became worthless. Simple Simon should report (before any limitations) a:
   a. $10,000 short-term capital loss
   b. $10,000 long-term capital loss
   c. $10,000 ordinary loss
   d. No gain or loss

_____ 2. Liz Roberts owns §1244 stock in X Corporation with a basis of $120,000. She acquired the stock three years ago. During the current year she sells the stock for $40,000. If Liz is single, as a result of the sale of the stock she should report (before any $3,000 annual capital loss limitation):
   a. $60,000 long-term capital loss
   b. $60,000 ordinary loss
   c. $50,000 long-term capital loss and $10,000 ordinary loss
   d. $50,000 ordinary loss and $30,000 long-term capital loss
   e. None of the above

_____ 3. For tax purposes, research and experimental expenses may be:
   a. Capitalized
   b. Expensed in the year paid or incurred
   c. Deferred and amortized over 60 months or more
   d. All of the above
   e. None of the above

_____ 4. Robert Chamberlain loaned his friend, Fred, $6,000. Fred used the money to

start a business. In the current year Fred went bankrupt and the debt became worthless. Assuming he has no other capital transactions, Robert should report (in the current year):
a. No deduction for the loss
b. $6,000 long-term capital loss
c. $3,000 short-term capital loss
d. $6,000 short-term capital loss
e. None of the above

_____ 5. Martha Altus had a deductible casualty loss of $10,000 in 19X1. Her taxable income for 19X1 was $55,000. In 19X2, Martha was reimbursed $7,000 for the casualty loss. How much income must Martha report in 19X2 for the reimbursement?
a. $-0-
b. $3,000
c. $7,000
d. $10,000
e. Some other amount

_____ 6. During the current year, Tim Kelley's house was robbed. His stereo and coin collection were taken. The stereo had a basis of $600 and a FMV of $250, while the coin collection's basis was $400 and its FMV was $500. What is Tim's theft loss deduction before the ten percent of adjusted gross income limitation?
a. $-0-
b. $550
c. $650
d. $450
e. Some other amount

_____ 7. Which of the following would be deductible as a personal casualty loss?
a. Rust on the panels of an automobile
b. Decrease in value of a personal residence because of the construction of a new sewer plant nearby .
c. Moth damage to clothes
d. Damage to the roof of a personal residence when a tree blows over in a storm
e. None of the above

_____ 8. Linda McKaig had a casualty gain of $6,000 in the current year and a casualty loss of $4,000 (after deducting the $100 floor). Her adjusted gross income for the year is $25,000. Both the casualties are from long-term capital assets.

Linda should report:
a. $2,000 ordinary income
b. $1,500 casualty loss and $6,000 ordinary income
c. $6,000 ordinary gain and $2,000 capital loss
d. $6,000 capital gain and $4,000 capital loss
e. No gain or loss should be reported

_____ 9. Craig McKasson had adjusted income of $70,000. During the year his personal winter home was completely destroyed by fire. Pertinent data with respect to the winter home is as follows:

Cost basis	$40,000
FMV before casualty	$55,000
FMV after casualty	$13,000

Craig received a $23,000 insurance settlement for the fire. What is Craig's allowable casualty loss?
a. $-0-
b. $16,900
c. $10,000
d. $9,900
e. Some other amount

_____ 10. Singing Hills Corporation incurred the following expenditures in connection with the development of a new product:

Salaries	$50,000
Materials	6,000
Marketing survey	4,000
Sales promotion	10,000

If the corporation elects to expense research and experimental expenditures, what amount is allowed as a deduction in the current year?
a. $50,000
b. $56,000
c. $60,000
d. $70,000
e. Some other amount

_____ 11. John Jensen has the following tax items for the current year:

Nonbusiness capital gains	$5,000

Nonbusiness capital losses	3,000
Dividend income	6,000
Itemized deductions (no casualty losses)	10,000

What amount would John add back to his taxable income in calculating his net operating loss for the year?

a. $2,000
b. $3,000
c. $4,000
d. $10,000
e. Some other amount

Problems

1. T, a married individual, had the following income and deductions for 1992:

Income:

Gross income from business	$71,720
Interest on savings account	600 — sub $72,320

Deductions:

NOL carryover from 1991	$ 300 — add	
Business expenses	75,000	
Net loss on rental property	1,000	
Personal exemptions (2)	4,600 — add	
Itemized deductions (no casualty loss)	16,000 — add	-96,900

Taxable income (loss)	-$24,580

Calculate T's NOL for 1992.

2. During 1992 T had the following casualty losses occurring in separate events:

Asset	Adjusted Basis	FMV Before	FMV After
A	$2,000	$3,000	-0-
B	$2,000	$1,800	-0-
C	$3,000	$2,000	-0-
D	$2,000	$3,000	$500

Assets A and B are personal assets while C and D were used in T's business at the time of the casualty. The assets were not covered by insurance. Determine the amount of the deductible casualty loss (disregarding the 10 percent of adjusted gross income limitation where applicable) for:

Asset A _____1800_____

Asset B _____1700_____

Asset C _____600_____

Asset D _____2000_____

Code Section Recognition

Indicate by number the appropriate Code Section where the following items are found.

_____ 1. Bad debt deduction.

_____ 2. Worthless securities.

_____ 3. Casualty and theft losses.

_____ 4. Research and experimental expenditures.

_____ 5. Net operating losses.

_____ 6. Losses between related parties.

_____ 7. Losses on small business stock.

SOLUTIONS TO CHAPTER 8

True or False

1.   True   (p. 8-2)

2.   True   (p. 8-2)

3.   False   Nonbusiness bad debts are deductible only when totally worthless. (p. 8-2)

4.   True   (p. 8-4)

5.   False   These expenditures do not qualify. (p. 8-15)

6.   True   (p. 8-5)

7.   False   Losses on worthless securities are usually treated as capital losses. (p. 8-5)

8.   True   (p. 8-5)

9.   True   (p. 8-7)

10.   False   The losses are ordinary losses. (p. 8-7)

11.   False   Business casualty loss deductions are not subject to the $100 floor. (p. 8-10)

12.   False   Rust is not sudden and unexpected. (p. 8)

13.   True   (p. 8-8)

14.   False   They may be deducted in the prior year. (p. 8-10)

15.   False   The deduction is equal to the *lesser* of the adjusted basis of the property or the decrease in FMV of the property. (p. 8-11)

16.   False   The carryforward period is 15 years. (p. 8-18)

17.   False   A deduction for personal and dependency exemptions is not allowed in arriving at the taxpayer's NOL. (p. 8-18)

18.   True   (p. 8-15)

19.   False   The maximum amount of loss on § 1244 stock that may be treated as an ordinary loss is $100,000 on a joint return. (p. 8-7)

20.   False   Preferred stock is included under § 1244. (p. 8-7)

21.   False   Net operating loss carryovers and carrybacks must be added back to taxable income in arriving at the current year net operating loss. (p. 8-19)

22.   True   (p. 8-22)

23.   True   (p. 8-7)

Fill-in-the-Blanks

1.   specific charge-off (p. 8-2)

2.   ordinary (p. 8-4)

3.   discovery (p. 8-9)

4.   expense (p. 8-15)

5.   sixty (p. 8-16)

6.   three, fifteen (p. 8-18)

7.   economic (p. 8-18)

8.   taxable (p. 8-21)

Multiple Choice

1.   B   (p. 8-6)

2.   D   (p. 8-7)

3.   D   (p. 8-15)

4.   C   (p. 8-4)

5.   C   The reimbursement is income to the extent the casualty loss deduction resulted in a tax benefit. (p. 8-10)

6.   B $250 (stereo) + $400 (TV) - $100 (limit) = $550. (p. 8-11)

7.   D   (p. 8-8)

8.   D   There is a net casualty gain, therefore all gains and losses are capital. (p. 8-13)

9.   D Fair market value before casualty $55,000
           Fair market value after casualty   -13,000
           Decrease in fair market value $42,000 ✓

           Lesser of decrease in FMV or adjusted basis $40,000
           Insurance recovery   -23,000
           Gross loss $17,000
           Per casualty limitation   -100
           Adjusted gross income limitation   -7,000
           Casualty loss deduction $ 9,900   (pp. 8-11)

10.   B $50,000 + 6,000 = $56,000. (p. 8-15)

11.   A $2,000 = $10,000 - [$6,000 + ($5,000 - 3,000)]. (p. 8-19)

Problems

1.   Taxable income (loss) for 1992   -$24,580

        Add:
        NOL from 1991 $ 300
        Personal exemptions   4,600
        Itemized deductions   16,000
        Less: Interest income   -600   15,400   20,300
        Net operating loss for 1992   -$ 4,280   (p. 8-18)

2.   Asset A $1,900 = Lesser of decrease in FMV ($3,000 - 0) or adjusted basis
                     ($2,000); $2,000 - 100 = $1,900.

        Asset B $1,700 = Lesser of decrease in FMV ($1,800) or adjusted basis
                     ($2,000); $1,800 - 100 = $1,700.

        Asset C $3,000 = Adjusted basis of $3,000. (Note, complete destruction)

        Asset D $2,000 = Lesser of decrease in FMV ($3,000 - 500) or adjusted basis
                     ($2,000); $2,000. (p. 8-10)

Code Section Recognition

1. § 166

2. § 165

3. § 165

4. § 174

5. § 172

6. § 267

7. § 1244

CHAPTER

9

DEPRECIATION, COST RECOVERY, AMORTIZATION, AND DEPLETION

CHAPTER HIGHLIGHTS

The tax law provides for the recovery of the cost of assets through depreciation, cost recovery, amortization or depletion. This chapter looks at the methods by which capitalized costs may be recovered under the Code. In addition, the types of assets that qualify for some form of capital recovery are discussed.

I.   DEPRECIATION AND AMORTIZATION

   A.   § 167 permits a deduction for depreciation in the form of a reasonable allowance for the exhaustion, wear and tear, and obsolescence of business property and property held for the production of income.

   The Regulations hold that tangible property is depreciable only to the extent that it is subject to wear and tear, to decay or decline from natural causes, to exhaustion and to obsolescence. Intangible property is not subject to depreciation unless the property has a definite and limited useful life, such as patents and copyrights. Goodwill is not amortizable because it does not have a measurable useful life.

   The basis for depreciation is generally the adjusted cost basis. However, personal use property converted to business or income-producing use will have a depreciable basis equal to the lower of its adjusted basis or fair market value when converted.

B.   Other Depreciation Considerations. Property placed in service before January 1, 1981 is subject to different rules than property placed in service after that date.

Before 1981, the taxpayer had a choice of the following allowable depreciation methods:

- The straight-line method (cost basis less salvage value divided by the estimated useful life).

- The declining balance method using a rate not more than twice the straight-line rate. Various classes of property were limited to a rate less than 200 percent declining balance. Salvage value is not taken into account in computing depreciation under the declining balance method. However, no further depreciation can be claimed once net book value and salvage value are equal.

- The sum-of-the-years' digits method.

- Any other consistent method which does not result in greater total depreciation being claimed during the first two thirds of the useful life than would have been allowable under the double declining balance method. Permissible methods included the machine-hours, and the units-of-production methods.

In determining the depreciable basis, the taxpayer must take into account the salvage value. However, salvage value of amounts not in excess of 10% of the basis of tangible personal property with an estimated useful life of three years or more, may be disregarded. This special provision does not apply to livestock.

In the Tax Reform Act of 1969 Congress placed limitations on the use of accelerated methods for certain types of assets. The following table summarizes the permitted methods of depreciation for real property acquired before January 1, 1981 and after July 24, 1969:

Before 1/1/81

	Nonresidential Realty	Residential Realty
New property	150% DB, SL	200% DB, SYD 150% DB, SL
Used property	SL	125% DB (if EUL is 20 years or more); SL

Limitations were also imposed on the use of accelerated depreciation methods for used tangible personalty. Neither the sum-of-the-years' digits method nor the 200 percent declining balance method was permitted for used tangible personalty acquired after July 24, 1969, but before January 1, 1981.

The Asset Depreciation Range (ADR) system established guideline lives for the depreciation of pre-1981 property.

II. ACCELERATED COST RECOVERY SYSTEM (ACRS)

A. General Considerations.

The accelerated cost recovery system applies to most property acquired after December 31, 1980. ACRS is designed to aid capital formation by providing a rapid write-off for capital goods. The recovery periods under ACRS are based on the classification of property into "classes". ACRS was revised by the Tax Reform Act of 1986, so that the classification of property depends on whether the property was placed in service before January 1, 1987 in which case the original ACRS rules apply, or after December 31, 1986, in which case the modified ACRS (MACRS) rules apply.

B. Personalty: Recovery Periods and Methods.

The cost of eligible personalty (and certain realty) is recovered based on the following recovery classes:

Pre-1987 Acquisitions

    3 year: Autos, light duty trucks, R&D equipment, and

certain horses.

5 year:	Property that is not in another class.
10 year:	Public utility property with an ADR life of greater than 18 but not more than 25 years.
15 year:	Public utility property with an ADR life over 25 years.

Post-1986 Acquisitions

3-year:	ADR midpoints of 4 years and less (except autos and light trucks), certain horses.
5-year:	ADR midpoints of more than 4 years and less than 10 years, autos, light trucks, R&D equipment, etc.
7-year:	Property that is not included in another class, includes office furniture, fixtures and equipment.
10-year:	ADR midpoints of 16 years or more but less than 20 years.
15-year:	ADR midpoints of 20 years or more but less than 25 years.
20-year:	ADR midpoints of 25 years or more.

The pre-1987 ACRS rates are based on the 150 percent declining-balance method, using the half-year convention in the year of acquisition and disregarding salvage value. No depreciation is permitted in the year of disposition.

The post-1986 ACRS rates are based on the 200 percent declining balance method (3-, 5-, 7-, and 10-year classes) or 150 percent declining balance method (15- and 20-year classes), using the half-year convention in both the year of acquisition and the year of disposition, and disregarding salvage value. In certain cases, a mid-quarter convention may be required.

C.   Realty: Recovery Periods and Methods.

Pre-1987 real estate under ACRS is written off over 15, 18, or 19 years depending on the date the property was placed in service. The pre-1987 rates are based on 175% declining balance. Depreciation for 15-year property and certain 18-year property uses a full month convention. Eighteen-year real property placed in service after June 22, 1984 and 19-year recovery property use a mid-month convention. (See text for the various ACRS tables).

Post-1986 real estate is written off over 15 years (land improvements), 27.5 years for residential realty, or 31.5 years for nonresidential realty. Residential and nonresidential realty can only use the straight-line method. Property depreciated under the 27.5-year or 31.5-year class uses a mid-month convention.

D.   Straight-Line Election Under ACRS and MACRS. Instead of using the accelerated methods under ACRS, taxpayers may elect to use the straight-line method of depreciation. The pre-1987 straight-line recovery periods are as follows:

3-year property: 3, 5, or 12 years
5-year property: 5, 12, or 25 years
10-year property: 10, 25, or 35 years
15-year property: 15, 35, or 45 years
18-year property: 18, 35, or 45 years
19-year property: 19, 35, or 45 years

The election of the straight-line method is a class-by-class election for other than real property in the 15-, 18-, or 19-year classes. For real property, the straight-line election was available on a property-by-property basis. The half-year, monthly, or mid-month conventions continue to apply when the straight-line election is made.

Depreciation under the post-1986 straight-line election is based on the property's class life using a half-year or mid-quarter convention, whichever is applicable. The straight-line method is required for real property acquired after 1986.

See the text for various tables for calculating straight-line ACRS or MACRS.

E.   Election to Expense. § 179 permits an election to expense a limited amount of the cost of certain depreciable assets used in a trade or business up to a

$10,000 annual limit. The amount expensed cannot exceed the taxable income derived from the taxpayer's trade or business. Furthermore, the amount expensed is reduced dollar-for-dollar when property placed in service exceeds $200,000 for the year.

F.   ACRS and MACRS Anti-churning Rules. To prevent transactions that attempt to change pre-1981 property into post-1980 recovery property without actually changing ownership, the ACRS provisions contain "anti-churning" rules. The taxpayer must use pre-1981 depreciation rules if the property was owned or used during 1980 by the taxpayer or a related person.

The modified accelerated cost recovery system applicable to post-1986 asset acquisitions uses rules similar to the pre-1987 ACRS anti-churning rules to prevent taxpayers from converting pre-1987 ACRS property into post-1986 MACRS property.

G.   Business and Personal Use of Autos and Other Listed Property. A taxpayer must show that listed property used for both business and personal use is used predominately for business (greater than 50%) in order to use the statutory percentage methods under ACRS or MACRS. If the property is not used predominately for business, the depreciable basis must be recovered using straight-line deprecation under the ADS. Recapture rules apply where the business usage of listed property depreciated under the statutory percentage method drops below the greater than 50 percent requirement.

Under the "luxury auto" rules, the deduction for depreciation expense on passenger automobiles for 1992 is limited to $2,660 in the first year, $4,300 for the second year, $2,550 for the third year, and $1,575 for each subsequent year. These limits are imposed before the percentage reduction for personal use of the automobile. Also, the annual limits apply to any election to expense under § 179.

H.   Alternative Depreciation System (ADS). For post-1986 property the ADS must be used in calculating depreciation expense for the following:

- the alternative minimum tax calculation

- property used outside the U.S.

- property leased or otherwise used by a tax-exempt entity

- property financed by tax-exempt bonds

- certain imported property

- determining earnings and profits

In most cases the ADS requires the use of the straight-line method, except with regard to the alternative minimum tax calculation of depreciation on personalty which uses the 150 percent declining balance method.

Taxpayers may elect to use the 150% declining balance method to compute the regular tax rather than the normal 200% MACRS method. Thus there will be no difference between regular and alternative minimum tax. (Note: the taxpayers must use the ADS recovery periods if this election is made).

See text for the ADS calculation.

III.   AMORTIZATION

A.   Intangible property used in a trade or business or for the production of income may be amortized if the property has a limited life that can be determined with a reasonable degree of accuracy. Patents and copyrights are example of intangibles with a definite useful life established by law and thus can be amortized.

B.   Intangibles that do not have a useful life that can be determined with reasonable accuracy (such as goodwill) may not be amortized. Also intangible property must have an ascertainable cost basis separate and distinct from goodwill.

IV.   DEPLETION

A.   Payment for natural resources is recovered through depletion. However, intangible drilling and development costs can be handled in one of two ways. Such costs can either be (1) expensed in the year incurred, or (2) capitalized (added to the depletable basis) and written off through depletion. These costs include the cost of making property ready for drilling, erecting derricks, and drilling the well.

B.   Depletion Methods. The owner of an interest in a wasting asset is entitled to a depletion deduction. The tax law allows for two types of depletion, cost and percentage.

Cost depletion is based on the adjusted basis of the asset. The basis is divided by the estimated recoverable units of the asset to arrive at a cost per unit. This cost is multiplied by the units sold to arrive at the deduction allowed. The cost per unit may be redetermined on a prospective basis, based on revised estimates of the recoverable units.

Percentage depletion is based on a percentage specified in the Code which is applied to the gross income from the property to arrive at the amount of depletion allowed. Such depletion may not exceed 50 percent of the taxable income from the property before the depletion allowance. Special limitations apply to the use of percentage depletion for certain oil and gas wells. The cost basis of the asset must be reduced by the percentage depletion claimed even though the calculation is made without reference to the basis of the asset.

If intangible drilling costs are capitalized, the basis for cost depletion is increased. If such costs are expensed, the 50 percent limit for the percentage depletion deduction will be decreased.

IV.   REPORTING PROCEDURES

A.   Sole proprietors engaged in a trade or business should file a Schedule C with their Form 1040. Part I of Schedule C is used for reporting items of income. Part II is used for reporting deductions such as bad debts, depletion, and depreciation.

B.   If depreciation is claimed, it generally should be supported on a Form 4562.

TEST FOR SELF-EVALUATION

True or False

Indicate which of the following statements are true or false by circling the correct answer.

 T (F) 1.   If depreciation is not claimed for a particular year, the basis for the asset remains unchanged.

T (F) 2.   An asset purchased in 1979 and depreciated using the straight-line method can be changed to the ACRS method provided the taxpayer uses the remaining cost recovery life.

T F 3.   The depreciable basis of personal use property converted to business use is the lower of its adjusted basis or fair market value on the date of conversion.

T F 4.   The alternative depreciation system must be used on all automobiles.

T F 5.   Cost depletion is determined by dividing the fair market value of the asset by the estimated recoverable units expected.

use adj basis

T F 6.   A taxpayer may disregard salvage value in applying the ACRS percentages.

T F 7.   The Accelerated Cost Recovery System contains provisions to prevent the conversion of non-ACRS property into ACRS property.

T F 8.   Assets that do not decline in value on a predictable basis are not depreciable under ACRS.

T F 9.   Under ACRS, realty may be depreciated using the component method.

no can't use

T F 10. Depreciation, depletion, and amortization are different words to describe the process of deducting the cost of an asset.

T F 11. Under MACRS an automobile acquired in 1992 and used in a business is seven-year recovery property.

5 yr

T F 12. The cost of residential rental real estate acquired after 1986 is written off over 27.5 years under MACRS.

T F 13. For 1992 the maximum amount that can be expensed under § 179 is $10,000.

T F 14. If more than 40 percent of the non-realty assets acquired during a year are acquired in the last quarter of the tax year, then the taxpayer must use the mid-quarter MACRS tables to calculate the cost recovery deduction for all personal property placed in service during the year.

T F 15. The annual limits for automobile depreciation do not apply to the election to expense under § 179.

T F 16. ACRS and other depreciation, amortization, and depletion are reported on

Form 4562.

T̶ (F)   17.   The § 179 expense election is ~~available~~ *not* for real property or for property
               used in the production of income.

(T) F   18.   A taxpayer who leases a passenger automobile must include an *inclusion
               amount* in gross income.

(T) F   19.   Intangible property used in a trade or business or for the production of
               income may be amortized if the property has a limited life that can be
               determined with a reasonable degree of accuracy.

(T) F   20.   Generally, intangible property is amortized using a straight-line method.

T   (F)   21.   Land can generally be depleted under the tax law.

Fill-in-the-Blanks

Complete the following statements with the appropriate word(s) or amount(s).

1.   Post-1986 nonresidential real estate is written off over ____31.5____ years.

2.   The taxpayer must have an ____economic____ interest in property in order to be
      entitled to a depletion deduction.

3.   Percentage depletion may not exceed ____50____ percent of the taxable income
      from the property before the allowance for depletion.

4.   An automobile acquired in 1992 is ____5____ year property under MACRS.

5.   The pre-1987 tables under ACRS for writing off realty are based on a ____175____
      percent declining balance depreciation method.

6.   Under the pre-1987 ACRS straight-line election, five year property may be written off
      over ____5____ , ____12____ , or ____25____ years.

7.   The maximum amount that can be expensed under § 179 is $____10,000____ .

8.   The two methods of depletion under the tax law are called ____cost____ depletion
      and ____%____ depletion.

9.   To use the statutory percentage method under MACRS on listed property such as an automobile, the business use of the property must be more than ___*50*___ percent.

Multiple Choice

Choose the best answer for each of the following questions.

_____   1.   § 167 permits a depreciation deduction for which of the following reasons?
  a. Exhaustion
  b. Wear and tear
  c. Obsolescence
  d. All the above

_____   2.   Which of the following is not depreciable for tax purposes?
  a. A delivery truck
  b. Goodwill
  c. An office building
  d. Office equipment
  e. None of the above

_____   3.   For non-ACRS property, salvage value is not used in calculating depreciation under which of the following methods?
  a. Declining-balance
  b. Straight-line
  c. Sum-of-the-years-digits
  d. Units-of-production
  e. None of the above

_____   4.   For new residential rental property acquired after July 24, 1969, and before 1981, the maximum depreciation rate that can be used is:
  a. Sum-of-the-years-digits
  b. 200% declining-balance
  c. 150% declining-balance
  d. 125% declining-balance
  e. None of the above

_____   5.   The Big Tex Oil Company purchases an oil lease for $1,000,000. After exploration, oil is discovered and it is estimated that 100,000 barrels of oil will be recovered from the lease. If during 1992 Big Tex produces 15,000 barrels of oil from the lease and sells 12,000 barrels, what is the amount of cost depletion allowed Big Tex?

    a. -0-
    b. $120,000
    c. $150,000
    d. $1,000,000
    e. Some other amount

6. The Pit Sulfur Company has gross income of $200,000 from certain property (not oil and gas property) subject to depletion. The expenses related to that property are $140,000, and a statutory depletion rate of 22 percent is applicable. What is the amount of depletion using percentage depletion?
    a. -0-
    b. $44,000
    c. $30,000
    d. $13,200
    e. Some other amount

7. On July 1, 1992 farmer John acquires a new tractor at a cost of $30,000. If John is married and files a joint return for 1992, what amount can John expense under § 179 and what amount is subject to regular MACRS depreciation (assuming John has adequate taxable income from his business of farming)?
    a. $0, $30,000
    b. $10,000, $30,000
    c. $5,000, $25,000
    d. $10,000, $20,000
    e. Some other amounts

8. Sun Corporation acquires $200,000 worth of three-year property and $210,000 worth of five-year property in 1992. If the election to expense is not made, what is Sun's MACRS deduction using the half-year convention?
    a. $108,660
    b. $101,500
    c. $81,500
    d. $97,205

9. For 1992, what is the maximum amount of qualified expense property that can be placed in service during the year without causing a reduction in the $10,000 expense ceiling?
    a. $100,000
    b. $125,000
    c. $150,000
    d. $200,000

e. Some other amount

10. For pre-1987 five-year class ACRS property, which of the following cannot be used as the recovery period under the straight-line election?
    a. 5 years
    b. 8 years   9-16
    c. 12 years
    d. 25 years
    e. None of the above

11. On September 1, 1992, Mike Shields places in service an automobile with a cost of $40,000. The car is used 90 percent for business and 10 percent for personal use. What is Mike's 1992 MACRS deduction?
    a. $2,660
    b. $2,394 $2660 \times .90 = 2354$
    c. $4,200
    d. $8,000
    e. Some other amount

12. Using the information in Question 11 above, and assuming the same business use percentage in 1993, what is Mike's MACRS deduction in 1993?
    a. $2,660
    b. $12,800 $4300 \times .90 = 3870$
    c. $4,200
    d. $3,870
    e. Some other amount

13. Maggie McCall acquires an apartment building on June 3, 1992 for $600,000. What is Maggie's cost recovery deduction for calculating earnings and profits during 1992 under the alternative depreciation system (ADS)?
    a. $8,124
    b. $10,769 $600,000$
    c. $7,993 $\times 1.354$
    d. $15,000   ————
    e. Some other amount 8124

14. The percentage depletion rate on coal is:
    a. 22%
    b. 15%
    c. 14%
    d. 10%
    e. 5%

_____ 15. Daniel Chamberlain purchases for $400,000 an apartment building in Canada. The apartment is purchased during March, 1992. What is Daniel's depreciation deduction for the first year?
a. $7,916
b. $11,516
c. $10,052
d. $8,742
e. Some other amount

_____ 16. For real property acquired in 1992 which of the following conventions is required to be used in calculating the MACRS deduction?
a. Mid-week
b. Mid-month
c. Mid-quarter
d. Mid-year
e. None of the above

_____ 17. T purchases a cellular telephone for his business automobile. Cellular telephones are listed property. The phone is used 80% for business calls and 20% for personal calls. What method of cost recovery must T use on the phone?
a. Straight-line reduced by personal use percentage
b. Straight-line subject to recovery limits ($2,660, etc.), reduced by personal use percentage
c. Statutory percentage reduced by personal use percentage
d. Statutory percentage subject to recovery limits ($2,660. etc.), reduced by personal use percentage
e. None of the above

_____ 18. G purchases office equipment at a cost of $50,000 on March 25, 1992. G does not elect § 179, however, he elects to use ADS 150 declining-balance cost recovery. What is T's cost recovery deduction for 1992?
a. $3,000
b. $3,750
c. $4,750
d. $5,000
e. Some other amount

_____ 19. H purchased a seven-year business asset (not listed property) on July 30, 1992, at a cost of $100,000. H did not elect to expense under § 179 nor did he elect straight-line cost recovery. H sold the asset on February 11, 1995. What is H's cost recovery for 1995?

a. $-0-
b. $12,490.00
c. $6,245.00
d. $3,122.50
e. Some other amount

20. K purchased an automobile on June 15, 1992 at a cost of $20,000. K used the car 75% for business use and 25% for personal use in 1992. In 1993 K used the automobile 40% for business and 60% for personal use. What is K's excess depreciation to be recaptured in 1993?
a. $-0-
b. $495
c. $1,500
d. $1,995
e. Some other amount

21. On February 11, 1992, Sheila leases and places in service a passenger automobile worth $40,000. The lease is for five years. During 1992 she uses the automobile 80% for business and 20% for personal use. Assuming the IRS table amount for 1992 is $267, how much must Sheila included in gross income for 1992?
a. $-0-
b. $267.00
c. $213.60
d. $194.87
e. Some other amount

22. On January 4 of the current year Byrne was granted a patent good for 17 years. The costs associated with the patent were $204,000. In the current year Byrne may amortized how much of the patent?
a. $-0-
b. $204,000
c. $12,000
e. $10,000
e. Some other amount

23. On January 3, 1992, Heather purchased land for $150,000. She plans to build an apartment building on the land. The apartment will have an estimated useful life of 30 years. She does in fact build the apartment in 1992 for $400,000. How much of the land cost can be depleted by Heather this year?
a. $-0-
b. $150,000

    c. $5,000

    d. $10,000

    e. Some other amount

Problems

1. Each of the following assets was acquired in 1992. Determine the appropriate MACRS recovery class for each.

    _____ a. A used delivery truck

    _____ b. A used office building

    _____ c. A new farm tractor

    _____ d. A new duplex held for rental

    _____ e. A used apartment building

    _____ f. A new computer

2. On August 8, 1992, Steve Brownell acquired an apartment building (27.5-year property) as an investment. The apartment cost $500,000 and has an estimated salvage value of $100,000. Using the table in the text, give the MACRS deduction for the first four years for this apartment.

    Year 1 _____

    Year 2 _____

    Year 3 _____

    Year 4 _____

Code Section Recognition

Indicate by number the appropriate Code Section where the following items are found.

    _____ 1. Depreciation deduction.

_____ 2. Accelerated Cost Recovery System (ACRS) or MACRS.

_____ 3. The election to expense.

_____ 4. Depletion deduction.

_____ 5. Percentage depletion.

SOLUTIONS TO CHAPTER 9

True or False

1.   False   The basis decreases by the amount of allowable depreciation. (p. 9-3)

2.   False   Taxpayers cannot benefit by converting non-ACRS property into ACRS property. (p. 9-19)

3.   True   (p. 9-4)

4.   False   The regular MACRS may be used for autos meeting the more than 50 percent business use test. (p. 9-20)

5.   False   Adjusted basis is used, not fair market value. (p. 9-28)

6.   True   (p. 9-9)

7.   True   (p. 9-19)

8.   True   (p. 9-8)

9.   False   The component method generally cannot be used. (p. 9-13)

10.   True   (p. 9-2)

11.   False   Automobiles are five-year property. (p. 9-10)

12.   True   (p. 9-14)

13.   True   (p. 9-18)

14.   True   (p. 9-11)

15.   False   The limit does apply to any amount expensed under § 179. (p. 9-21)

16.   True   (p. 9-31)

17.   False   The election under § 179 is not available. (p. 9-18)

18.   True   (p. 9-23)

19.   True   (p. 9-26)

20.   True   (p. 9-26)

21.   False   Land can not be depleted. (p. 9-27)

Fill-in-the-Blanks

1.   31.5 (p. 9-15)

2.   economic (p. 9-27)

3.   fifty (p. 9-29)

4.   five (p. 9-10)

5.   175 (p. 9-13)

6.   five, twelve, twenty-five (p. 9-16)

7. $10,000 (p. 9-18)

8.   cost, percentage (p. 9-28)

9.   fifty (p. 9-20)

Multiple Choice

1.   D   (p. 9-2)

2.   B   (p. 9-2)

3.   A   (p. 9-5)

4.   B   (p. 9-6)

5.   B   ($1,000,000/100,000 barrels) x 12,000 barrels = $120,000. (p. 9-28)

6.   C   ($200,000 - 140,000) x 50% = $30,000 maximum. (p. 9-29)

7.   D   (p. 9-18)

8.   A   ($200,000 x 33.33%) + ($210,000 x 20%) = $108,660. (p. 9-38)

9.   D   (p. 9-18)

10.   B   (p. 9-16)

11.   B $2,660 (max) x 90% = $2,394. (p. 9-21)

12.   D $4,300 (max) x 90% = $3,870. (p. 9-22)

13.   A $600,000 x 1.354% = $8,124, Table 9-12. (pp. 9-26, 9-46)

14.   D   (p. 9-30)

15.   A $400,000 x 1.979% = $7,916, Table 9-12. (pp. 9-26, 9-46)

16.   B   (p. 9-15)

17.   C   (p. 9-20)

18.   B $50,000 x 7.5% = $3,750, Table 9-10. (pp. 9-26, 9-45)

19.   C $100,000 x 12.49% x 1/2 = $6,245, Table 9-2. (pp. 9-11, 9-38)

20.   B   MACRS for 1992 $2,660 x 75% = $1,995
          Straight-line for 1992 $20,000 x .10 x 75% =   -1,500
          Recapture amount $ 495
          Table 9-11, (pp. 9-20, 9-21, 9-22)

21.   D $267 x (333 days/365 days) x 80% = $194.87   (p. 9-23)

22.   C $204,000 ÷ 17 = $12,000   (p. 9-26)

23.   A   Land cannot be depleted.   (p. 9-27)

Problems

1.   a.   5-year

      b.   31.5-year

      c.   7-year

      d.   27.5-year

      e.   27.5-year

      f.   5-year   (p. 9-12)

2.   Year 1 $500,000 x 1.364% = $6,820

      Year 2 $500,000 x 3.636% = $18,180

      Year 3 $500,000 x 3.636% = $18,180

      Year 4 $500,000 x 3.636% = $18,180   (Table 9-7)

Code Section Recognition

1.   § 167

2.   § 168

3.   § 179

4.   § 611

5.   § 613

CHAPTER

10

DEDUCTIONS: EMPLOYEE EXPENSES

CHAPTER HIGHLIGHTS

This chapter identifies and categorizes employee expenses. In certain situations, employee expenses are treated as expenses incurred in a trade or business and thus are deductions *for* adjusted gross income (AGI). Most employee business expenses are deductible *from* adjusted gross income as itemized deductions. The factors that determine whether an individual is an employee or self-employed are also discussed.

I.   CLASSIFICATION OF EMPLOYMENT RELATED EXPENSES

A.   Self-employed Versus Employee Status.

One major problem in taxation is to determine if an employer-employee relationship exists or if an individual is self-employed. An employer-employee relationship exists when the employer has the right to specify the result and the ways and means by which the result will be obtained.

A self-employed person is required to file a Schedule C and all allowable expenses incurred will be deductions for adjusted gross income. In addition, statutory employees are allowed to file a Schedule C and deduct these expenses for AGI.

B.   Deductions for or from AGI.

Employee expenses reimbursed under an accountable plan are deductions *for* adjusted gross income. Unreimbursed employee expenses are deductible *from* adjusted gross income

C. Itemized Deductions.

After classifying deductions as *for* or *from* AGI, it is necessary to group the itemized (deductions from AGI)) deductions into two groups. The deductions in the first group are deductible in full for taxpayers who itemize while the second group of deductions are added together and reduced by 2% of AGI.

Miscellaneous itemized deductions subject to the 2% of AGI limitation include:

- All § 212 expenses other than rent and royalty expenses
- All unreimbursed employee expenses (after a 20% reduction, if applicable)
- Professional dues and subscriptions
- Union dues and work uniforms
- Employment-related education expenses
- Malpractice insurance premiums
- Job hunting expenses
- Office in the home and outside sales expenses
- Legal, accounting, and tax return fees
- Hobby expenses
- Investment expenses
- Custodial fees for income-producing property or IRAs
- Collection fees for interest and dividends
- Appraisal fees for establishing the amount of casualty losses or charitable deductions

Miscellaneous itemized deductions not subject to the 2% of AGI limitation are:

- Work-related handicapped expenses
- Certain estate taxes
- Certain claim of right adjustments
- Certain amortizable bond premiums
- Gambling losses to the extent of gambling winnings
- Certain short sale deductions
- Certain terminated annuity payments
- Certain cooperative housing costs

D. Percentage Reduction for Meals and Entertainment.

Deductions for meals and entertainment (including facilities) are limited to 80% of the otherwise allowable amount. This rule applies to taxes and tips relating to meals and entertainment. Cover charges, parking, and room rental fees are also subject to the 80% rule.

Transportation expenses are not affected by this provision. If meals and entertainment are part of luxury water travel and are not separately stated, then the 80% rule does not apply.

The 80% rule does not apply in the following cases:

- Compensation of employees
- Income of independent contractors
- Meals and entertainment in a subsidized eating facility
- Where the de minimis rule applies
- Where employees are fully reimbursed for business and entertainment (the 20% reduction applies to the person making the reimbursement)
- Certain employer-paid recreation expenses

II. EMPLOYEE BUSINESS EXPENSES

A. Accountable Plans. Employee expenses are reimbursed under accountable plans or nonaccountable plans. For a plan to be accountable two requirements must be met. The employee must:

- Adequately account for (substantiate) the expenses, and

- Return any excess reimbursement or allowance.

B. Substantiation requires the employee provide the following to the employer:

- The amount of the expense

- The time and place of travel or entertainment (or date of gift)

- The business purpose of such expense

- The business relationship of the person entertained (or receiving the gift)

C. The amount of an expenditure can be substantiated by a deemed substantiation (per diem) method. By using such a method the amount of the expense is proved. The maximum amount deemed substantiated is equal to the lesser of the per diem allowance or the Federal per diem rate, which varies by area and location. A simplified high-low method may be used which specifies a single rate for high cost locations and all other locations have a single lower rate. When the per diem method is used, the place, date, business purpose and business relationship must still be substantiated in the normal manner.

D. Nonaccountable Plan. Under a nonaccountable plan an adequate accounting or reimbursement is not required. In such plans any reimbursement is reported in its entirety as wages on the employee's W-2. Any allowable expenses are treated in the same manner as unreimbursed expenses. Thus the employee is subject to the 80% limit on meals and entertainment, the 2% miscellaneous itemized deduction limit, etc.

E. Reporting Procedures. The reporting requirements for employee expenses depend upon whether the amount is reimbursed or unreimbursed and whether the amount is paid under an accountable plan or a nonaccountable plan.

III. TRANSPORTATION EXPENSES

A. Qualified Expenditures. A taxpayer is permitted a deduction from AGI subject to the 2% floor for unreimbursed, employment-related transportation expenses. An example of such expenses would include those incurred by an employee commuting to a second job from a first job. However, the cost of commuting from home to work and back is not deductible.

B. Computation of Automobile Expenses. In computing automobile expenses a taxpayer has two choices, actual cost or an automatic mileage method. In 1992, under the automatic mileage method a taxpayer can deduct 27.5 cents per mile for all business miles. Parking fees and tolls can be deducted in addition to the amount calculated under the automatic mileage method.

See the text for restrictions which apply to changing from one method to another, the use of a fully depreciated vehicle, and the use of more than one vehicle for business purposes.

IV. TRAVEL EXPENSES

    A.   Definition of Travel Expenses. An employee may be allowed a deduction for unreimbursed travel expenses subject to the 2% of adjusted gross income limitation. Travel expenses include transportation costs and meals (80%) and lodging while away from home in the pursuit of a trade or business, along with reasonable laundry and incidental expenses. Entertainment expenses are not included as travel and are discussed elsewhere.

    B.   Away-from-Home Requirement. To meet the away from home test, an employee must be away from home overnight. An overnight stay is a period substantially longer than an ordinary day's work and requires rest, sleep or relief from the work period. To be in travel status a taxpayer must be away from his tax home for a temporary period. Generally, if a taxpayer has a work assignment of less than one year it is regarded as temporary. If the work assignment is more than two years it is regarded as indefinite. For periods between one and two years, the facts and circumstances determine each specific case.

    C.   Disallowed and Limited Travel.

        Expenses related to attending a convention, seminar, or similar meeting are disallowed unless the expenses are related to a trade or business of the taxpayer.

        The deduction of expenses for luxury water travel is limited to twice the highest amount generally allowable for a day of travel for federal employees serving in the United States.

        No deduction is allowed for travel that, by itself, is deemed to be educational by the taxpayer. This rule does not apply with respect to a deduction for travel necessary to engage in an activity that gives rise to a business deduction related to education.

        Expenses incurred to attend conventions outside North America are disallowed unless the taxpayer can show that it is as reasonable for the convention to be held in a foreign location as in the North American area.

    D.   Combined Business and Pleasure Travel. If a trip combines both business and pleasure and is within the United States, transportation is deductible only if the trip is primarily for business. If the trip is primarily a vacation, expenses relating to business, other than transportation, are still deductible. Special rules apply for trips outside the United States.

V.   MOVING EXPENSES

A.   Moving expenses are deductible by employees from (not subject to the 2% limit) adjusted gross income. Reimbursements from the employer must be included in gross income. The two basic tests that must be met for moving expenses to be deductible are the distance test and the time requirement test.

B.   Distance Test. The distance test requires that the taxpayer's new job location be at least 35 miles farther from the taxpayer's old residence than the old residence was from the former place of employment.

C.   Time Requirements. A time requirement is also necessary for an employee to qualify for the moving expense deduction. An employee must be employed full time at the new location for 39 weeks in the twelve month period following the move and a self-employed individual must work in the new location for 78 weeks during the next two years.

D.   When Deductible. Moving expenses are deductible in the year of payment. However, if the employee is to be reimbursed for the expenses in the following year, an election can be made to deduct the expenses in that year.

E.   Classification of Moving Expenses. There are limits on various classes of moving expense deductions. The five classes are:

1)   Expense of moving household and personal belongings

2)   Expense of travel to the new residence (meals are limited to 80%)

3)   Expense of house-hunting trips (meals are limited to 80%)

4)   Temporary living expenses (meals are limited to 80%)

5)   Certain residential buying, selling, or leasing expenses

There is no dollar limit on classes 1 and 2. Classes 3 and 4 combined are limited to $1,500. For classes 3, 4, and 5 the total limit is $3,000.

VI.   EDUCATION EXPENSES

A. General Requirements. An employee may deduct expenses (subject to the 2% limit) for education as ordinary and necessary business expenses provided such items were incurred either (1) to maintain or improve existing skills required in the present job, or (2) to meet the express requirements of the employer or the requirements imposed by law to retain the employment status. However, expenses are not deductible if they are required to meet the minimum educational standards for the taxpayer's job or if they qualify the taxpayer for a new trade or business.

B. Requirements Imposed by Law or by the Employer for Retention of Employment. Many states require that teachers take additional courses to retain their position. Such expenses would qualify as deductible since they are incurred in meeting requirements imposed by law or the employer for retention of employment.

C. Maintaining or Improving Existing Skills. The deductibility of educational expenses said to "maintain or improve existing skills" is a heavily litigated subject. The deduction is disallowed in cases where the deduction qualifies the taxpayer for a new trade or business. For example, the expenses of a business executive or accountant incurred in obtaining a law degree are specifically not deductible under this provision.

VII. ENTERTAINMENT EXPENSES

A. Classification of Expenses. Entertainment expenses can be categorized as those "directly related to" business and those "associated with" business. "Directly related to" expenses are those related to an actual business meeting or discussion. "Associated with" expenses are those that promote the general goodwill of the business; however, the entertainment must serve a specific business purpose.

B. Restrictions upon Deductibility. Business meals are 80% deductible if the following conditions are met:

- The meal is directly related to or associated with the active conduct of a trade or business,

- The expense is not lavish or extravagant, and

- The taxpayer (or an employee) is present at the meal.

The deduction of costs related to entertainment facilities is strictly limited. If a country club is used greater than 50 percent for business use (both directly related and associated with), the taxpayer may be entitled to a deduction for dues based on the ratio of the days of directly-related business use and the total days of use of the facility.

A deduction for the cost of a ticket for an entertainment activity is limited to the face value of the ticket. Deductions for skyboxes at sports arenas are generally disallowed except to the extent of the cost of a regular ticket.

Business gifts are limited to $25 per donee per year. Excluded from the $25 limit are certain gifts costing $4 or less, gifts used for advertising, and gifts or awards for employees for length of service, etc. that cost $400 or less.

VIII. OTHER EMPLOYEE EXPENSES

A. Office in the Home. There is no deduction for an office in the home unless it is used exclusively and on a regular basis as the taxpayer's principal place of business or as a place of business which is used by patients, clients, or customers. If the office is used in connection with the taxpayer's business as an employee, the use of the office must also be for the convenience of the employer. The deductions for an office in the home cannot exceed gross income from the business activity reduced by all other deductible expenses attributable to the business but not allocable to the use of the home itself (unless the item would otherwise be deductible).

B. Miscellaneous Employee Expenses. Miscellaneous employee expenses such as special clothing, union dues, and professional expenses are deductible subject to the 2% of AGI limitation.

TEST FOR SELF-EVALUATION

True or False

Indicate which of the following statements are true or false by circling the correct answer.

(T)   F   1.   Expenses of self-employed taxpayers are deductible for adjusted gross income as trade or business expenses.

(T)   F   2.   An employer-employee relationship exists if the employer has the right to specify the result and the ways and means by which the result is to be attained.

(T) F 3. A self-employed individual is required to file Schedule C of Form 1040.

(T) F 4. Unreimbursed employee travel expenses are a deduction from adjusted gross income.

(T) F 5. All miscellaneous deductions are subject to the 2 percent of AGI limitation.

T (F) 6. To the extent employee expenses are reimbursed under an accountable plan, they are deductions for adjusted gross income.

(T) (F) 7. If an employer reimburses an employee for more than his or her expenses, the excess is not income to the employee.

(T) (F) 8. Travel and transportation expenses are defined in the same manner for tax purposes.

(T) F 9. Commuting expenses from home to one's place of employment are not deductible.

(T) F 10. An employee will be allowed a deduction for the cost of commuting from a primary job to a second job.

T (F) 11. Taxpayers must always use the automatic mileage method to determine an automobile expense deduction.

T (F) 12. If a taxpayer has two or more vehicles in use at the same time, he or she may use the automatic mileage method.

(T) F 13. A taxpayer cannot change to the automatic mileage method if the election to expense has been made or accelerated depreciation has previously been taken.

(T) F 14. Unreimbursed travel expenses are a deduction from adjusted gross income (subject to the 2% floor).

(T) F 15. Union dues are deductible (subject to the 2% of adjusted gross income limitation) for tax purposes.

(T)   F   16.   To be deductible, a home office must be used exclusively and on a regular basis as the taxpayer's principal place of business or as a place which is used by patients, clients, or customers.

T   (F)   17.   All business gift deductions are limited to $25 per donee.

T   (F)   18.   Law school expenses are always deductible.

T   (F)   19.   The cost of a Bar or CPA exam review course is generally deductible.

(T)   F   20.   The moving expense mileage deduction is 9 cents per mile for 1992.

(T)   F   21.   Expenses of moving household and personal belongings are not subject to a dollar limitation.

(T)   F   22.   Qualified business meals are only 80 percent deductible.

(T)   (F)   23.   Luxury water travel is limited to three times the Federal employee daily travel rate.

(T)   F   24.   Travel as a form of education is not allowed as a deduction for individual taxpayers.

(T)   F   25.   If per diem or milage reimbursements paid under an accountable plan exceed the government rate, then the excess is reported on the employee's W-2 subject to withholding and employment taxes.

(T)   T   26.   If an employee receives reimbursement under a nonaccountable plan, then reimbursement is reported on the employee's W-2 and any allowable expenses are deductible in the same manner as unreimbursed expenses.

(T)   (F)   27.   A taxpayer may switch to the automatic mileage method on an automobile if in prior year he had used MACRS or § 179 expensing on that automobile.

Fill-in-the-Blanks

Complete the following statements with the appropriate word(s) or amount(s).

1.   In order to claim a deduction for travel expenses, a taxpayer must be away from home for a ___Temp___ period.

2.   To qualify for a moving expense deduction, the taxpayer's new job location must be at least _____35_____ miles farther from the taxpayer's old residence than the old residence was from the former place of employment.

3.   To satisfy the time requirement for the moving expense deduction, a self-employed individual must work in the new location for _____78_____ weeks during the next two years and an employee must be employed for _____39_____ weeks during the next 12 months.

4.   The total expenses for house-hunting trips and temporary living quarters cannot exceed _____1500_____ dollars.

5.   If an education expense qualifies the taxpayer for a ___new___ trade or business the amount is not deductible.

6.   If a convention is held outside ___N America___ , the deduction of the convention expenses may be limited.

7.   Educational expenses incurred to maintain or improve ___existing___ skills or to meet the requirements of an ___employer___ are usually deductible.

8.   Entertainment expense deductions are categorized as those ___directly___ related to business and those ___associated___ with business.

9.   For an office in the home to be deductible, it must be used exclusively and on a regular basis as the taxpayer's ___principal___ place of business, or a place which is used by ___patients___, ___clients___, or ___customers___.

10. The cost of special clothing specifically required as a condition of ___employment___ and not adaptable to ___regular___ wear is deductible.

Multiple Choice

Choose the best answer for each of the following questions.

_____   1.   Which of the following educational expenses would be deductible?
        a. Travel expenses for general knowledge.
        b. CPA review course expenses.
        c. Law school educational expenses.
        d. Expenses of a senior in college who has already accepted a job.
        e. None of the above are deductible

_____ 2. The substantiation requirements for business entertainment under § 274 do not include:
   a. The amount
   b. Credit card receipts
   c. The business purpose
   d. The business relationship
   e. None of the above

_____ 3. In 1992, an employee drove her automobile 20,000 miles on business. Using the automatic mileage method, her deduction for unreimbursed expenses (before any 2% limit) is:
   a. $5,500 for AGI
   b. $5,500 from AGI
   c. $5,200 from AGI
   d. $1,800 from AGI
   e. Some other amount

_____ 4. Which of the following miscellaneous expenses is not subject to the 2 percent of adjusted gross income limitation?
   a. Unreimbursed employee expenses
   b. Outside sales expenses
   c. Union dues
   d. Investment expenses
   e. Certain amortizable bond premiums

_____ 5. Cathy McGrath is a high school teacher. She has set aside one room in her house as a home office where she grades papers, prepares for class, etc. No revenue is produced from this activity. Depreciation and maintenance are $400 on the home office. How much of the expenses are deductible by Cathy?
   a. -0-
   b. $400
   c. $500
   d. $900
   e. Some other amount

_____ 6. T is self-employed and while traveling spends $120 on meals and $200 on transportation and lodging. What is the amount of T's deduction for these expenditures?
   a. $296
   b. $320
   c. $256
   d. $280

e. Some other amount

_____ 7. T, an employee of an accounting firm, spent $600 on dues to professional organizations and $250 for subscriptions to professional journals. T's AGI is $30,000. Assuming T itemizes deductions, how much (after the 2% limit) may she deduct?
a. $-0-
b. $850
c. $600
d. $250
e. Some other amount

_____ 8. Which of the following would be an employer-employee relationship?
a. A plumber who comes to your home to do work
b. A CPA who prepares a tax return
c. A physician who pays a nurse to help him in his office
d. A gardener who takes care of individual lawns for a monthly fee
e. None of the above

_____ 9. A self-employed CPA moves from California to Texas to establish a new practice. To qualify for a moving expense deduction, which of the following must be true?
a. He must work for another CPA in Texas for one year
b. He must have been in practice for three years in California
c. He must obtain a license to practice from the state of Texas
d. He must work full-time in the new location for 78 weeks during the next two years
e. None of the above

_____ 10. Fran Huffman is a CPA who has a small tax practice in her home in addition to working her regular job. The gross income from this practice is $5,500 for the year. Based on square footage, the portion of mortgage interest and real estate taxes allocable to the business amount to $3,000. The allocable portion of maintenance, utilities, and depreciation is $3,500. Assuming no other expenses related to the business were incurred, what amount of the maintenance, utilities, and depreciation is deductible by Fran?
a. $-0-
b. $3,500
c. $2,500
d. $500
e. Some other amount

10-27

_____ 11. Mike Reynolds, a staff accountant for a CPA firm, incurred the following expenses:

Travel	$200
Transportation	$500
Dues and Subscriptions	$300

Mike gave his employer an adequate accounting and received a reimbursement under an accountable plan of $1,000 to cover these expenses. What amount is deductible from adjusted gross income?
a. $-0-
b. $60
c. $300
d. $700
e. Some other amount

_____ 12. In 1992, Rachel Mollering, an employee of the Big CPA firm, spent $3,000 for business expenses (none of which are subject to the 80% limitation). She was reimbursed $4,000 for these expenses. *An adequate accounting was not made to her employer.* If Rachel's AGI was $50,000 for the year and her employer included $4,000 on her W-2, what amount of the employee business expenses may she deduct as an itemized deduction?
a. $-0-
b. $2,000
c. $3,000
d. $5,000
e. Some other amount

_____ 13. U had travel expenses of $1,500 substantiated by credit card receipts. He has a diary that provides the business purpose and relationship for $800 of these expenses. How much will U be allowed as a deduction, before considering any limitation based on adjusted gross income?
a. a maximum of $25 per day
b. $700
c. $800
d. $1,500
e. Some other amount

_____ 14. Under the deemed substantiation method of accounting for expenses, what is the maximum amount that taxpayers are allowed as a deduction without being required to substantiate the amount of the expense?
a. The federal per diem amount

　　b. $138 per day
　　c. All expenses up to $25 per day
　　d. The state per diem rate of the state in which they live
　　e. None of the above

15. Statutory employees report income and deductions on which of the following Forms or Schedules?
　　a. Form 2106
　　b. Schedule B
　　c. Schedule E
　　d. Form 2106 and Schedule A
　　e. None of above

16. K, a self-employed CPA, attended a two-day course on auditing. She incurred the following expenses:

Airfare	$ 500
Taxi	40
Meals	200
Lodging	300
Laundry	20
Total	$1,060

How much can K claim as a deduction *for* AGI?
　　a. $-0-
　　b. $1,060
　　c. $1,020
　　d. $1,040
　　e. Some other amount

17. J, a professor of history at a local university, attended an investment seminar. He incurred the following expenses:

Airfare	$300
Meals	100
Lodging	200
Total	$600

What is J's miscellaneous itemized deduction (before any 2% limit)?
　　a. $-0-
　　b. $540
　　c. $580

d. $600
e. Some other amount

_____ 18. T incurred the following unreimbursed expenses in connection with his employment:

Annual dues to country club	$3,000	
Business meals (directly related)	2,000	1600
Personal meals	1,000	1800
Days of business use (directly related)	60	3400
Days of personal use	40	

What is T's entertainment deduction before any 2% limitation?
a. $6,000
b. $4,800
c. $4,000
d. $3,040
e. Some other amount

_____ 19. T purchased her automobile in 1991 for $15,000. It was used 80% for business purposes. T drove the car for 10,000 business miles in 1991. What is T's basis in the business portion of the automobile at the beginning of 1992.
a. $15,000
b. $12,000
c. $10,900
d. $8,000
e. Some other amount

_____ 20. The foreign convention expense limitation rules would apply to a convention held in which of the following?
a. Mexico
b. Hawaii
c. Alaska
d. Guam
e. Venezuela

Problems

1.   In 1992, Dorothy Hicks was transferred from San Francisco to San Diego. She paid

$4,000 to have her personal and household goods moved. In addition, she had temporary living expenses of $900 (including meals of $300) and qualified house-hunting expenses of $800 (including meals of $200). During the move, Dorothy drove the 500 miles to San Diego, incurring lodging expenses of $150 and meal expenses of $50. In selling her residence Dorothy incurred $6,500 in qualified selling expenses. Dorothy received no reimbursement for her moving expenses. Calculate Dorothy's moving expense deduction using the following worksheet.

Moving household goods $_____

Travel, meals and lodging $_____

House-hunting expenses $_____

Temporary living expenses $_____

Total $_____

Amount of house-hunting and
temporary living expenses allowed $_____

Qualified house sale expenses $_____

Total $_____

Amount of house-hunting, temporary living,
and house sale expenses allowed $_____

Moving expense deduction $_____

2.   Ray Whittington, a college professor, incurred the following business-related expenses for which he was not reimbursed.

Mileage	16,500 miles
Travel (includes meals of $200)	$750
Air transportation	$600

Calculate Ray's employee business expense deduction for 1992 (before the 2% limitation).

Mileage	$_____
Travel	$_____
Transportation	$_____
Total	$_____

3. Chee Chow, a college professor, accepted a position with the IRS in Washington D.C. The assignment was designated as temporary and was for a 12-month period. Chee left his wife and children in Houston and rented an apartment in Washington during his employment. Chee's AGI for the year is $50,000. He incurred the following expenses, none of which were reimbursed by the IRS.

Air fare to and from Washington D.C. $2,000
Rent on Washington apartment $10,000
Meals, in Washington $5,000

What amount is deductible by Chee? Is the deduction for AGI or from AGI?

Code Section Recognition

Indicate, by number, the appropriate Code Section where the following items are found.

_____ 1. Deductions for adjusted gross income.

_____ 2. Transportation expenses.

_____ 3. Travel expenses.

_____ 4. Moving expense deduction.

_____ 5. Entertainment expenses deductions and limitations.

_____ 6. Office in the home.

SOLUTIONS TO CHAPTER 10

True or False

1. True   (p. 10-2)

2. True   (p. 10-2)

3. True   (p. 10-3)

4. True   (p. 10-4)

5. False   Only certain deductions are subject to the 2% limitation. (p. 10-4)

6. True   (p. 10-3)

7. False   The amount is income. (p. 10-10)

8. False   They are different categories of deductions. (pp. 10-11, 14)

9. True   (p. 10-11)

10. True   (p. 10-12)

11. False   They may use actual operating costs. (p. 10-13)

12. False   Employees with two vehicles must use actual operating costs. (p. 10-14)

13. True   (p. 10-14)

14. True   (p. 10-14)

15. True   (p. 10-29)

16. True   (p. 10-27)

17. False   Employees may be given awards costing up to $400 if the gift is for retire-ment, etc. (p. 10-270)

18. False   The taxpayer is being qualified for a new trade or business; therefore, the education expenses are not deductible. (p. 10-24)

19.   False   The taxpayer has not met the minimum standards for the job. (p. 10-23)

20.   True   (p. 10-21)

21.   True   (p. 10-21)

22.   True   (p. 10-5)

23.   False   The limit is based on two times the federal employee travel rate. (p. 10-17)

24.   True   (p. 10-17)

25.   True   (p. 10-10)

26.   True   (p. 10-10)

27.   False   Taxpayers may not switch to the automatic mileage method. (p. 1-14)

Fill-in-the-Blanks

1.   temporary (p. 10-15)

2.   35 (p. 10-19)

3.   78, 39 (p. 10-20)

4. $1,500 (p. 10-22)

5.   new (p. 10-23)

6.   North America (p. 10-19)

7.   existing, employer (p. 10-23)

8.   directly, associated (p. 10-25)

9.   principal, patients, clients, customers (p. 10-27)

10.   employment, regular (p. 10-29)

Multiple Choice

1.   E   (p. 10-23)

2.   B   (p. 10-8)

3.   B   20,000 miles x $.275 = $5,500 from AGI. (p. 10-13)

4.   E   (p. 10-4)

5.   A   (p. 10-27)

6.   A   (80% of $120) + $200 = $296. (pp. 10-5, 10-14)

7.   D $600 + 250 - (2% of $30,000) = $250. (p. 10-29)

8.   C   (p. 10-2)

9.   D   (p. 10-20)

10.   C $5,500 - 3,000 = $2,500. (p. 10-27)

11.   A   All of the expenses are reimbursed. (p. 10-10)

12.   B $3,000 - (2% of $50,000) = $2,000. (p. 10-10)

13.   C   (p. 10-8)

14.   A   (p. 10-8)

15.   E   Statutory employees report on Schedule C. (p. 10-3)

16.   C $500 + 40 + (80% x $200) + 300 + 20 = $1,020. (pp. 10-3, 14)

17.   A   Investment seminar expenses are not deductible. (p. 10-16)

18.   D   [(60% x $3,000) + $2,000] x 80% = $3,040. (pp. 10-5, 10-25)

19.   C   ($15,000 x 80%) - ($.11 x 10,000) = $10,900. (p. 10-14)

20.   E   (p. 10-18)

Problems

1.   Moving household goods $4,000
        Travel, meals and lodging
          $150 + (80% x $50) + ($.09 x 500)   235

        House-hunting expenses
          $600 + (80% x $200) $760
        Temporary living expenses
          $600 + (80% x $300)   _840_
        Total $1,600

        Max amount of house-hunting and
        temporary living expenses allowed $1,500
        Qualified house sale expenses   _6,500_
        Total $8,000

        Max amount of house-hunting, temporary living,
        and house sale expenses allowed   _3,000_
        Moving expense deduction $7,235
        (p. 10-22)

2.   Mileage 16,500 x $.275 $4,538
        Travel (80% of $200) + $550 710
        Transportation   _600_
        Total $5,848
        (p. 10-13)

3.   The expenses are deductible from AGI, subject to the 2% limit. Chee's total deduc-
        tion would be as follows:

                   Air fare $ 2,000
                   Rent   10,000
                   Meals 80%($5,000)   _4,000_
                   Total $16,000
                   2% of $50,000   _-1,000_
                   Deduction $15,000
                   (p. 10-15)

Code Section Recognition

1.   § 62

2.   § 162

3.   § 162

4.   § 217

5.   § 274

6.   § 280A

CHAPTER

□
11
□

DEDUCTIONS AND LOSSES: CERTAIN ITEMIZED DEDUCTIONS

CHAPTER HIGHLIGHTS

Personal expenses are generally disallowed as deductions. However, Congress has identified certain personal expenses which are allowed as itemized deductions. This chapter summarizes the provisions which allow deductions for medical expenses, state and local taxes, certain interest expense, and charitable contributions. The limitations which apply to these deductions are also discussed.

I. MEDICAL EXPENSES

    A. General Requirements. Taxpayers are allowed a deduction for medical expenses (net of any reimbursement) for the care of the taxpayer, spouse, and dependents. Medical expenses are deductible only to the extent that they exceed 7.5 percent of adjusted gross income.

    B. Medical Expenses Defined. The term medical care means expenditures incurred for the "diagnosis, cure, mitigation, treatment, or prevention of disease," or for "affecting any structure or function of the body."

        Expenses to improve the taxpayer's general health such as programs to stop smoking or to lose weight are not deductible. Expenses for unnecessary cosmetic surgery are not deductible.

        If a patient is placed in a nursing home for personal or family reasons, expenses are deductible only to the extent of actual medical or nursing attention received. If the patient is placed in the home primarily for medical reasons, the expenses are fully deductible.

The expenses of keeping a dependent at a special school for the mentally or physically handicapped may be deductible as medical expenses.

C. Capital Expenditures for Medical Purposes. Capital expenditures for medical care are deductible to the extent that the cost exceeds the increase in value of the related property. However, the cost of capital expenditures that enable a handicapped individual to live independently and productively are fully deductible subject to the 7.5 percent of adjusted gross income limitation.

D. Transportation and Lodging Expenses for Medical Treatment. Expenditures for transportation to and from the point of treatment are deductible as medical expenses. If a taxpayer uses a personal automobile, a mileage allowance of 9 cents per mile may be claimed as a medical expense or the taxpayer may use actual out-of-pocket costs. Qualified lodging that is part of medical care is deductible up to $50 per night per person.

E. Amounts paid for Medical Insurance Premiums. Medical insurance premiums are included in medical expenses subject to the 7.5 percent limitation. A self-employed person who is not covered under a medical plan may deduct as a business expense (*for* AGI) up to 25 percent of medical insurance premiums paid for coverage for his or her family. Any excess can be claimed as a medical expense.

F. Medical Expenses Incurred for Spouse and Dependents. Medical expenses for dependents are deductible if they are legitimate medical expenses. The gross income test and joint return test need not be met for a dependent to qualify for the medical deduction.

G. Year of Deduction. Medical expenses are deductible in the year paid by the taxpayer.

H. Reimbursements. If a taxpayer receives an insurance reimbursement for medical expenses deducted in a previous year, the reimbursement must be included as income in the year of receipt. The reimbursement is income only if the expense provided a tax benefit in the previous year.

If the taxpayer used the standard deduction amount in the year the medical expenses were paid instead of itemizing deductions, any reimbursements received need not be included in gross income.

II. TAXES

A. Deductibility as a Tax. Taxpayers are allowed a deduction for the payment of certain state and local taxes to reduce the effect of multiple taxation. The law defines a tax as an enforced contribution exacted under legislative authority. Under § 164, the following taxes are deductible:

- State, local, and foreign real property taxes

- State, and local personal property taxes

- State, local, and foreign income taxes

- The environmental tax

Federal income taxes, employee FICA taxes, estate, inheritance, and gift taxes, general sales taxes, and excise taxes cannot be deducted under this section.

B. Property Taxes, Assessments, and Apportionment of Taxes.

For personal property taxes to be deductible, they must be ad valorem (assessed in relation to the value of the property).

As a general rule, assessments for local benefits are not deductible and are added to the adjusted basis of the property.

Real estate taxes are apportioned between the buyer and seller on the basis of the number of days the property was held by each. This apportionment is required without regard to whether the tax is paid by the buyer or seller.

C. Income Taxes.

State and local taxes are deductible in the year paid by a cash basis taxpayer. Withholding and actual payments are deductible under this rule and state and local tax refunds are included in gross income, providing there was a tax benefit in the prior year.

State and local income taxes imposed on an individual are itemized deductions even if the source of the taxable income is from a trade or business or the production of income.

III.   INTEREST

A.   Disallowed and Allowed Items. Taxpayers are allowed a deduction within limits for the following kinds of interest:

- Trade or business interest

- Investment interest

- Interest on passive activities

- Qualified residence interest

After 1990, personal interest is not deductible.

B.   Investment interest is deductible only to the extent of net investment income. Disallowed investment interest may be carried over and deducted in future years.

C.   Qualified residence interest includes acquisition indebtedness up to a maximum of $1,000,000 ($500,000, if married filing separately) on a taxpayer's first and second residences, and interest on home equity borrowing of up to $100,000 ($50,000, if married filing separately).

D.   Classification of Interest Expense. Interest expense can be either a deduction for or a deduction from adjusted gross income, depending on whether the loan is for business (other than that as an employee), investment, or personal purposes. Deductions for interest charges on personal indebtedness are reported as itemized deductions on Schedule A of Form 1040 (subject to limitations).

IV.   CHARITABLE CONTRIBUTIONS

A.   The Code permits the deduction of contributions made to qualified charitable organizations. The deduction is justified as a social consideration in the tax law.

B. Criteria for a Gift. To qualify as a charitable contribution, the gift must be made to a qualified organization. The major elements needed for a gift to be deductible are a donative intent, the absence of consideration, and acceptance by the donee.

If a contribution to a college or university carries the right to purchase athletic tickets, then 80% of the amount of the contribution is deductible.

Contributions of services are not allowed as a deduction. Out-of-pocket expenses incurred in the performance of donated services are allowed if there is no significant element of personal pleasure, recreation, or vacation in the donated services.

C. Qualified Organizations. A qualified organization is:

- A state or possession of the United States or any subdivision thereof

- An organization situated in the United States and operated exclusively for religious, charitable, scientific, literary, or educational purposes or for the prevention of cruelty to children or animals

- A veterans' organization

- A fraternal organization operating under the lodge system

- A cemetery

D. Time of Deduction. Charitable contributions are deductible in the year paid for both cash and accrual basis taxpayers. However, an accrual basis corporation can pledge a contribution at the end of the year and deduct it if the amount is paid within two and one-half months after the close of the tax year.

E. Recordkeeping and Valuation Requirements. As a general rule contributions of property are deducted at the fair market value of the property. Taxpayers must have one of the following to substantiate each charitable contribution of money:

- A canceled check,

- A receipt from the donee, or

- Other reliable written evidence.

For contributions of property valued at $500 or less, the taxpayer must have a receipt from the organization showing the donee, date, location and description of the property. The taxpayer must also have written evidence of the fair market value and certain other items with respect to the contribution. For gifts of property valued at over $500, additional information is required and the taxpayer must complete Form 8283 (either Part A or B).

F. Limitations on Charitable Contribution Deductions.

There are limitations placed on the amount of charitable contributions. For individuals, the general AGI limitations are:

- 50 percent for contributions to certain public charities, all private operating foundations, and certain private nonoperating foundations.

- 30 percent for contributions of cash and ordinary income property to private nonoperating foundations and contributions of appreciated capital gain property to 50 percent organizations. If the value of the capital gain property is reduced by any appreciation on the property, then the 50 percent limit applies.

- 20 percent for contributions of long-term capital gain property to certain private nonoperating foundations. See text for calculation of limits.

If ordinary income property is contributed, the deduction is equal to the fair market value of the property less the amount of ordinary income which would have been reported if the property were sold.

Generally, contributions may be carried over for five years. Contributions made during the carryover years are deducted before carryover amounts are applied.

V.   MISCELLANEOUS DEDUCTIONS

A. Taxpayers are allowed certain miscellaneous deductions if they exceed two percent of AGI. Examples of such deductions are:

- Professional dues
- Uniforms
- Tax return preparation fees

- Job hunting expenses
- Safe-deposit box fees
- Investment expenses
- Appraisals for casualty losses, donated property, etc.
- Hobby loss expenses

Miscellaneous deductions not subject to the two percent limitation include:

- Moving expenses
- Gambling losses
- Certain handicapped work expenses
- Certain casualty and theft losses (10% of AGI limitation)
- Certain unrecovered annuity investments

VI.   OVERALL LIMITATION ON CERTAIN ITEMIZED DEDUCTIONS

Effective in 1991, itemized deductions, other than medical expenses, investment interest expense, casualty and theft losses, and wagering losses to the extent of wagering gains, are phased out when adjusted gross income reaches a certain level. The applicable itemized deductions are reduced by an amount equal to three percent of the excess of adjusted gross income over $100,000 ($50,000 for married filing separately). Certain applicable itemized deductions cannot be reduced by more than 80 percent.

TEST FOR SELF-EVALUATION

True or False

Indicate which of the following statements are true or false by circling the correct answer.

T F 1. For medical expenses to be deductible, they must be for the taxpayer, spouse or dependents.

T F 2. The term "medical care expenditure" would include expenses that are not related to a particular ailment.

T **F** 3. Nursing home expenditures are always deductible as medical expenses.

T F 4. Under certain circumstances, capital expenditures can be deducted as medical expenses.

T F 5. The cost of special schools for the mentally or physically handicapped may be deductible as a medical expense.

T F 6. For other than self-employed taxpayers, 100 percent of medical insurance premiums are subject to the 7.5 percent of adjusted gross income floor.

T F 7. The term "medicine and drugs" does not include toothpaste, shaving lotion, deodorants, and hand lotions.

T F 8. The expense of unnecessary cosmetic surgery are not deductible as a medical expense.

T F 9. All medicine and drugs are deductible.

T F 10. If a taxpayer is reimbursed for medical expenses that were paid in a previous year, he or she must always include that amount in income.

T F 11. All amounts paid to a government are deductible under § 164 as a tax.

T F 12. The IRS defines a tax as "an enforced contribution exacted under legislative authority in the exercise of taxing power, and imposed and collected for raising revenue to be used for public or governmental purposes."

T F 13. State, local, and foreign income taxes are deductible for Federal tax purposes.

T F 14. For personal property taxes to be deductible, they must be ad valorem, that is, assessed in relation to the value of the property.

T F 15. Real property taxes include taxes assessed for local benefits such as new streets and sidewalks.

T F 16. Real property taxes are apportioned between the buyer and seller on the basis of the number of days each held the property.

T F 17. State income taxes are always deducted on the accrual method.

T F 18. For 1992, personal interest is not deductible by taxpayers.

T (F) 19. Cash contributions to needy individuals are deductible charitable contributions.

(T) F 20. Property donated to a charity is generally valued at fair market value at the time of the gift.

T (F) 21. Any charitable contribution is deductible for tax purposes.

T (F) 22. Interest on a principal residence mortgage is not deductible.

(T) F 23. For 1992, the investment interest expense deduction is limited to net investment income.

T (F) 24. The interest deduction is always a deduction for adjusted gross income.

(T) (F) 25. The estate and gift taxes are deductible for income tax purposes.

Fill-in-the-Blanks

Complete the following statements with the appropriate word(s) or amount(s).

1. Interest has been defined by the Supreme Court as __compensation__ for the use or forbearance of money.

2. For an interest payment to be deductible by the taxpayer, the debt must be the taxpayer's __obligation__.

3. The tax law requires that prepaid interest except for "points" on a personal residence be __accrued__ and allocated to the subsequent periods to which the interest payments relate.

4. Excess annual contributions to public charities subject to the 50 percent limitation are carried forward for ___5___ years.

5. Fees paid to mortgage loan companies for finding, placing, or processing a mortgage loan are commonly called __points__.

6. To be deductible, a charitable contribution must be to a __qualified__ organization.

7. Property donated to a charity is generally valued at fair __market__ value.

8.   The maximum limitation on charitable contributions for individuals is _____50_____ percent of adjusted gross income.

Multiple Choice

Choose the best answer for each of the following questions.

_____ 1. Steve Linberg borrows $150,000 at 10% interest on January 3, 1992. The proceeds are used to purchase $100,000 worth of raw land and $50,000 worth of stock in Exxon. During 1992 the stock pays dividends of $2,500. Steve has deductible expenses on this investment property of $500 (after considering the 2% of adjusted gross income limitation). Assuming Steve pays interest of $15,000 (10% of $150,000) in 1992, how much is deductible?
   a. $2,000
   b. $12,500
   c. $2,500
   d. $15,000
   e. Some other amount

_____ 2. During 1992 Mary Adams had adjusted gross income of $30,000 and she paid the following medical expenses:

Medical insurance	560
Dentist's charges	600
Physicians' charges	1,000
Prescription drugs	100
Hospital costs	400

Assuming Mary itemizes deductions, what is Mary's medical expense deduction?
   a. $-0-
   b. $2,660
   c. $410
   d. $1,160
   e. Some other amount

_____ 3. During the current year, T paid $66 for California license plates for his automobile. California plates are sold at a fee of $24 plus $2 per hundred dollar valuation of the automobile. Assuming T itemizes his deductions, how much, if any, may T claim as a deduction for taxes?
   a. $-0-

b. $26
c. $42
d. $66
e. Some other amount

For Questions 4 through 8, indicate the amount of the charitable contribution deduction T would be allowed in each of the independent situations.

_____ 4. In 1992 T donated an art object to Goodwill Industries, a qualified charity. The art object cost T $2,000 five months ago and has a fair market value of $3,000 on the date of donation.
a. $-0-
b. $2,000
c. $2,500
d. $3,000
e. Some other amount

_____ 5. Assume the same situation as in Question 4, except the art object possesses a fair market value of $1,800 (not $3,000) on the date of donation.
a. $-0-
b. $1,800
c. $2,000
d. $1,600
e. Some other amount

_____ 6. T donated shares of Texaco stock to his church in satisfaction of last year's church pledge. T purchased the stock as an investment two years ago. The stock cost T $2,300 and possessed a fair market value of $2,700 on the date of donation.
a. $-0-
b. $2,300
c. $2,700
d. $2,500
e. Some other amount

_____ 7. T donated $650 of his time as a painter and paint with a cost basis to him of $200, to help fix up his church. How much can he deduct?
a. $-0-
b. $850
c. $650
d. $200
e. Some other amount

_____ 8. T works for the American Red Cross for free during each month of the current year. He would normally charge $400 per month for the type of work performed. What is T's charitable deduction?
     a. $-0-
     b. $400
     c. $4,800
     d. Some other amount

_____ 9. What is the maximum amount of property contributions that a taxpayer may make to qualified organizations without being required to complete Form 8283?
     a. $-0-
     b. $200
     c. $500
     d. $3,000
     e. Some other amount

_____ 10. Pat Sbarbaro is a cash basis taxpayer who had $1,000 of state income tax withheld from her salary in 1992. In addition, during 1992 she received a refund of 1991 state income taxes of $250. During 1992, Pat also made estimated state income tax payments of $600. For 1992, Pat's state income tax deduction is
     a. $-0-
     b. $1,350
     c. $1,000
     d. $1,600
     e. Some other amount

_____ 11. Gene Hallner owns his own home which he bought several years ago. His original mortgage, which was used to buy the house, is $150,000. In the current year he obtains a home equity loan on the house of $90,000. The interest on the original mortgage is $15,000 and on the new loan is $10,000. The fair market value of the house is $325,000. How much of this interest is deductible as "qualified residence interest"?
     a. $-0-
     b. $10,000
     c. $15,000
     d. $25,000
     e. Some other amount

_____ 12. Which of the following items will not qualify as medical expense deduction?

    a. Eyeglasses
    b. Insulin
    c. A trip to Arizona for the general improvement of the taxpayer's health
    d. Transportation to and from a doctor's office
    e. None of the above

13. The prepaid interest rules of § 461(g) apply to all prepaid interest payments except which of the following?
    a. "Points" on a rental house
    b. Construction loans
    c. Bank auto loans
    d. "Points" paid by a buyer of a personal residence
    e. None of the above

14. Big Booster gives $1,000 to his alma mater's athletic department. The contribution entitles him to four football tickets worth $50 each. How much is Big's charitable contribution deduction?
    a. $-0-
    b. $1,000
    c. $800
    d. $640
    e. Some other amount

Questions 15 to 17 use the following information.

Eric Ross, who is single and has no dependents, had adjusted gross income of $80,000 in 1992, comprised of the following:

10 000

Salary	$74,000
Net investment income	6,000

During 1992, uninsured art objects owned by Eric, with a basis of $50,000 and a fair market value of $70,000, sustained casualty fire damage reducing the fair market value to $60,000. Also during 1992, Eric made the following payments:

Interest on margin account to stockbroker	$18,000
Real estate taxes on condominium (owned by Eric's mother, in which Eric resides)	3,000
State and city gasoline taxes	180
Medical insurance premiums	300
Unreimbursed dental expenses	4,500
Contribution to political committee	

of elected public official   500

Eric elected to itemize his deductions for 1992. (CPA adapted)

_____ 15. How much can Eric claim as taxes in itemized deductions on his 1992 return?
    a. $0
    b. $180
    c. $3,000
    d. $3,180
    e. Some other amount

_____ 16. How much can Eric claim in his itemized deductions for medical and dental expenses on his 1992 return?
    a. $2,400
    b. $800
    c. $300
    d. $-0-
    e. Some other amount

_____ 17. How much can Eric claim in his itemized deductions for the casualty loss on his 1992 return?
    a. $-0-
    b. $1,900
    c. $2,000
    d. $9,900
    e. Some other amount

_____ 18. Carol Hirai, a resident of San Diego, travels with her dependent sick mother to see a specialist in San Francisco for medical treatment. The cost of the trip includes $400 ($200 each) for airfare and $450 for lodging in San Francisco for 3 nights. Disregarding the percentage limitation, what is Carol's medical deduction for this trip?
    a. $-0-
    b. $400
    c. $850
    d. $700
    e. Some other amount

_____ 19. X would otherwise qualify as Z's dependent except for the joint return test. During 1992, Z paid the following medical expenses:

Operation for X $2,000

Prescription drugs for Z	1,200
Z's dentists bills	3,000
X's membership in health spa	2,500
Total	$8,700

Disregarding the percentage limitation, what is the total of Z's deductible medical expenses?
a. $8,700
b. $6,200
c. $5,000
d. $4,200
e. Some other amount

20. During 1992 S, a self-employed individual taxpayer, paid the following amounts:

State income tax	$2,000 ✓
Federal income tax	$4,000
Real estate tax on land in Ireland	$1,000 ✓
State sales tax	$500
CPA license fee	$150

What amount can S deduct as an itemized deduction for taxes on Schedule A of Form 1040?
a. $3,500
b. $3,000
c. $2,000
d. $1,000
e. Some other amount

21. During 1992, C is a resident of a state that imposes a state income tax. During the year, C had the following transactions in regards to his state income taxes:

Taxes withheld	$6,000
Last year's state income tax refund	1,000
Estimated payments	2,000
Deficiency paid related to 2 years ago	3,000

If C itemizes his deductions, how much may be claimed as a deduction for taxes on Schedule A?
a. $5,000
b. $8,000
b. $10,000

d. $11,000
e. Some other amount

_____ 22. During 1992, S sells his home to B for $200,000. After the sale B pays the real estate taxes of $3,600 for the calendar year. For income tax purposes the deduction is apportioned $2,100 to S and $1,500 to B. Assuming the real estate taxes are not prorated in escrow, what is B's basis in the residence?
a. $200,000
b. $201,500
c. $202,100
d. $198,500
e. Some other amount

_____ 23. T purchase a new residence in January 1992 for $150,000 and paid points of $4,500 to obtain mortgage financing. The mortgage is for 30 years. Her regular interest on the mortgage for the year was $6,500. What is the maximum amount T can deduct for interest on her home in 1992?
a. $4,500
b. $6,500
c. $6,650
d. $11,000
e. Some other amount

Problem

1.   Ted and Joyce Skekel, both employees of Zeran Corporation, had the following items of income and expense for 1992:

Adjusted gross income	$31,500
Medical insurance	500
Doctor bills	1,000
Prescription drugs	200
Hospital bills	1,000
Medical insurance reimbursement	1,200
State income tax	950
Real estate taxes	775
Qualified residence interest	7,150
Personal interest	625
Contribution to church (by check)	450
Tax return preparation fee	225
Professional dues	600

      Contribution of used goods to Goodwill   150
      Contribution carryover from 1991   625

They file a joint return. Calculate Ted and Joyce's itemized deductions using the worksheet below.

Medical expenses   _____

Insurance reimbursement   _____

   Total   _____

Less 7.5% of A.G.I.   _____

Medical Deduction   _____

Taxes   _____

Interest   _____

Contributions   _____

Miscellaneous   _____

Total Deductions   _____

Code Section Recognition

Indicate, by number, the appropriate Code Section where the following items are found.

_____   1.   Disallowance of personal expenditures.

_____   2.   Medical expense deduction.

_____   3.   Deduction for taxes.

_____   4.   The interest deduction.

_____   5.   Deduction for charitable contributions.

SOLUTIONS TO CHAPTER 11

True or False

1.   True   (p. 11-2)

2.   True   (p. 11-2)

3.   False   The expenditure must be primarily for medical reasons. (p. 11-3)

4.   True   (p. 11-4)

5.   True   (p. 11-3)

6.   True   (p. 11-6)

7.   True   (p. 11-3)

8.   True   (p. 11-2)

9.   False   Only prescription drugs and insulin are deductible. (p. 11-3)

10.   False   The reimbursement is included in income only to the extent of the tax benefit derived in the prior year. (p. 11-8)

11.   False   Fees, unless incurred in a trade or business or as an investment expense, are not deductible. (p. 11-8)

12.   True   (p. 11-8)

13.   True   (p. 11-9)

14.   True   (p. 11-9)

15.   False   Assessments usually increase the value of the property and are added to the taxpayer's basis of the property. (p. 11-9)

16.   True   (p. 11-10)

17.   False   Individuals deduct state income taxes on the cash method. (p. 11-11)

18.   True   (p. 11-11)

19.   False   Contributions must be made to qualifying organizations. (p. 11-19)

20.   True   (p. 11-20)

21.   False   There are limits based on 50%, 30% and 20% of AGI. (p. 11-21)

22.   False   Qualified interest on residence mortgages is deductible. (p. 11-13)

23.   True   (p. 11-12)

24.   False   Interest for personal use is a deduction from AGI. (p. 11-17)

25.   False   Estate and gift taxes are not deductible. (p. 11-9)

Fill-in-the-Blanks

1.   compensation (p. 11-12)

2.   obligation (p. 11-16)

3.   accrued (p. 11-16)

4.   five (p. 11-21)

5.   "points" (p. 11-15)

6.   qualified (p. 11-17)

7.   market (p. 11-20)

8.   50 (p. 11-21)

Multiple Choice

1.   A   The deduction is limited to net investment income. (p. 11-12)

2.   C

Drugs	$ 100
Insurance	560
Dentists	600
Physicians	1,000

Hospitals	400
Total	$2,660
Less 7.5% (AGI)	-2,250
Medical deduction	$ 410 (pp. 11-2, 3)

3.   C $66 - 24 = $42. (p. 11-8)

4.   B $3,000 - ($3,000 - 2,000) = $2,000 since the property contributed is ordinary income property. (p. 11-21)

5.   B $1,800 - 0 = $1,800. (p. 11-21)

6.   C   Fair market value is used provided the stock is not contributed to a private nonoperating foundation. (p. 11-22)

7.   D   The donation of one's services is not deductible. (p. 11-18)

8.   A   The donation of free services is not deductible. (p. 11-18)

9.   C   (p. 11-20)

10.   D $1,000 + 600 = $1,600 (p. 11-11)

11.   D   All of the debt is considered qualified residence interest. (p. 11-14)

12.   C   (p. 11-3)

13.   D   (p. 11-16)

14.   D   ($1,000 - 200) x 80% = $640 (p. 11-18)

15.   A   A taxpayer must own real estate to deduct any taxes on it. (p. 11-9)

16.   D $4,500 + 300 - 7.5% ($80,000) = $-0-. (p. 11-2)

17.   B $10,000 - 100 - 10% ($80,000) = $1,900. (see previous chapter)

18.   D $400 (airfare) + (3 (nights) x $50 (per person) x 2 persons) = $700. (p. 11-5)

19.   B $2,000 + 1,200 + 3,000 = $6,200. (pp. 11-3)

20.   B $2,000 + 1,000 = $3,000. (p. 11-9)

21.   D $6,000 + 2,000 + 3,000 = $11,000. (p. 11-11)

22.   C $200,000 + 2,100 = $202,100. (p. 11-10)

23.   D $4,500 (points) + $6,500 (regular interest) = $11,000.   (p. 11-15)

Problem

1.   Medical expenses

($500 + 1,000 + 1,000 + 200)	$2,700
Insurance reimbursement	-1,200
Total	$1,500
Less 7.5% of A.G.I.	-2,363
Medical Deduction	-0-

Taxes ($950 + 775)	1,725
Interest	7,150
Contributions ($450 + 150 + 625)	1,225
Miscellaneous [$225 + 600 - (2% of AGI)]	195
Total Deductions	$10,295

Code Section Recognition

1.   § 262

2.   § 213

3.   § 164

4.   § 163

5.   § 170

CHAPTER

12

ALTERNATIVE MINIMUM TAX

CHAPTER HIGHLIGHTS

This chapter deals with those situations where there is an alternative computation of tax liability for individuals and corporations, the alternative minimum tax. The purpose of the alternative minimum tax is to ensure taxpayers with economic income pay some tax. In general, the alternative minimum tax is a special tax on "loopholes" that keeps taxpayers from using several tax preferences in combination to avoid most of their tax liability.

I. THE INDIVIDUAL ALTERNATIVE MINIMUM TAX

    A. The alternative minimum tax (AMT) must be paid if it produces a greater tax liability than an individual taxpayer would otherwise pay. This "extra" tax prevents certain taxpayers from completely avoiding the Federal income tax through the use of special favorable tax provisions.

    B. The first step in the calculation of the AMT is the determination of alternative minimum taxable income (AMTI). AMTI is defined as:

> Taxable income
> Plus: Positive AMT adjustments
> Minus: Negative AMT adjustments
> Plus: Tax preferences
> Equals: Alternative minimum taxable income

As shown in the AMTI formula, taxable income is increased by positive adjustments and decreased by negative adjustments. Many of the positive adjustments arise because of timing differences related to the deferral of income or the acceleration of deductions. When these timing differences are reversed, negative adjustments are made.

C.   The AMT adjustments include:

- Circulation expenditures
- Certain depreciation on post-1986 real property
- Certain depreciation on post-1986 personal property
- Adjusted gains or losses on asset dispositions
- Certain excess amortization on post-1986 pollution control facilities
- Mining exploration costs
- Research and experimental expenditures
- Incentive stock options
- Passive activity losses, recomputed
- Passive farm losses
- Long-term contract timing differences
- Alternative tax NOL deduction
- Certain itemized deductions
- The standard deduction (if taxpayer did not itemize)
- The personal and dependency exemptions

D.   The AMT tax preferences are always an addition to taxable income. Tax preferences include the following:

- Certain excess depreciation on pre-1987 real property
- Certain excess depreciation on pre-1987 leased personal property
- Excess percentage depletion
- Excess intangible drilling costs
- Net appreciation on certain charitable contributions of appreciated property (certain exceptions apply for related use long-term tangible personal property until June 30, 1992, see text)
- Interest on certain private activity bonds
- Certain excess amortization on pre-1987 pollution control facilities

E.   The complete formula for computing the alternative minimum tax is as follows:

Regular taxable income:

+/-:	Adjustments
Plus:	Tax Preferences
Equals:	Alternative minimum taxable income
Minus:	Exemption
Equals:	Alternative minimum tax base
Times:	24% alternative minimum tax rate
Equals:	Tentative minimum tax before foreign tax credit
Minus:	Alternative minimum tax foreign tax credit
Equals:	Tentative minimum tax
Minus:	Regular tax liability
Equals:	Alternative minimum tax

F.   AMT Credit.   To provide equity for taxpayers when timing differences reverse, the regular tax liability may be reduced by a tax credit for prior years' minimum tax liability attributable to timing differences. The credit may be carried over indefinitely.

G.   The alternative minimum tax exemption is equal to $40,000 for married taxpayers filing joint returns, $30,000 for single taxpayers, and $20,000 for married taxpayers filing separate returns. The 25 percent phase-out of the exemption begins when alternative minimum taxable income exceeds the following levels:

- $112,500 for single taxpayers

- $150,000 for married taxpayers filing jointly

- $75,000 for married taxpayers filing separately

II.   THE CORPORATE ALTERNATIVE MINIMUM TAX

A.   The corporate alternative minimum tax is similar to the individual AMT. The tax preferences that apply to the calculation of the alternative minimum tax for individual taxpayers also apply to corporations. However, corporations have certain adjustments which differ from those that apply to individuals. The AMT rate for corporations is 20% instead of 24%. The corporate AMT tax formula is:

Taxable income:
Plus: Income tax NOLs
+/-: AMT adjustments
Plus: Tax preferences
Equals: AMTI before ATNOL
Minus: ATNOL (limited to 90%)
Equals: Alternative minimum taxable income (AMTI)
Minus: Exemption
Equals: Alternative minimum tax base
Times: 20% alternative minimum tax rate
Equals: AMT before AMT foreign tax credit
Minus: AMT foreign tax credit (may be limited to 90%)
Equals: Tentative AMT
Minus: Regular tax before credits less the regular foreign tax credit
Equals: Alternative minimum tax

B. Corporate AMT adjustments include the following:

- Certain depreciation on post-1986 real and personal property

- Certain excess mining exploration costs

- Certain long-term contract timing differences

- Differences in gains and losses for asset dispositions

- Certain amortization on pollution control facilities

- Alternative tax net operating loss

- Adjusted current earnings (ACE) adjustment

The adjusted current earnings (ACE) adjustment is equal to 75% of the difference between adjusted current earnings and unadjusted AMTI.

C. The exemption amount for corporations is $40,000, reduced by 25% of the amount by which AMTI exceeds $150,000.

TEST FOR SELF-EVALUATION

True or False

Indicate which of the following statements are true or false by circling the correct answer.

T   F   1.   The alternative minimum tax is beneficial to most high-income individual taxpayers.

T   F   2.   For 1992, the rate for the individual alternative minimum tax is 24 percent.

T   F   3.   The AMT exemption for single taxpayers is $30,000 before any phase out.

T   F   4.   The AMT exemption is reduced 25 cents on the dollar for AMTI above specified amounts.

T   F   5.   Casualty losses are allowed in calculating alternative minimum taxable income for individuals.

T   F   6.   Tentative AMT less the regular tax liability is the AMT due.

T   F   7.   Net appreciation on contributed capital gain property is not a tax preference under the AMT.

T   F   8.   The alternative tax net operating loss cannot offset more than 90% of alternative minimum taxable income.

T   F   9.   The difference between modified ACRS depreciation and the ADS (alternative depreciation system) is an adjustment for AMT purposes, arising as a result of a timing difference.

T   F   10.   Intangible drilling costs in excess of 50% of net income from oil, gas, and geothermal properties is an AMT tax preference.

T   F   11.   For AMT purposes, the cost of certified pollution control facilities placed in service after 1986 must be depreciated using the ADS over the appropriate class life.

T   F   12.   Qualified housing interest is deductible in calculating the alternative minimum tax.

T   F   13.   The corporate AMT tax rate is 25%.

T   F   14.   The ACE adjustment may be either positive or negative.

T   F   15.   For 1992, losses from passive activities are not deductible in computing either the regular income tax or the AMT.

T   F   16.   For long-term contracts entered into after March 1, 1986, the AMT computation requires that taxpayers use the percentage-of-completion method.

T   F   17.   For the individual AMT calculation, medical expenses are deductible to the extent they exceed 7.5 percent of AGI.

T   F   18.   In arriving at alternative minimum taxable income, alternative minimum tax adjustments may either increase or decrease taxable income.

T   F   19.   An individual's regular tax liability may be reduced by a credit for prior years' minimum tax liability attributable to timing differences.

T   F   20.   The corporate AMT exemption is $40,000 reduced by 25% of the excess of AMTI over $100,000.

T   F   21.   A passive loss computed for regular income tax purposes may differ from the passive loss computed for AMT purposes.

Fill-in-the-Blanks

Complete the following statements with the appropriate word(s) or amount(s).

1.   The individual alternative minimum tax rate for 1992 is _____ percent.

2.   The corporate AMT foreign tax credit may be limited to _____ percent of AMT liability before the AMT foreign tax credit.

3.   The _____ _____ _____ adjustment is a special alternative minimum tax adjustment for corporate taxpayers which attempts to indirectly impose conformity between tax accounting and financial accounting methods.

4.   Form _____ is the individual AMT form.

5.   The individual AMT credit may be carried forward _____.

6.   The alternative minimum tax exemption amount for married taxpayers filing jointly is $_____ for 1992.

Multiple Choice

Choose the best answer for each of the following questions.

_____ 1. For 1992, Carolyn Glasner's taxable income is $300,000. She has tax prefer-
ences of $75,000 and positive adjustments of $40,000. If she is a single
taxpayer, what is Carolyn's alternative minimum taxable income?
   a. $300,000
   b. $375,000
   c. $415,000
   d. $340,000
   e. Some other amount

_____ 2. For question number 1, what is Carolyn's tentative minimum tax?
   a. $-0-
   b. $99,600
   c. $87,150
   d. $78,750
   e. Some other amount

_____ 3. Which of the following is not allowed as a deduction in computing the
alternative minimum tax?
   a. Gambling losses (to the extent of winnings)
   b. State income taxes
   c. Charitable contributions
   d. Casualty losses

_____ 4. Carol Smith is single and has AMTI of $140,000. What is Carol's exemption
amount for the AMT?
   a. $-0-
   b. $20,000
   c. $23,125
   d. $30,000
   e. Some other amount

_____ 5. On nonresidential real property placed in service after 1986 the AMT
depreciation (ADS) is based on a life of how many years?
   a. 27.5
   b. 31.5
   c. 35
   d. 40

e. None of the above

_____ 6. In 1992, T incurs mine exploration costs of $200,000 which are deducted for regular income tax purposes. What is T's adjustment in computing AMTI for 1992?
   a. $-0-
   b. $200,000 positive
   c. $180,000 positive
   d. $160,000 negative
   e. Some other amount

_____ 7. For question number 6, what is T's adjustment for 1993, assuming no additional mine exploration costs were incurred in 1993?
   a. $-0-
   b. $20,000 negative
   c. $40,000 negative
   d. $200,000 positive
   e. Some other amount

_____ 8. For 1992 T Corporation has adjusted current earnings of $400,000 and the corporation has unadjusted alternative minimum taxable income of $100,000. What is T Corporation's adjusted current earning adjustment for the AMT?
   a. $-0-
   b. $300,000 positive
   c. $225,000 positive
   d. $150,000 positive
   e. Some other amount

_____ 9. In 1992, T incurred a net operating loss of $200,000. T had no AMT adjustments, but deducted tax preferences of $30,000. What is T's ATNOL carryover into 1993?
   a. $30,000
   b. $170,000
   c. $200,000
   d. $230,000
   e. Some other amount

_____ 10. T, whose AGI is $70,000, incurred medical expenses of $10,000 during the year. What is T's adjustment, if any, for the individual AMT?
   a. $-0-
   b. $1,750 negative
   c. $1,750 positive

d. $7,000 negative

e. Some other amount

_____ 11. In the current year, Fern Hilger has modified ACRS depreciation of $30,420 on a nonresidential building placed in service last year. Her AMT depreciation under ADS is $23,960. Fern's adjustment for computing AMTI is?
a. $6,460 positive
b. $6,460 negative
c. $23,960 positive
d. $30,420 negative
e. Some other adjustment

_____ 12. Bob Yetman owns a rental duplex. His basis for regular tax purposes is $93,000 while the basis for AMT purposes is $95,000. Bob sells the duplex for $105,000 for an income tax gain of $12,000 and an AMT gain of $10,000. What is Bob's AMT adjustment from the sale?
a. $-0-
b. $2,000 positive
c. $2,000 negative
d. $10,000 positive
e. $10,000 negative

_____ 13. The corporate alternative minimum tax ACE adjustment applies to which of the following?
a. S corporations
b. C corporations
c. Regulated investment companies
d. Real estate investment trusts
e. The ACE adjustment applies to all of the above

_____ 14. For regular income tax purposes, A had net investment income of $30,000 before deducting investment interest. He incurred investment interest of $45,000 during the year. Also, A had interest income on private activity bonds of $12,000. What is A's investment interest deduction for AMT purposes?
a. $-0-
b. $12,000
c. $30,000
d. $42,000
e. Some other amount

_____ 15. The AMT credit is available for which of the following differences between regular taxable income and AMTI?

a. Circulation expenditures
b. Standard deduction
c. Personal exemptions
d. Charitable contribution preference
e. None of the above

_____ 16. D owns mineral property that qualifies for a 15 percent depletion rate. At the beginning of 1992 the basis of the property is $5,000. Gross income from the property during the year was $120,000. What is D's tax preference generated by the property?
a. $-0-
b. $5,000
c. $13,000
d. $18,000
e. Some other amount

_____ 17. W Corporation, a calendar year taxpayer, has alternative minimum taxable income (before the ACE adjustment) of $500,000 for 1992. If X's adjusted current earnings (ACE) are $1,200,000. What is the amount of X Corporation's ACE adjustment?
a. $-0-
b. $525,000 positive
c. $375,000 positive
d. $900,000 negative
e. Some other amount

_____ 18. Using the information in question 17, what is X Corporation's tentative minimum tax for 1992?
a. $-0-
b. $205,000
c. $215,250
d. $240,000
e. Some other amount

_____ 19. In 1992, U Corporation (a calendar year taxpayer) had the following transactions:

Taxable income	$500,000
Expensed mine exploration costs	90,000
Interest on private activity bonds (issued in 1988)	60,000
Excess percentage depletion	150,000

What is U Corporation's AMTI for 1992?
a. $791,000
b. $800,000
c. $641,000
d. $650,000
e. Some other amount

_____ 20. Sarajane has total nonrefundable credits of $20,000, regular tax liability of $66,000, and tentative AMT of $50,000. How much of the nonrefundable credits can Sarajane claim in the current year?
a. $-0-
b. $16,000
c. $20,000
d. $4,000
e. Some other amount

Problem

1. Tim and Mary Kelley are married taxpayers who file a joint tax return. For the current tax year, the Kelley's have AGI of $70,000 (including $30,000 of investment income). They have excess accelerated depreciation on personal property of $60,000 and excess depreciation on realty of $20,000. The amount of their investment interest expense for the year is $25,000, and they made charitable contributions of $5,000. If the Kelley's regular taxable income for the current year is $29,000, determine the following amounts.

a. What is the amount of their regular income tax? _____

b. What is the amount of their tentative minimum tax? _____

c. What is the Kelly's total tax liability? _____

Code Section Recognition

Indicate, by number, the appropriate Code Section where each of the following items are found.

_____ 1. Alternative minimum tax.

_____ 2. The tax preferences.

_____ 3. The alternative minimum tax adjustments.

SOLUTIONS TO CHAPTER 12

True or False

1. False The AMT ensures that high-income taxpayers pay some amount of tax. (p. 12-3)

2. True (p. 12-20)

3. True (p. 12-20)

4. True (p. 12-20)

5. True (p. 12-13)

6. True (p. 12-19)

7. False Appreciation on contributions of certain long-term capital gain property is a tax preference item. (p. 12-5)

8. True (p. 12-25)

9. True (p. 12-4)

10. False Intangible drilling costs in excess of 65% of net income from such properties is an AMT tax preference. (p. 12-5)

11. True (p. 12-7)

12. True (p. 12-14)

13. False   The rate is 20%. (p. 12-24)

14. True   (p. 12-26)

15. True   (p. 12-9)

16. True   (p. 12-10)

17. False   The percent of AGI is 10%. (p. 12-13)

18. True   (p. 12-3)

19. True   (p. 12-22)

20. False   The adjustment to the exemption is for AMTI over $150,000. (p. 12-24)

21. True   (p. 12-9)

Fill-in-the-Blanks

1. 24 (p. 12-19)

2. 90 (p. 12-24)

3. adjusted current earnings (p. 12-25)

4. 6251 (Appendix B)

5. indefinitely (p. 12-22)

6. $40,000 (p. 12-20)

Multiple Choice

1. C $300,000 + 75,000 + 40,000 = $415,000. (p. 12-19)

2. B $415,000 x 24% = $99,600. (p. 12-19)

3. B   (p. 12-13)

4.   C $30,000 - 25% ($140,000 - 112,500) = $23,125. (p. 12-20)

5.   D   (p. 12-6)

6.   C $200,000 - ($200,000/10 years) = $180,000. (p. 12-8)

7.   B $0 - ($200,000/10 years) = ($20,000). (p. 12-8)

8.   C   ($400,000 - 100,000) x 75% = $225,000. (p. 12-25)

9.   B $200,000 - 30,000 = $170,000. (p. 12-12)

10.   C   [$10,000 - 7.5%($70,000)] - [$10,000 - 10%($70,000)] = $1,750. (p. 12-13)

11.   A $30,420 - 23,960 = $6,460 positive. (p. 12-6)

12.   C $12,000 income tax gain - $10,000 AMT gain = $2,000 AMT negative adjustment. (p. 12-12)

13.   B   See footnote 25. (p. 12-25)

14.   D $30,000 + 12,000 = $42,000. (p. 12-15)

15.   A   (p. 12-22)

16.   C   (15% x $120,000) - $5,000 = $13,000. (p. 12-16)

17.   B   75% x ($1,200,000 - 500,000) = $525,000. (p. 12-25)

18.   B   ($500,000 + 525,000) x 20% = $205,000. (p. 12-24)

19.   A   Mine exploration costs adjustment: $90,000 - 9,000 = $81,000 positive
            AMTI: $500,000 + 81,000 + 60,000 + 150,000 = $791,000. (pp. 12-5, 7, 16, 18)

20.   B $66,000 - $50,000 = $16,000   (p. 12-21)

Problem

1.   a. $4,350 = 15% x $29,000

       b. $19,200 = 24% x ($70,000 + 60,000 + 20,000 - 25,000 - 5,000 - 40,000)

c. $19,200 = $4,350 regular tax + $14,850 alternative minimum tax   (p. 12-19)

Code Section Recognition

1.   § 55

2.   § 57

3.   § 56

13

TAX CREDITS AND PAYMENT PROCEDURES

CHAPTER HIGHLIGHTS

I. OVERVIEW AND PRIORITY OF CREDITS

    A. Refundable Versus Nonrefundable Credits. Certain credits are refundable while others are nonrefundable. Refundable credits are refunded to the taxpayer even if the amount of the credit exceeds the taxpayer's tax liability.

    The refundable credits are:

- Taxes withheld on wages

- Earned income credit

- Tax withheld at the source on nonresident aliens and foreign corporations

- Credit for certain gasoline use and special fuels

    All other credits are nonrefundable. See Figure 13-1 of the text for a complete list.

    B. General Business Credit. Special rules apply to the general business credit. First, any unused credit must be carried back 3 years and forward 15 years. Second, for any tax year, the general business credit is limited to the taxpayer's *net income tax* reduced by the greater of:

- The *tentative minimum tax*, or

- 25% of the *net regular tax liability* over $25,000.

C   Unused General Business Credits. Unused credits are carried back three years and forward 15 years on a FIFO basis.

See text for the general business-related tax credits that comprise the general business credit.

II.   SPECIFIC BUSINESS-RELATED TAX CREDIT PROVISIONS

A.   Investment Tax Credit Introduction.

The investment tax credit (ITC) was designed to spur investment in capital goods. It is comprised of three components: the regular ITC, the credit for rehabilitation expenditures, and the business energy credit. The regular ITC was repealed for most tangible property placed in service after 1985. The latter two components are discussed later.

B.   Regular Investment Tax Credit. If ITC property is prematurely disposed of or ceases to be qualified ITC property, all or a portion of the investment credit previously taken will be recaptured. The portion that is recaptured is added to the taxpayer's regular tax liability for the recapture year. Recapture is triggered by the following events if they take place before the required holding period:

- Disposition of property through sale, exchange, or sale-and-lease-back transactions

- Retirement or abandonment of property or conversion to personal use

- Gifts of ITC property

- Transfers to partnerships and corporations (unless certain conditions are met)

- Like-kind exchanges (unless certain conditions are met)

Recapture does not occur as a result of the following events:

- A transfer by reason of death

- A transfer under certain tax-free reorganizations

- A liquidation of a subsidiary corporation where the assets are transferred to the parent without a change in basis

- A transfer of property between spouses or incident to divorce

C. Tax Credit for Rehabilitation Expenditures.

Taxpayers are allowed a credit for rehabilitating industrial and commercial buildings and certified historic structures. Currently, the credit is 10 percent for nonresidential buildings, other than certified historic structures, originally placed in service before 1936 and 20 percent for residential and nonresidential certified historic structures. To qualify for the credit, the expenditure must exceed the greater of the adjusted basis of the property before the rehabilitation or $5,000.

The rehabilitation credit must be recaptured if the property is disposed of prematurely or if it ceases to be qualifying property.

D. Business Energy Credits. Two business energy credits remain through June 30, 1992 to encourage the conservation of natural resources and to develop alternate energy sources. These are the credits for solar energy property (10%) and geothermal property (10%).

E. Reporting the Investment Tax Credit. Form 3468 is used to calculate the investment tax credit for the current year. Form 4255 is used to determine the amount of investment tax credit recapture on the early disposition of investment tax credit property. If the taxpayer has other business credits, Form 3800 must be used to determine the overall limitations and any general business credit carryovers or carrybacks.

F. Jobs Credit.

Taxpayers may take a jobs credit for employees hired before June 30, 1992. The jobs credit is equal to 40 percent of the first $6,000 of wages per employee for the first year of employment. Eligible employees include certain disadvantaged individuals (e.g. youth from low-income families, ex-convicts, and handicapped individuals). The wage expense deduction is reduced by the amount of the credit claimed. The credit is allowed for qualified summer youth employees. The maximum wages eligible for this credit are $3,000 per employee at a tax credit rate of 40 percent.

G.   Incremental Research Activities Credit.

To encourage research and experimentation, taxpayers are allowed a 20 percent credit for qualifying incremental expenditures. The credit only applies to qualified expenditures which exceed a base amount, determined by multiplying the average annual gross receipts of the taxpayer for the four preceding tax years by the taxpayer's "fixed base" percentage. The base amount may not be less than 50 percent of the qualified research expenses in the credit year. This credit is available through June 30, 1992.

The following conditions must be met for the expenditure to qualify:

- The expenditure must qualify as an expense under § 174

- The research must be technological in nature

- The research must be intended to be useful in the development of a new or improved business component of the taxpayer

A business component is any product, process, computer software, technique, formula, or invention that is to be held for sale, lease, or license, or used by the taxpayer in a trade or business.

Basic Research Credit. Corporations (other than S Corporations) are allowed an additional 20 percent credit for basic research expenditure amounts paid to a qualified research organization, in excess of a base amount.

H.   Low-Income Housing Credit. Owners of qualified low-income housing projects are allowed a credit based on the qualified basis of the property.

I.   Disabled Access Credit. This credit is available for eligible access expenditures paid or incurred by an eligible small business after November 5, 1990. The credit is 50% of the eligible expenditures that exceed $250 but do not exceed $10,250. An eligible small business must satisfy one of the following:

- Had gross receipts for the previous year of $1,000,000 or less, or

- Had no more than 30 full-time employees during the previous year.

The depreciable basis of the access property is reduced by the amount of the credit.

III.   OTHER TAX CREDITS

A.   Earned Income Credit.

The earned income credit is designed to help certain low income taxpayers. The earned income credit includes three components: the basic earned income credit, the supplemental young child credit, and the supplemental health insurance credit.

- The basic earned income credit is determined by multiplying a maximum amount of earned income ($7,520 in 1992) by the appropriate earned income credit percentage. The earned income credit rate is increased over a four-year period from 1991 through 1994 and a higher percentage rate applies if the taxpayer has two or more qualifying children. The credit is subject to phase out as the taxpayer's adjusted gross income or earned income reaches a certain level ($11,840 in 1992) and once the taxpayer's earned income or adjusted gross income exceeds a certain amount ($22,373 in 1992), no credit is available. See the text, Figure 13-3, for the credit percentages and phase-out percentages.

- The supplemental young child credit is for taxpayers with a child who has not attained the age of one at the end of the tax year. The credit is calculated by increasing the basic earned income credit percentage by 5 percentage points and the phase-out percentage by 3.57 percentage points. If a taxpayer elects to claim the supplemental young child credit then the child may not be considered a qualifying individual for purposes of the child and dependent care credit for that year.

- The supplemental health insurance credit is in addition to the basic earned income credit. This credit is limited to the cost of health insurance coverage on one or more qualifying children. The method of calculation is the same as the basic earned income credit except the credit percentage is 6% and the phase-out is at 4.285% of the taxpayer's adjusted gross income or earned income, if greater, over $11,840 (for 1992).

The taxpayer must have a qualifying child to claim the credit. A qualifying child must meet a relationship test, a residency test, and an age test.

The earned income credit is a form of negative income tax because a taxpayer can receive a credit (refund) even if no tax is due.

B.   Tax Credit for Elderly or Disabled Taxpayers.

To qualify for the credit for the elderly, the taxpayer must be 65 years old, or if under 65 must be retired with a permanent and total disability and have income from a public or private employer because of the disability. For taxpayers age 65 or older, the maximum credit is equal to 15 percent of $5,000 (single taxpayers or one spouse over 65), $7,500 (married with both spouses over 65), or $3,750 (married filing separately). The base amount is reduced by excluded social security and railroad retirement benefit payments, and one-half of adjusted gross income over certain amounts ($7,500 for single taxpayers, head of household and surviving spouse; $10,000 for married filing jointly; and $5,000 for married filing separately).

C.   Foreign Tax Credit.

Individual and corporate taxpayers may claim a tax credit for foreign income tax paid on income earned and subject to tax in another country or U.S. possession. Unused foreign tax credits may be carried back two years and forward five years.

An overall limitation on the foreign tax credit is based on the following formula:

$$\frac{\text{Foreign taxable income}}{\text{Total taxable income}} \times \text{U.S. tax liability before the FTC}$$

D.   Credit for Child and Dependent Care Expenses.

Taxpayers are allowed a credit for employment-related child and dependent care expenses. The credit is 30 percent of unreimbursed expenses reduced by one percent for every $2,000 (or fraction thereof) of AGI over $10,000, but not below 20 percent. The maximum qualifying expenses in any one year are $2,400 for one qualifying individual and $4,800 for two or more individuals. The eligible expenses are further limited to the taxpayer's earned income. For married taxpayers, the limitation applies to the spouse with the least amount of earned income. A taxpayer qualifies for the credit if he or she maintains a household for either of the following:

- A dependent under age 13

- A dependent or spouse who is physically or mentally incapacitated

Special rules allow taxpayers with spouses who are students to qualify for the credit. A spouse who is a full-time student is deemed to have earned income of $200 per month for one qualifying individual or $400 per month if there are two or more qualifying individuals in the household.

Taxpayers are not allowed to use amounts reimbursed to the taxpayer by an employer for dependent care and excluded from gross income. See Chapter 5 for this exclusion.

The taxpayer must provide the name, address, and taxpayer identification number of the provider of the child or dependent care.

IV. PAYMENT PROCEDURES

A. Procedures Applicable to Employers.

Employers are required to withhold Federal income tax and the employees' share of FICA tax from employees' paychecks. The IRS publishes a list of which employees and wages require Federal income and employment tax withholding. The procedure for determining federal income tax withholding involves the following three steps.

Step 1   Have the employee complete Form W-4.

Step 2   Determine the employee's payroll period.

Step 3   Compute the amount to be withheld using the wage-bracket table or the percentage method.

The percentage method of calculating withholding requires the following procedures:

- Multiply the amount of one allowance (see text) by the employee's total allowances.

- Reduce the employee's wages by the amount in step a.

- Use the results in step b. to compute the withholding using the proper percentage-method table (see text).

Reporting and payment procedures require that the employer file the following forms with the IRS:

- Form SS-4 provides the employer with an identification number which must be used on all forms filed with the IRS and the Social Security Administration.

- Form W-2 is a summary of each employee's wages and the amount of federal income tax and FICA tax withheld. The Form W-2 must be furnished to the employee no later than January 31 of the following year.

- Form W-3 is a summary of withholdings for all employees and is filed with the Social Security Administration along with a copy of each Form W-2.

- Form 940 or 940EZ is used for the employer's annual accounting for FUTA.

- Form 941 must be filed quarterly summarizing employment taxes for the quarter. Any undeposited amounts must be deposited or accompany this form.

Withholding on Pensions. Income tax withholding for pension payments is mandatory under the tax law unless the taxpayer elects to have no tax withheld.

Backup Withholding. Certain taxpayers may be subject to "backup withholding" on interest and dividend payments. The backup withholding is designed to make sure that taxpayers report all their investment income. For example backup withholding applies if a taxpayer does not give his or her identification number to a bank so that any income can be reported on Form 1099.

B. Procedures Applicable to Self-Employed Persons.

Taxpayers who have income other than wages or who are self-employed may be required to make estimated tax payments (Form 1040ES). One-fourth of the required annual payment is due on April 15, June 15, and September 15 of the current year and January 15 of the following year. The required annual payment is the lesser of the following amounts:

- 90 percent of the current year's tax

- 100 percent of last year's tax

- 90 percent of the current year's tax, including the alternative minimum tax and self-employment tax determined by computing taxable income on an annualized basis.

No payment is required if the estimated tax is under $500. An under-payment occurs when any installment is less than 25 percent of the required annual payment.

The Self-Employment (SE) Tax. Self-employed taxpayers are required to pay a self-employment tax, which is to provide for Social Security benefits. Individuals with net earnings from self-employment of $400 or more are subject to this tax. For 1992, the SE tax consists of two separate portions, the old age, survivors, and disability insurance (OASDI) and the medicare insurance. Each portion consists of a rate and a ceiling amount. For 1992 these are:

	Rate	Ceiling Amount
OASDI	12.4%	$55,500
Hospital	2.9%	$130,200
Total rate	15.3%	

Taxpayers are allowed an income tax deduction for one-half of the self-employment tax paid and a deduction at one-half the self-employment tax rate for purposes of determining the self-employment tax.

The ceiling amounts are reduced by any wages the taxpayer has that are subject to the regular Social Security tax (FICA). Schedule SE is used to calculate the self-employment tax.

TEST FOR SELF-EVALUATION

True or False

Indicate which of the following statements are true or false by circling the correct answer.

T　　F　　1.　　In general, the investment tax credit has been repealed for tax years after 1985.

T　　F　　2.　　The basic research credit is 25 percent for basic research payments in excess of a base amount.

T　　F　　3.　　The rate for the low-income housing credit is set monthly by the IRS.

T　　F　　4.　　If investment credit property is prematurely disposed of or ceases to qualify as investment credit property, the investment credit which was previously taken must be recaptured in whole or in part.

T　　F　　5.　　A transfer of property to a partnership or a corporation will not cause the recapture of any investment credit.

T　　F　　6.　　For 1992, the earned income credit is the appropriate percentage of the first $7,520 of earned income, reduced by the appropriate percentage of adjusted gross income (or, if greater, earned income) over $11,840.

T　　F　　7.　　A married individual must file a joint return to receive the benefits of the earned income credit.

T　　F　　8.　　The earned income credit is a form of negative income tax and can be refunded even if no tax is due.

T　　F　　9.　　To be eligible for the earned income credit, an individual must maintain a household which is the principal abode of a qualifying child.

T　　F　　10.　　The tax credit for the elderly is 20 percent of the § 22 amount, reduced by excluded social security, railroad retirement benefits, and certain pension amounts.

T　　F　　11.　　The maximum dependent care credit for three qualifying children is $800.

T　　F　　12.　　Amounts spent for the care of a taxpayer's spouse may qualify for the dependent care credit.

T F 13. A transfer of property to a qualified basic research organization does not qualify for the 20 percent basic research credit.

T F 14. The maximum amount of general business credit than can be taken in one year is equal to the taxpayer's net income tax reduced by the greater of the tentative minimum tax or 25% of net regular tax over $25,000.

T F 15. If an employee has no regular payroll period, then he or she is considered to be paid on a daily basis.

T F 16. The wage bracket method of withholding calculation requires more computation than the percentage method.

T F 17. Employers can always wait until the end of their taxable year before filing the required form for payroll withholding, and they do not have to deposit the withholding until the end of the year.

T F 18. The penalty for underpayment of estimated tax may be avoided if timely filed quarterly payments (including amounts withheld) are equal to or exceed the prior year's tax liability.

T F 19. Individuals with net earnings from self-employment of $200 or more are subject to the self-employment tax.

T F 20. The backup withholding rate is 20 percent.

T F 21. Starting in 1992, self employment tax is 60 percent deductible for income tax purposes.

Fill-in-the-Blanks

Complete the following statements with the appropriate word(s) or amount(s).

1. The purpose of the foreign tax credit is to mitigate _____ taxation.

2. The foreign tax credit calculation is based on an _____ limitation.

3. The maximum employment-related child and dependent care expenses that may be considered in calculating the child and dependent care credit is _____ for one qualifying individual and _____ for two or more qualifying individuals.

4. A full-time student is deemed to have earned income of _____ per month for one qualifying individual for purposes of the child care credit.

5. The regular jobs credit is equal to 40 percent of the first _____ of wages per eligible employee for the first year of employment.

6. For 1992, individuals with net earnings from self-employment of $400 or more, are subject to an OASDI portion of the self-employment tax which is 12.4% of self-employment income up to _____ and a hospital insurance portion of the self-employment tax of 2.9% of self employment income up to _____.

7. Form _____ is the Employer's Quarterly Federal Tax Return.

Multiple Choice

Choose the best answer for each of the following questions.

_____ 1. T and his wife, W, pay $3,000 to keep their son, T Jr., in a day care center. T Jr. is five years old. T's earnings are $12,000 and W's earnings are $15,000, What is the child care credit T and W can claim on a joint return assuming no other income or losses for the year?
   a. $-0-
   b. $480
   c. $504
   d. $900
   e. None of the above

_____ 2. Given the same situation as in Question 1, except W's earnings are only $1,500, what is the child care credit T and W can claim on a joint return?
   a. $-0-
   b. $315
   c. $504
   d. $420
   e. None of the above

_____ 3. T is 68 years old and single. He has adjusted gross income of $5,000 and does not receive any social security benefits. What is T's tax credit for the elderly?
   a. $-0-
   b. $375
   c. $750
   d. None of the above

_____ 4. Given the same situation as in Question 3, except T's adjusted gross income is $13,000, what is T's elderly tax credit?
   a. $-0-
   b. $750.00
   c. $337.50
   d. None of the above

_____ 5. T maintains a household for her child, who is 13 years old. T's adjusted gross income is $5,000, all from salary. How much is T's 1992 basic earned income credit?
   a. $-0-
   b. $880
   c. $920
   d. $905
   e. Some other amount

_____ 6. For 1992, Cary Corporation has $110,000 worth of excess qualified incremental research expenditures. What is Cary's incremental research credit?
   a. -0-
   b. $20,000
   c. $55,000
   d. $22,000
   e. None of the above

_____ 7. Bill and Betty Brown have one child, Bobby, who is 6 years old. Bill's earnings are $15,000 and Betty's are $14,000. Other income includes interest on a savings account at San Diego Federal Savings and Loan of $450. The Brown's paid $2,600 to the Tiny Tot Day Care Center to keep Bobby so they could both work. What is the Browns' child care credit?
   a. $-0-
   b. $480
   c. $520
   d. $2,600
   e. Some other amount

_____ 8. The basic research credit rate is:
   a. 10%
   b. 15%
   c. 20%
   d. 22%
   e. Some other amount

_____ 9. Sheila spends $60,000 to rehabilitate a commercial building originally placed in service in 1910. The building is not a certified historic structure. What is Sheila's rehabilitation credit on the building?
   a. $-0-
   b. $6,000
   c. $9,000
   d. $12,000
   e. Some other amount

_____ 10. Same as the above question, what is Sheila's rehabilitation credit if the building is a certified historic structure?
   a. $-0-
   b. $6,000
   c. $9,000
   d. $12,000
   e. Some other amount

_____ 11. T has net earnings from self-employment of $30,000. What is T's social security (OASDI) portion of the self-employment tax for 1992?
   a. $4,239
   b. $3,435
   c. $2,295
   d. $1,860
   e. Some other amount

_____ 12. T has net earnings from self-employment of $75,000. What is T's social security (OASDI) portion of the self-employment tax for 1992?
   a. $6,882
   b. $9,300
   c. $8,415
   d. $11,475
   e. Some other amount

_____ 13. Same as number 12. What is T's medicare insurance portion of the self-employment tax for 1992?
   a. $-0-
   b. $2,175
   c. $2,009
   d. $11,475
   e. Some other amount

_____ 14. Which of the following taxpayers would not be subject to the penalty for the

underpayment of estimated tax?
a. The taxpayer did not have the cash to make the payments
b. The taxpayer's estimated payments this year exceed his tax liability for the prior year
c. The taxpayer's CPA forgets to fill out the appropriate forms and send them to the taxpayer
d. The estimated payments this year are equal to 70% of the current tax liability
e. None of the above

15. Which of the following forms is the Employer's Annual Federal Unemployment Tax Return?
a. Form SS-4
b. W-2
c. 940 or 940EZ
d. 941
e. None of the above

16. Joyce Smith is married and earns a monthly salary of $2,050 in June 1992. If she claims two exemptions, how much must be withheld from her salary using the wage bracket tables found in the text?
a. $205
b. $148
c. $171
d. $177
e. Some other amount

17. Adrian Wong is married and earns a salary of $2,000 per month in March 1992. If he claims two exemptions, calculate Adrian's withholding using the percentage method.
a. $185.49
b. $208.64
c. $167.50
d. $207.71
e. Some other amount

18. Backup withholding can apply in all of the following situations, except where:
a. The taxpayer does not give his or her identification number to a bank
b. The taxpayer fails to certify that he or she is not subject to backup withholding
c. The IRS notifies a bank that the taxpayer's identification number is incorrect

d. Interest is earned on money in a foreign bank

_____ 19. In 1992, H, an eligible small business, made $12,000 of capital improvements that qualify for the disabled access credit. What is the amount of H's credit?
   a. $-0-
   b. $5,000
   c. $6,000
   d. $5,875
   e. Some other amount

_____ 20. During 1992, F incurred the following research expenditures:

In-house	$100,000
Paid to Tech University for research	$60,000

What is the total of F's qualified research expenditures for 1992?
   a. $-0-
   b. $60,000
   c. $139,000
   d. $160,000
   e. Some other amount

_____ 21. During 1992, J earned $45,000 in wages subject to FICA. J also had net earnings of $20,000 from an outside consulting business. J sold IBM stock for a gain of $4,000 during the year. What is the amount of J's net earnings from self-employment for purposes of determining the OASDI portion of the self-employment tax?
   a. $-0-
   b. $10,500
   c. $20,000
   d. $24,000
   e. Some other amount

Code Section Recognition

Indicate, by number, the appropriate Code Section where the following items are found.

_____ 1. Definition of net earnings from self-employment.

_____ 2. Research and experimentation credit.

_____ 3. Child care credit.

_____ 4. Earned income credit.

SOLUTIONS TO CHAPTER 13

True or False

1.   True   (p. 13-6)

2.   False   The credit is 20%. (p. 13-15)

3.   True   (p. 13-16)

4.   True   (p. 13-8)

5.   True   (p. 13-8)

6.   True   (p. 13-18)

7.   True   (p. 13-20)

8.   True   (p. 13-20)

9.   True   (p. 13-20)

10. False   The credit is 15 percent. (p. 13-21)

11. False   The maximum credit is 30% x \$4,800 = \$1,440. (p. 13-24)

12. True   (p. 13-23)

13. True   (p. 13-15)

14. True   (p. 13-4)

15. True   (p. 13-29)

16. False   The wage bracket method is where the amount is simply looked up using the appropriate table. (p. 13-31)

17. False   Employers must deposit employment taxes at least quarterly. (p. 13-33)

18. True   (p. 13-34)

19. False   Individuals with net earnings from self-employment of $400 or more are subject to the self-employment tax. (p. 13-35)

20. True   (p. 13-33)

21. False   It is 50% deductible. (p. 13-35)

Fill-in-the-Blanks

1. double (p. 13-22)

2. overall (p. 13-22)

3. $2,400, $4,800 (p. 13-24)

4. $200 (p. 13-24)

5. $6,000 (p. 13-11)

6. $55,500, $130,200 (p. 13-35)

7. 941 (p. 13-33)

Multiple Choice

1. C   Credit from text: 21% of $2,400 (maximum) = $504. (pp. 13-24)

2. D   28% of $1,500 = $420. (pp. 13-24)

3. C   15% of $5,000 = $750. (p. 13-21)

4. C   15% of ($5,000 - (($13,000 - 7,500)/2)) = $337.50. (pp. 13-21)

5. B   17.6% of $5,000 = $880. (p. 13-18)

6. D   (20% x $110,000) = $22,000. (pp. 13-14)

7.   B $2,400 x 20% = $480. (pp. 13-24)

8.   C   (p. 13-15)

9.   B $60,000 x 10% = $6,000. (p. 13-19)

10.   D $60,000 x 20% = $12,000. (p. 13-9)

11.   B $30,000 x 92.35% = $27,705 x 12.4% = $3,435. (p. 13-35)

12.   A $75,000 x 92.35% = $69,262 limited to: $55,500 x 12.4% = $6,882. (p. 13-35)

13.   C $75,000 x 92.35% = $69,262 x 2.9% = $2,009. (p. 13-36)

14.   B   (p. 13-34)

15.   C   (p. 13-33)

16.   D   See table in text. (p. 13-30)

17.   C   15% x ($2,000.00 - (2 x $191.67) - $500) = $167.50 (p. 13-31)

18.   D   (p. 13-33)

19.   B   50% x ($10,250 maximum - 250) = $5,000. (p. 13-17)

20.   C $100,000 + (65% x $60,000) = $139,000. (p. 13-13)

21.   B $55,500 - 45,000 = $10,500. (p. 13-35)

Code Section Recognition

1.   § 1402

2.   § 41

3.   § 21

4.   § 32

14

PROPERTY TRANSACTIONS: DETERMINATION OF GAIN OR LOSS AND BASIS CONSIDERATIONS

CHAPTER HIGHLIGHTS

When a taxpayer disposes of property, the following four questions should be answered:

- Is there a realized gain or loss?
- If so, is the gain or loss recognized?
- If the gain or loss is recognized, is it ordinary or capital?
- What is the basis of any replacement property?

This chapter and the next deal with the determination of realized and recognized gain or loss and the determination of the basis of replacement property. Chapters 16 and 17 address the classification of gain or loss as either ordinary or capital.

I.   DETERMINATION OF GAIN OR LOSS

A.   Realized Gain or Loss.

The realized gain or loss is the difference between the amount realized and the adjusted basis of the property.

The term "sale or other disposition" is defined broadly in the tax law. The term includes virtually all dispositions of property such as trade-ins, casualties, condemnations, and bond retirements.

The "amount realized" from the sale or other disposition of property is the sum of money received plus the fair market value of other property received reduced by the costs of transferring the property. The amount realized includes any liability (including nonrecourse debt) on the property assumed by the buyer.

The "adjusted basis" of the property disposed of is its original cost basis adjusted to the date of disposition. The adjustments consist of adding capital additions and subtracting capital recoveries. Capital additions include the cost of capital improvements and betterments made to the property and amortization of bond discounts. The major capital recoveries are depreciation, certain corporate distributions, and amortization of bond premiums.

The basis in property must be reduced by the amount of any deductible casualty or theft loss. The basis is also reduced by any insurance proceeds received. In addition, if the insurance proceeds result in the recognition of gain, the basis must be increased by the recognized gain.

B.   Recognized Gain or Loss. Recognized gain is the amount of the realized gain that is included in the taxpayer's gross income. A recognized loss is deductible for tax purposes. As a general rule, the entire gain or loss realized will be recognized unless specific relief is found in the Code.

C.   Nonrecognition of Gain or Loss.

In certain cases, realized gain or loss is not recognized for tax purposes. Several such exceptions include nontaxable exchanges, losses on the sale, exchange, or condemnation of personal use assets, gains on the sale of a personal residence by taxpayers 55 years old or older, and certain transactions between related parties.

Losses realized on the sale, exchange, or condemnation of personal use property are not recognized for tax purposes, whereas gains realized on such property are generally fully taxable.

D.   Recovery of Capital Doctrine.

The recovery of capital doctrine states that a taxpayer is entitled to recover the cost or other basis of property acquired and is not taxed on that amount. The cost of depreciable property is recovered through annual depreciation deductions and the basis is reduced by the amount of the depreciation taken.

The relationship between the recovery of capital doctrine and the concepts of realized and recognized gain or loss can be summarized as follows:

- A realized gain (or loss) that is never recognized results in the permanent recovery of more (or less) than the taxpayer's cost or other basis for tax purposes.

- When recognition of a realized gain (or loss) is postponed, a temporary recovery of more (or less) than the taxpayer's cost or other basis results for tax purposes.

II. BASIS CONSIDERATIONS

A. Determination of Cost Basis.

The basis of property is generally its cost, where cost is the amount paid for the property in cash or other property. The basis of property acquired in a "bargain purchase" is its fair market value.

The Regulations require that taxpayers must adequately identify stock that is sold. If the stock cannot be identified, the IRS will assume FIFO for determining the basis of the shares sold.

When a taxpayer acquires multiple assets in a lump-sum purchase, it is necessary to allocate the total cost among the individual assets. This allocation is on the basis of the relative fair market value of the individual assets acquired. Special allocation rules apply when the purchase involves a business with goodwill as one of the assets purchased.

Shares of common or preferred stock received as nontaxable stock dividends must be allocated a part of the basis of the common stock owned. This allocation is done on the basis of relative fair market value.

If a taxpayer receives nontaxable rights to purchase additional stock and the fair market value of the rights is less than 15 percent of the fair market value of the stock with respect to which they were distributed, the basis in the rights is zero unless the taxpayer elects to allocate a portion of the cost of the stock to the rights. If the value of the rights is 15 percent or more of the fair market value of the stock, then the rights must be allocated part of the stock's basis using relative fair market values. The holding period of nontaxable rights received includes the holding period of the stock on which the rights were distributed. However, if the rights are exercised, the holding period of the new stock begins the day the rights are exercised.

B.   Gift Basis.

When property owned by a taxpayer is received by gift, there is no cost basis, so a basis must be assigned to the asset. If the gift of the property was made before 1921, the property has a basis equal to the fair market value on the date of gift. For gifts received after 1920, the basis for dispositions that result in a gain is the donor's adjusted basis. If the property is disposed of at a loss, the basis to the donee is the lower of the donor's adjusted basis or fair market value on the date of the gift. If property is disposed of at an amount that falls between the basis for gain and the basis for loss, no gain or loss is realized. This post-1921 gift property is referred to as "dual basis" property.

An adjustment to the basis of property acquired by gift may be required for gift tax paid. For gifts before 1977, the full amount of the gift tax is added to the donor's basis up to the fair market value of the property. The following formula is used to calculate the donee's gain basis for gifts after 1976:

Donee's gain basis = donor's adjusted basis   +   {unrealized appreciation ÷ fair market value}
     x gift tax paid

The holding period of property acquired by gift begins on the date the property was acquired by the donor if the gain basis rule applies. Otherwise, if the loss basis rule (FMV) for gifts applies, the holding period starts on the date of the gift.

C.   Property Acquired from a Decedent.

The basis of property acquired from a decedent is generally its fair market value at the date of death or the alternate valuation date. The alternate valuation date is six months after the date of death and may be elected only if the value of the gross estate and estate tax liability will be reduced.

The holding period for property acquired from a decedent is always long-term.

The basis of community property at the time of death of one spouse becomes the fair market value of the entire amount of the property, not just the decedent's share.

D.   Disallowed Losses.

Under § 267, realized losses from sales or exchanges of property, directly or indirectly, between certain related parties are not recognized. If property is acquired in such a transaction, the basis is the property's cost to the transferee. However, if a subsequent sale or other disposition of the property results in a realized gain, the amount of the gain is reduced by the loss which was previously disallowed. If the original sale involves a personal use asset, any gain realized in a subsequent sale is not reduced by the previously disallowed loss.

The most common related party transactions are those between family members, and those between an individual and a corporation in which the individual owns directly or indirectly more than 50 percent of the stock.

If a taxpayer acquires stock or securities in a "wash sale" under § 1091, any loss on the sale of the stock replaced by the substantially identical stock or securities will be disallowed. The basis in the replacement stock or securities will be the cost plus any disallowed loss. A wash sale occurs when a taxpayer sells or exchanges stock or securities and within 30 days before or after such sale or exchange acquires substantially identical stock or securities. If the taxpayer acquires less than the number of shares sold in a wash sale any loss must be prorated on the basis of the number of shares acquired relative to the number of shares sold.

A recognized loss on "tax straddles", such as buy and sell orders in the same commodity, is limited to the amount by which the realized loss exceeds any unrealized gain on the offsetting position. Losses which are not recognized are treated as having occurred in the following taxable year.

E. Conversion of Property from Personal to Business or Income-Producing Use.

The basis for loss and depreciation for property converted from personal to business or income-producing use is the lower of the property's adjusted basis or fair market value on the date of conversion. The basis for gain is the adjusted basis on the date of conversion.

Depreciation is calculated for tax purposes using the basis for loss. The basis for gain, however, must also be adjusted for depreciation to determine the gain or loss on disposition.

TEST FOR SELF-EVALUATION

True or False

Indicate which of the following statements are true or false by circling the correct answer.

T (F) 1. A realized gain and a recognized gain are the same thing.

(T) (F) 2. Trade-ins are not dispositions and would not cause a gain or loss to be recognized.

(T) F 3. The amount realized from a sale or disposition of property includes property received at fair market value.

T (F) 4. The amount realized from a sale or disposition of property does not include any liability assumed by the buyer.

(T) F 5. The term fair market value is defined by the courts as the price at which property will change hands between a willing seller and a willing buyer when neither is compelled to sell or buy.

(T) F 6. The amount realized is reduced by the costs to transfer the property.

T (F) 7. The adjusted basis of property is the original basis plus capital recoveries, less capital additions.

(T) F 8. Depreciation is an example of capital recovery.

(T) F 9. The Code assumes all gains that are realized will be recognized unless otherwise stated.

(T) (F) 10. A realized loss from the sale or disposition of a personal use asset is not recognized for tax purposes.

(T) (F) 11. Under the cost recovery doctrine, a taxpayer may recover the cost of property acquired and will be taxed on that amount.

(T) F 12. The cost of depreciable property is recovered through annual depreciation deductions.

(T) F 13. The original basis of property is generally its cost, which is paid for by cash or other property.

T (F) 14. The basis of property acquired in a bargain purchase is its cost.

T (F) 15. If stock lots cannot be identified, the Regulations make a LIFO presumption.

(T) F 16. A lump sum cost is allocated on the basis of relative fair market values of the individual assets acquired.

(T) F 17. For gifts acquired before 1921, the basis to the donee for income tax purposes is the fair market value at the date of the gift.

(T) F 18. If stock rights are exercised, the holding period of the newly acquired stock begins with the date the rights are exercised.

T (F) 19. The basis of property converted to business use is always fair market value on the date of conversion.

(T) (F) 20. The wash sale provision applies to both gains and losses.

(T) F 21. A loss on the sale of stock to which the wash sale provisions apply, will be disallowed if substantially identical stock or securities are acquired within thirty days before or after the date of the sale or exchange.

(T) (F) 22. Both the decedent's share and the surviving spouse's share of community property have a basis equal to the fair market value on the date of death.

Fill-in-the-Blanks

Complete the following statements with the appropriate word(s).

1. For gifts made after 1920, if no gift tax is paid, the basis for gain is the same as the donor's __adj__ __basis__.

2. For gifts made after 1920, the basis for loss is the lesser of the donor's adjusted basis or ____f____ ____m____ ____v____ on the date of the gift.

3. For gifts made after 1920, but before 1977, the gift tax paid is __added__ to the donor's basis up to the fair market value of the property.

4. For gifts made after 1976, the basis of the gifted property must be increased by the amount of gift taxes paid that are due to the net unrealized __basis__ of the gifted
__appreciation__

property.

5. The basis of property acquired from a decedent is its fair market value at the date of _____death_____ or the alternate valuation date.

6. In a wash sale, the realized loss that is not recognized is _____added_____ to the basis of the replacement stock.

7. If property is converted from personal to business or income-producing use, the basis for loss and depreciation is the lesser of the property's adjusted _____basis_____ or fair market value on the date of conversion, while the basis for gain is the adjusted basis on the date of _____sale conversion_____.

Multiple Choice

Choose the best answer for each of the following questions.

_____ 1. In 1984, D acquired Texaco stock at a cost of $300,000. This stock was worth $275,000 on the date of D's death, March 1, 1992. Nine months prior to D's death the stock was worth $400,000. The alternate valuation date is not used. If the securities are sold by D's heirs, the basis for determining gain or loss is:

  a. -0-
  b. $275,000
  c. $300,000
  d. $400,000
  e. Some other amount

_____ 2. Under the Internal Revenue Code, the holding period for property acquired from a decedent is always:

  a. Long-term
  b. Short-term
  c. Determined by the date acquired by the decedent
  d. Determined by the date of death
  e. Some other amount

_____ 3. On January 2, 1992, T converts his house into rental property. The basis of the house is $100,000 and its fair market value on the date of conversion is $88,000. T's basis for depreciation is:

  a. -0-
  b. $88,000

    c. $100,000

    d. $12,000

    e. Some other amount

_____ 4. Assume the same situation as in Question 3. T's basis for gain in the event the property is later sold would be:

    a. $88,000 less any depreciation

    b. $100,000 less any depreciation

    c. $88,000 with no depreciation allowed

    d. Some other amount

_____ 5. Assume the same situation as in Question 3. T's basis for loss in the event the property is later sold would be:

    a. $88,000 less any depreciation

    b. $60,000 less any depreciation

    c. $60,000

    d. Some other amount

_____ 6. On July 1, 1992, T sells 100 shares of Green Burrito, Inc. stock (basis of $4,000) for $3,500. On July 18, 1992, he purchases 50 shares for $1,800. T's recognized loss on the sale is:

    a. -0-

    b. $500

    c. $250

    d. Some other amount

_____ 7. Assume the same situation as in Question 6. T's basis in the 50 shares purchased on July 18, 1992, would be:

    a. -0-

    b. $1,800

    c. $2,300

    d. $2,050

    e. Some other amount

_____ 8. John Deaux of Lake Charles, Louisiana, sold common stock acquired two years ago to his brother, Don, at the current market price of $6,000. John's basis in the stock is $8,000. He should report:

    a. Neither a gain nor a loss

    b. A long-term capital loss of $2,000

    c. An ordinary loss of $2,000

    d. A short-term capital loss of $2,000

    e. A § 1231 gain of $2,000

_____ 9. Assume the same situation as in Question 8. The stock market recovered rapidly and later Don Deaux sold the stock to an unrelated third party for $9,000. His recognized gain would be:

    a. -0-
    b. $3,000
    c. $1,000
    d. $2,000
    e. Some other amount

_____ 10. During 1992, T received a gift of property with a fair market value of $8,000. The property had an adjusted basis to the donor of $8,500. There was no gift tax paid on the transfer. If T sold the property for $8,700, the gain or (loss) would be:

    a. $200
    b. $700
    c. $500
    d. Some other amount

_____ 11. Assume the same situation as in Question 10, except the property is sold for $7,500. What is the gain or (loss)?

    a. $500 gain
    b. $500 loss
    c. $1,000 loss
    d. Some other amount

_____ 12. Assume the same situation as in Question 10, except that the property is sold for $8,200. What is the gain or (loss)?

    a. No gain or loss
    b. $300 loss
    c. $200 gain
    d. Some other amount

_____ 13. T sells his house with a basis of $40,000 for $50,000 in cash. The buyer assumes T's mortgage of $60,000. The amount of gain realized on this transaction is:

    a. -0-
    b. $10,000
    c. $20,000
    d. $70,000
    e. Some other amount

_____ 14. T buys an automobile from her employer for $8,000. The fair market value of the car is $12,000 and its basis to the employer is $14,000. T's basis in the automobile is:

    a. $4,000
    b. $8,000
    c. $12,000
    d. $14,000
    e. Some other amount

15. T has a "straddle" in silver futures. In 1992 he sells his short position for a $5,000 loss. He has an unrealized gain of $5,000 on the offsetting position which is not liquidated. For 1992, what is T's recognized loss?
    a. -0-
    b. $5,000
    c. $10,000
    d. $15,000
    e. Some other amount

16. An asset used in a trade or business is damaged by a fire. The adjusted basis of the asset before the fire is $25,000 and the fair market value is $15,000 after the fire. No insurance proceeds are received. The amount of the casualty loss deduction is $10,000. What is the adjusted basis of the asset after the fire?
    a. -0-
    b. $10,000
    c. $15,000
    d. $25,000
    e. Some other amount.

17. Van Ballew purchases a rental house and land for $90,000 in a depressed real estate market. Appraisals place the value of the house at $70,000 and the land at $30,000 (a total of $100,000). What is Van's basis in the house?
    a. $63,000
    b. $70,000
    c. $90,000
    d. $100,000
    e. Some other amount.

18. On March 1, 1992, Harry Beech received a gift of income-producing real estate having a donor's adjusted basis of $50,000 at the date of the gift. Fair market value of the property at the date of gift was $40,000. No gift tax was paid on the transfer. Beech sold the property for $46,000 on August 1, 1992. How much gain or loss should Beech report for 1992?
    a. No gain or loss

　　b. $6,000 short-term capital gain
　　c. $4,000 short-term capital loss
　　d. $4,000 ordinary loss　　　　　　(CPA adapted)

Use the following information for questions 19 through 21.

On March 1, 1992, Lois Rice learned that she was bequeathed 1,000 shares of Elin Corp. common stock under the will of her uncle, Pat Prevor. Pat had paid $5,000 for the Elin stock in 1984. Fair market value of Elin stock on March 1, 1992, the date of Pat's death, was $8,000. Lois sold the Elin stock for $9,000 on May 1, 1992, the date that the executor distributed the stock to her. (CPA adapted)

_____ 19. How much should Lois include in her 1992 individual income tax return for the inheritance of the 1,000 shares of Elin stock which she received from Pat's estate?
　　a. $0
　　b. $5,000
　　c. $8,000
　　d. $9,000

_____ 20. Lois' basis for gain or loss on the sale of the Elin stock is:
　　a. $5,000
　　b. $8,000
　　c. $9,000
　　d. $0

_____ 21. Lois should treat the 1,000 shares of Elin stock as a:
　　a. Short-term § 1231 asset
　　b. Long-term § 1231 asset
　　c. Short-term capital asset
　　d. Long-term capital asset.

_____ 22. T owns land with an adjusted basis of $100,000, subject to a mortgage of $50,000. On May 1, 1992 T sells the land for $200,000 in cash, a note for $300,000, and property with a fair market value of $60,000. The $50,000 mortgage is assumed by the purchaser. What is the amount realized from this transaction?
　　a. $500,000
　　b. $550,000
　　c. $560,000
　　d. $610,000

e. Some other amount

_____ 23. The bank forecloses on K's office building. The property had been pledged as security on a nonrecourse mortgage, whose principle amount at the date of foreclosure is $600,000. The adjusted basis of the office building is $350,000 and the fair market value is $500,000. What is K's recognized gain or loss?

   a. $-0-
   b. $100,000
   © $250,000
   ⓓ $150,000
   e. Some other amount

(handwritten: 600,000 realized / 350,000 basis / 250,000 recog)

_____ 24. L owns City of San Diego bonds with a face amount of $10,000. L purchased the bonds on January 1, 1992, for $12,000. The maturity date is December 31, 1996, (five years later). Assuming annual amortization of the bond premium is $400 and the annual interest rate on the bonds is 8 percent, what is L's adjusted basis in the bonds as of the end of 1992?

   a. $10,000
   b. $10,400
   ⓒ $11,600
   d. $12,000
   e. Some other amount

_____ 25. G was given a residence in 1992. At the time of the gift, the residence had an adjusted basis to the donor of $100,000 and a fair market value of $250,000. The donor paid gift tax of $15,000 on the gift. What is G's basis for gain in the residence?

   a. $100,000
   ⓑ $109,000
   ⓒ $115,000
   d. $250,000
   e. Some other amount

(handwritten: adj basis / FMV gift tax / 100 + (150 ÷ 250 × 15))

Code Section Recognition

Indicate, by number, the appropriate Code Section where the following items are found.

_____ 1. Cost basis.

_____ 2. Adjustments to basis.

_____ 3. Basis of property acquired from a decedent.

_____ 4. Gift basis.

_____ 5. Wash sales.

_____ 6. Reduction of gain for previously disallowed losses.

SOLUTIONS TO CHAPTER 14

True or False

1. False "Recognized" is a term used for tax purposes only and refers to the amount of realized gain that is included in gross income or the amount of realized loss that is deductible for tax purposes. (p. 14-5)

2. False Trade-ins are dispositions. (p. 14-2)

3. True (p. 14-2)

4. False Liabilities are included in determining the amount realized. (p. 14-3)

5. True (p. 14-3)

6. True (p. 14-3)

7. False The adjusted basis is the original basis less capital recoveries, plus capital additions. (p. 14-3)

8. True (p. 14-4)

9. True (p. 14-6)

10. True (p. 14-6)

11. False Taxpayers are not taxed on the recovery of the cost or other basis of property. (p. 14-7)

12. True (p. 14-7)

13. True   (p. 14-8)

14. False   The basis of property acquired in a bargain purchase is FMV. (p. 14-8)

15. False   The Regulations assume FIFO. (p. 14-8)

16. True   (p. 14-8)

17. True   (p. 14-11)

18. True   (p. 14-10)

19. False   The basis (for loss) of converted property is the lesser of the property's adjusted basis or FMV on the date of conversion. (p. 14-18)

20. False   The wash sale provision only applies to losses. (p. 14-16)

21. True   (p. 14-17)

22. True   (p. 14-15)

Fill-in-the-Blanks

1. adjusted basis (p. 14-11)

2. fair market value (p. 14-11)

3. added (p. 14-12)

4. appreciation (p. 14-12)

5. death (p. 14-13)

6. added (p. 14-17)

7. basis, conversion (p. 14-18)

Multiple Choice

1. B   (p. 14-13)

2.   A   (p. 14-15)

3.   B   The basis for depreciation is the lesser of the adjusted basis or **FMV** on the date
          of conversion. (p. 14-19)

4.   B   (p. 14-18)

5.   A   (p. 14-18)

6.   C $3,500 - 4,000 = ($500), less 50% wash sale = ($250) loss allowed. (p. 14-17)

7.   D $1,800 + 250 = $2,050. (p. 14-17)

8.   A   (p. 14-15)

9.   C $9,000 - 6,000 = $3,000, less (2,000) disallowed loss = 1,000 recognized gain. (p.
          14-16)

10.   A $8,700 - 8,500 = $200. (p. 14-11)

11.   B $7,500 - 8,000 = ($500). (p. 14-11)

12.   A   (p. 14-12)

13.   D $50,000 + 60,000 - 40,000 = $70,000. (p. 14-2, 3)

14.   C   (p. 14-8)

15.   A   The recognized loss is limited to the excess of the realized loss over the
          unrealized gain. (p. 14-18)

16.   C $25,000 - 10,000 = $15,000. (p. 14-4)

17.   A   ($70,000 ÷ $100,000) x $90,000 = $63,000. (p. 14-8)

18.   A   (p. 14-12)

19 . A   (p. 14-14), previous chapter.

20.   B   (p. 14-14)

21.   D   (p. 14-15)

22.	D	Cash received	$200,000	
		Note	300,000	
		Property received	60,000	
		Mortgage assumed by purchaser	50,000	
		Total	$610,000	(p. 14-2,3)

23.	C	Amount realized (mortgage)	$600,000	
		Less: Adjusted basis	-350,000	
		Realized gain	$250,000	
		Recognized gain	$250,000	(p. 14-3)

24.	C	Cost of bonds	$12,000	
		Less: 1992 amortization	-400	
		Basis at end of 1992	$11,600	(p. 14-5)

25. B $109,000 = $100,000 + ($150,000 ÷ 250,000 x $15,000). (p. 14-12)

Code Section Recognition

1.   § 1012

2.   § 1016

3.   § 1014

4.   § 1015

5.   § 1091

6.   § 267

CHAPTER

15

PROPERTY TRANSACTIONS: NONTAXABLE EXCHANGES

CHAPTER HIGHLIGHTS

Realized gains and losses arising from certain exchanges are not recognized for tax purposes. In general, new property is viewed as substantially a continuation of an old investment, so the taxpayer is in the same relative economic position. The recognition of gain or loss is postponed until the property received in the exchange is disposed of in a taxable transaction. This chapter discusses several of the major types of transactions which receive nontaxable exchange treatment. Chapter 20 covers nontaxable contributions for partnership or corporate formation.

I.   LIKE-KIND EXCHANGES -- § 1031

Under § 1031, gain or loss on a like-kind exchange will not be recognized if property held for investment or for productive use in a trade or business is exchanged for like-kind property. This provision is mandatory rather than elective.

A.   Like-Kind Property. The term like-kind is intended to be interpreted broadly. However, the following three general limitations are placed on what qualifies as like-kind property:

- livestock involved in an exchange must be of the same sex

- realty must be exchanged for realty

- personalty must be exchanged for personalty

Real property includes rental buildings, office and store buildings, manufacturing plants, and land. Personalty consists primarily of machines, equipment, trucks, automobiles, furniture and fixtures. Exchanges of real property located in the United States and foreign real property is not considered like-kind property.

If the exchange involves a multiple asset business (e.g. a car dealership for a car dealership) the determination of the whether assets qualify as like-kind will not be made at business level, instead the underlying assets must be evaluated.

Also, depreciable personalty used in a business must be exchanged for property within the same *general business class* or the *same product class*. Examples of general business classes are:

- Office furniture, fixtures, and equipment

- Information systems (computers and peripheral equipment)

- Airplanes

- Automobiles and taxis

- Buses

- Light general-purpose trucks

- Heavy general purpose trucks

B.   Exchange Requirement. To qualify for the like-kind treatment, property must be part of an exchange not a sale and repurchase. In certain situations, taxpayers may want to avoid § 1031 in order to receive a higher basis for depreciation purposes, to recognize a realized loss, or to recognize a gain which will receive favorable capital gain treatment or be available to offset passive activity losses.

C.   Boot. On a like-kind exchange, gain realized will be recognized to the extent of boot received. However, the receipt of boot will not trigger the recognition of a realized loss. If boot is given, gain or loss is recognized only if the boot is appreciated or depreciated property.

D.   Basis of Property Received.   The basis of like-kind property received is equal to the fair market value of the like-kind property reduced by any postponed gain or increased by any postponed loss.   Alternatively the basis may be determined as follows:

> Adjusted basis of like-kind property surrendered
> + Adjusted basis of boot given
> + Gain recognized
> - Fair market value of boot received
> - <u>Loss recognized</u>
> = Basis of like-kind property received

The holding period of the property surrendered in the exchange carries over and "tacks on" to the holding period of the like-kind property received. Depreciation recapture potential also carries over to the property received.

The amount of any liability assumed by the transferee is treated as boot received by the transferor and boot given by the transferee.

II.   INVOLUNTARY CONVERSIONS -- § 1033

A.   General Scheme.   Under § 1033, a taxpayer who suffers an involuntary conversion may postpone the recognition of *gain* realized from the conversion if certain conditions are met. In general, gain is recognized to the extent that the amount realized is not reinvested in replacement property.

B.   Involuntary Conversion Defined.   An involuntary conversion is the result of destruction (complete or partial), theft, seizure, requisition, condemnation, or the sale or exchange under threat or imminence of requisition or condemnation of the taxpayer's property. Most involuntary conversions are casualties or condemnations.

C.   Computing the Amount Realized. The amount realized from a condemnation of property usually includes only the amount received as compensation for the property. It does not generally include amounts designated as severance damages which usually occurs when only part of the property is condemned.

D.   Replacement Property.   The replacement property for an involuntary conversion must be similar or related in service or use to the property involuntarily converted. To qualify, owner-investors must meet the taxpayer use test and owner-users must pass the functional use test for replacement property. Business or investment real property which is condemned is subject to the broader replacement rules for like-kind exchanges, which means that the taxpayer has more flexibility in selecting replacement property.

E. Time Limitation on Replacement. A taxpayer normally has two years after the close of the tax year in which any gain is realized to replace the property. For condemnations of trade or investment real property the taxpayer has three years instead of two.

F. Nonrecognition of Gain. If the conversion is directly into replacement property then the nonrecognition of gain is mandatory. The taxpayer's basis in the converted property carries over to the new property.

If the conversion is into money, a taxpayer may elect to postpone the gain or the gain may be recognized. If the election to postpone gain is made by the taxpayer, gain still must be recognized to the extent the amount realized exceeds the cost of replacement property. The basis of the replacement property purchased is its cost less any postponed gain. The holding period includes that of the converted property if postponement of the gain is elected.

§ 1033 does not modify the general rules for loss recognition. Therefore losses from involuntary conversions of business or income producing property are recognized, whereas conversion losses (other than casualty losses) related to personal use assets are not recognized.

G. Involuntary Conversion of a Personal Residence. An involuntary conversion of a personal residence can have several tax treatments. In a loss situation, if the conversion is a condemnation, the loss realized is not recognized. If the conversion is a casualty, the taxpayer may recognize the loss subject to the personal casualty loss limitations. In a gain situation, if the conversion is a condemnation, the gain can be postponed under § 1033 or § 1034. If the conversion is a casualty, the gain can be postponed only under § 1033.

H. Reporting Considerations. Supporting details should be included with the taxpayer's return in the year a gain is realized, and also in the year the property is replaced. If the property is not replaced within the time allotted, or it is replaced at a lower cost than anticipated, an amended return must be filed for the year the gain was realized.

III.   SALE OF A RESIDENCE -- § 1034

A loss on the sale of a personal residence cannot be recognized. However, gain is taxable unless the taxpayer purchases (or constructs) a qualified new residence within the required time period.

A.   Replacement Period. For nonrecognition treatment to apply, the old residence must be replaced with a new residence within a period beginning two years before and ending two years after the date of sale of the old residence. The taxpayer must use and occupy the new residence during this time period.

B.   Principal Residence. To qualify for nonrecognition under § 1034, both the old and new residence must be the taxpayer's principal residence. However, temporarily renting out the old or new residence does not necessarily terminate its status as the taxpayer's principal residence.

C.   Nonrecognition of Gain Requirements. The realized gain from the sale of an old residence is not recognized if a taxpayer reinvests an amount at least equal to the adjusted sales price of the old residence. Realized gain is recognized to the extent that the taxpayer does not reinvest the adjusted sales price in a new residence. The adjusted sales price is the amount realized less any qualified fixing-up expenses. The amount realized is the selling price less selling expenses.

Fixing-up expenses are those personal expenses incurred by the taxpayer in getting the old residence ready for sale including ordinary repairs, painting, wallpapering, etc. They must be incurred during the 90-day period ending on the date of the contract to sell, must be paid within 30 days after the date of the sale, and must not be capital expenditures. While fixing-up expenses reduce the adjusted sales price for purposes of determining the required reinvestment, they do not reduce the amount of gain realized.

D.   Basis of the New Residence. The basis of the new residence is its cost reduced by any realized gain which is not recognized due to the nonrecognition provision. The cost of the new residence includes any qualified capital expenditures incurred within the replacement period. If there is any postponed gain, the holding period of the old residence attaches to the new residence.

E.   Reporting Procedures. The taxpayer must report the details of the sale transaction on Form 2119 in the year gain is realized. If the old residence is not replaced within the allotted time period, or recognized gain results, an amended return must be filed for the year in which the sale took place.

IV.   SALE OF A RESIDENCE -- § 121

   A.   Requirements. Taxpayers age 55 or over who sell or exchange their principal residence may elect to exclude up to $125,000 ($62,500 for married filing separately) of realized gain from the sale or exchange. The election can only be made once. To qualify for this election, the residence must have been the taxpayer's principal residence for at least three of the previous five years. If the residence is jointly owned by a husband and wife and a joint return is filed, only one spouse must meet the requirements.

   B.   Relationship to Other Provisions. Taxpayers may treat an involuntary conversion of a principal residence as a sale for purposes of § 121. If a qualified new residence is purchased, any gain not excluded under § 121 can be postponed under § 1033 or § 1034 (condemnation only).

   C.   Making and Revoking the Election. The election not to recognize gain under § 121 may be made or revoked at any time before the statute of limitations expires. The election is made on Form 2119.

V.   OTHER NONRECOGNITION PROVISIONS

   A.   Exchanges of Stock for Property - § 1032. No gain or loss is recognized by a corporation dealing in its own stock, including treasury stock.

   B.   Certain Exchanges of Insurance Policies - § 1035. Under § 1035 of the Code certain insurance contracts qualify for nonrecognition of gain or loss when exchanged.

   C.   Exchange of Stock for Stock of the Same Corporation - § 1036. No gain or loss is recognized by a shareholder from the exchange of common stock for common stock, or preferred stock for preferred stock of the same corporation. An exchange of common stock for preferred stock is generally a taxable event.

   D.   Certain Reacquisitions of Real Property - § 1038. When property sold on the installment basis is repossessed only limited gain may be recognized and no loss is recognized.

E. Transfers of Property Between Spouses or Incident to Divorce - § 1041. Transfers of property between spouses or former spouses incident to divorce or between spouses during marriage are nontaxable events. The basis of the property is carried over to the recipient.

F. Sale of Stock to Stock Ownership Plans or Certain Cooperatives - § 1042. If a taxpayer has realized gain on securities sold to an employee stock ownership plan (ESOP) or a worker-owned cooperative, such gain will not be recognized if qualified replacement property is acquired by the seller within a specified time period.

TEST FOR SELF-EVALUATION

True or False

Indicate which of the following statements are true or false by circling the correct answer.

T F 1. Raw land held for investment does not qualify for a § 1031 like-kind exchange.

T F 2. A store building could be exchanged for a delivery truck and qualify for a like-kind exchange.

T F 3. In a like-kind exchange, gain realized will be recognized to the extent boot is received.

T F 4. The § 1031 like-kind exchange provision is elective, not mandatory.

T F 5. If a liability is assumed in a like-kind exchange, it will be treated as boot given by the party assuming the liability.

T F 6. For nonrecognition treatment to apply under § 1034, a replacement residence must be acquired within the two year period before or the two year period after the sale of the old residence.

T F 7. The holding period of like-kind property received begins on the day the exchange takes place.

T F 8. The involuntary conversion provisions under § 1033 apply to gains and not to losses.

T   F   9.   The § 1033 involuntary conversion provision is always elective.

T   F   10. In an involuntary conversion, realized gain is recognized to the extent that the proceeds are not reinvested in property that is similar or related in service or use.

T   F   11. Livestock destroyed because of disease will qualify as an involuntary conversion.

T   F   12. § 1033 applies to condemnation payments if they are designated as severance damages.

T   F   13. Owner-investors must conform to the functional use test to postpone gain under § 1033.

T   F   14. To qualify for nonrecognition of gain under § 1033, taxpayers have two years from the date property is involuntarily converted to replace it.

T   F   15. A loss on an involuntary conversion that is a casualty of a personal residence, can be recognized subject to the personal casualty loss limitations.

T   F   16. If an involuntary conversion of a personal residence is the result of a casualty, a realized gain can only be postponed under the involuntary conversion provisions of § 1033.

T   F   17. A realized loss from the sale of a personal residence can be recognized for tax purposes.

T   F   18. § 1034 is mandatory, not elective.

T   F   19. To qualify for the one-time $125,000 exclusion on the sale of a personal residence, the taxpayer must be at least 65 years old.

T   F   20. If gain is deferred on a personal residence, the basis of the new residence is equal to the cost of the new residence.

Fill-in-the-Blanks

Complete the following statements with the appropriate word(s) or amount(s).

1. Under § 1034, a new residence must be purchased within _____~_____ year(s) before or after the date of sale of the old residence.

2. For nonrecognition treatment under § 1034 to apply, the taxpayer must ___buy occupy___ _ the replacement residence within the required time period.

3. Gain realized from the sale of an old residence is not recognized if the taxpayer reinvests an amount at least equal to the ___~~realized~~ adj___ sales price of the old residence.

4. The adjusted sales price is the amount realized less the ___~~selling~~ fix up___ expenses.

5. Fixing-up expenses must be incurred for work performed during the ___90___ day period ending on the date of sale, be paid within ___30___ day(s) after the date of sale, and not be capital expenditures.

6. Under § 1034, the basis of the newly acquired residence is equal to the cost of the new residence less any ___~~realized~~ unrecognized___ gain.

7. Taxpayers 55 years or over who sell or exchange their personal residences may elect to exclude up to ___125,000___ of realized gain.

8. To qualify under § 121, the taxpayer must have owned and used the home as a personal residence for at least ___3___ of the last ___5___ years.

Multiple Choice

Choose the best answer for each of the following questions.

120 110
~~98~~
32

_____ 1. On May 11, 1992, Vern Odmark, age 40, sold his personal residence for a net sales price (after selling expenses) of $120,000. The house had been purchased several years ago at a cost of $88,000. To be able to sell it, Vern painted the house in April 1992 at a cost of $2,000 which he paid in April. On June 12, 1992, Vern purchased a duplex for $220,000. He rented one-half of the duplex and used the other half as a personal residence. For 1992, what is Vern's recognized gain?
   a. $-0-
   b. $4,000
   ⓒ $8,000
   d. $16,000
   e. Some other amount

_____ 2. During the current year, T and X exchange real estate investments. T gives up property with an adjusted basis of $250,000 (fair market value of $300,000) which is subject to a mortgage of $50,000 (assumed by X). In return for this property, T receives property with a fair market value of $225,000 and $25,000 cash. What is T's realized gain?

    a. $-0-
    b. $50,000
    c. $75,000
    d. $100,000
    e. Some other amount

_____ 3. Assuming the same situation as in Question 2, what is T's recognized gain on the exchange?

    a. $-0-
    b. $50,000
    c. $75,000
    d. $100,000
    e. Some other amount

_____ 4. Assuming the same situation as in Question 2, what is T's basis in the new property?

    a. $225,000
    b. $250,000
    c. $275,000
    d. Some other amount

_____ 5. T's building, which has an adjusted basis of $100,000, is destroyed by fire in 1992. During 1992, T receives $250,000 of insurance proceeds for the loss. T invests $160,000 in a qualified replacement building. By what date must T make a new investment to come within the nonrecognition provision of § 1033?

    a. December 31, 1992
    b. December 31, 1993
    c. December 31, 1994
    d. December 31, 1995
    e. None of the above

_____ 6. Assuming the same situation as in Question 5 and assuming the replacement building is acquired within the required time period, what is T's realized gain on the involuntary conversion?

    a. $-0-
    b. $90,000

    c. $60,000

    ⓓ $150,000

    e. Some other amount

_____ 7. Assuming the same situation as in Question 5 and assuming the replacement building is acquired within the required time period, what is T's recognized gain on the involuntary conversion providing T elects to be covered by § 1033?

    a. $-0-

    b. $150,000

    ⓒ $90,000

    d. $60,000

    e. Some other amount

_____ 8. T is 60 years old and sells her personal residence for $180,000 (adjusted basis of $50,000). If T elects § 121 and does not replace the residence, she would have a recognized gain of:

    a. $-0-

    ⓑ $5,000

    c. $130,000

    d. $55,000

    e. Some other amount

_____ 9. Which of the following exchanges would not qualify for like-kind exchange treatment under § 1031?

    a. Land held as an investment is exchanged for a rental house

    b. A light-duty Ford business truck is exchanged for a light-duty Dodge business truck

    ⓒ A personal automobile is exchanged for a business automobile

    d. A computer is exchanged for a laser printer, both are used in a business

    e. All of the above would qualify

_____ 10. Three years ago T acquired a capital asset for $10,000. The asset is worth $20,000 today. This property was exchanged for another capital asset worth $20,000 in a qualified § 1031 exchange. Five months later the new property was sold for $28,000. On this latest sale T should report:

    a. $10,000 long-term capital gain

    b. $10,000 short-term capital gain

    ⓒ $18,000 long-term capital gain

    d. $8,000 short-term capital gain

    e. None of the above

_____ 11. § 1031, the like-kind exchange provision, applies to both gains and losses, and the § 1033 involuntary conversion provision applies to:

a. Gains only
b. Losses only
c. Gains and losses
d. Capital gains only
e. None of the above

_____ 12. Indicate which of the following would not qualify for involuntary conversion treatment under § 1033:

a. A personal residence burns down
b. Inventory is damaged by a flood
c. A taxpayer sells his house because it is on a flood plain
d. Livestock is destroyed by disease
e. None of the above

_____ 13. The § 1033 involuntary conversion provision is:

a. Always elective
b. Never elective
c. Mandatory for direct conversions
d. Mandatory for conversions into money
e. None of the above

_____ 14. Which of the following does not qualify as a selling expense under § 1034?

a. Title transfer fees
b. Painting a house to make it ready for sale
c. Real estate commissions
d. Advertising the property for sale
e. All of the above qualify

_____ 15. If a qualified taxpayer elects § 121 on the sale of his or her personal residence, he or she may:

a. Still use § 1034
b. Not use § 1034
c. Not use § 1033
d. Still use § 1033
e. None of the above

_____ 16. In May of 1992, Jim Williamson sold his former residence for $140,000 and realized a gain of $60,000. On June 15, 1992 he moved into his new residence. This new residence is sold in November 1992 for $160,000 for a realized gain of $30,000 and Jim occupies his new (a third) residence which cost $170,000. During 1992 Jim should recognize a gain of:

    a. $-0-
    b. $60,000
    c. $30,000
    d. $130,000
    e. Some other amount

17. Ray Ballew transfers a house to his ex-wife in a divorce settlement. The house has a basis to Ray of $70,000 and a fair market value of $120,000 on the date of the transfer. From this transaction Ray should recognize a gain of:
    a. $-0-
    b. $50,000
    c. $70,000
    d. $120,000
    e. Some other amount.

18. On July 1, 1992 Louis Herr exchanged an office building having a fair market value of $400,000, for cash of $80,000 plus another office building having a fair market value of $320,000. Herr's adjusted basis for the office building given up in the exchange was $250,000. How much gain should Herr recognize in his 1992 income tax return?
    a. $-0-
    b. $80,000
    c. $150,000
    d. $330,000   (CPA adapted)

19. For taxpayers on active duty outside the United States with the United States Armed Forces, the time period for reinvesting in a new personal residence is extended to a maximum of:
    a. four years
    b. five years
    c. six years
    d. eight years

20. Under the proposed regulations, in order for depreciable tangible property to qualify for like-kind exchange treatment under § 1031, the property must be:
    a. in the same general business class or the same product class
    b. held for at least five years prior to the exchange
    c. similar in service or use
    d. functionally similar
    e. None of the above

21. Part of a taxpayer's land (basis $50,000, FMV $90,000) is condemned to build

a new state building. Another part of the land is rendered useless by the condemnation. The taxpayer receives $15,000 in severance damages for the condemnation. What is the taxpayer's basis in the land?

a. $-0-
b. $35,000
c. $50,000
d. $75,000
e. Some other amount

_____ 22. During 1992, U Corporation sold 2,000 ($10 par value) shares of its treasury stock for $50,000. The stock was acquired five years ago for $30,000. The stock was originally issued for $20 per share. How much is U Corporation's recognized gain from this sale of stock?

a. $-0-
b. $10,000
c. $20,000
d. $30,000
e. Some other amount

_____ 23. During 1992, G, age 65, sold his principal residence for a net sales price (sales price less selling expenses) of $400,000. The residence had an adjusted basis of $140,000. Also during 1992, G purchased a new residence for $180,000. G elected the § 121 exclusion. What is G's recognized gain on the sale of his residence?

a. $-0-
b. $135,000
c. $260,000
d. $95,000
e. Some other amount

_____ 24. H exchanges a rental cottage at the beach with an adjusted basis of $90,000 and a FMV of $80,000 for a rental condo in the mountains with a FMV of $60,000 plus cash of $20,000. What (if any) is H's recognized gain or loss on this like-kind exchange?

a. $-0-
b. $10,000
c. ($10,000)
d. ($20,000)
e. Some other amount

Problem

1. Maureen Motsinger, age 28, sells her personal residence on July 1, 1992 for $68,000. Selling expenses amount to $4,100. She pays qualified fixing-up expenses of $2,000. Her basis in the old residence is $42,000. On June 19, 1992 she purchases and occupies a new residence which cost $72,000. Calculate Maureen's realized gain, recognized gain, and the adjusted basis of her new residence using the following worksheet.

    a. Amount Realized *68000 - 4100*   63900

        Less: Adjusted Basis   42000

        Realized Gain   24,900

    b. Adjusted Sales Price   61900

        Less: Cost of New Residence   - 72000

        Recognized Gain   0

    c. Cost of New Residence   72000

        Less: Unrecognized Gain   21900

        Basis of New Residence   50,100

Code Section Recognition

Indicate, by number, the appropriate Code Section where each of the following items are found.

_____ 1. Like-kind exchanges.

_____ 2. Involuntary conversions.

_____ 3. Sale of a personal residence.

_____ 4. Exclusion on sale of a residence for certain taxpayers 55 years old or over.

SOLUTIONS TO CHAPTER 15

True or False

1. False Realty held for investment would qualify for a like-kind exchange. (p.15-3)

2. False Real estate cannot be exchanged for personal property. (p. 15-3)

3. True (p. 15-5)

4. False § 1031 is not elective. (p. 15-3)

5. True (p. 15-8)

6. True (p. 15-15)

7. False The holding period of the newly acquired property begins on the date the original property was acquired. (p. 15-7)

8. True (p. 15-9)

9. False For direct conversions into replacement property, § 1033 is mandatory. (p. 15-12)

10. True (pp. 15-9)

11. True (p. 15-9)

12. False § 1033 does not apply to amounts designated as severance damages. (p. 15-10)

13. False Owner-investors must conform to the taxpayer use test. (p. 15-10)

14. False Taxpayers have until two years after the close of the tax year in which gain was realized. (p. 15-11)

15. True (p. 15-14)

16. True (p. 15-14)

17. False Losses on personal assets are not deductible. (p. 15-15)

18.   True   (p. 15-15)

19.   False   The taxpayer must be at least 55 years old. (p. 15-21)

20.   False   The basis of the new residence is its cost less the realized gain that was not recognized. (p. 15-19)

Fill-in-the-Blanks

1.   two (p. 15-15)

2.   occupy (p. 15-15)

3.   adjusted (p. 15-18)

4.   fixing-up (p. 15-18)

5.   ninety, thirty (p. 15-18)

6.   unrecognized (p. 15-19)

7. $125,000 (p. 15-21)

8.   three, five (p. 15-21)

Multiple Choice

1.   C $120,000 - 2,000 = $118,000 adjusted sales price
$120,000 - 88,000 = $32,000 gain realized
$118,000 - ($220,000 ÷ 2) = $8,000 gain recognized. (p. 15-18)

2.   B $225,000 + 25,000 + 50,000 - 250,000 = $50,000. (p. 15-5)

3.   B   Lesser of gain realized, $50,000, or boot received, $75,000. (p. 15-5)

4.   A $250,000 + 0 + 50,000 - 75,000 = $225,000. (p. 15-6)

5.   C   (p. 15-11)

6.   D $250,000 - 100,000 = $150,000. (p. 15-9)

7.   C $250,000 - 160,000 = $90,000. (p. 15-13)

8.   B $180,000 - 50,000 = $130,000 - 125,000 = $5,000. (p. 15-21)

9.   C   (p. 15-3)

10.   C $28,000 - 10,000 = $18,000 LTCG. (pp. 15-6)

11.   A   (p. 15-9)

12.   C   (p. 15-9)

13.   C   (p. 15-12)

14.   B   (p. 15-18)

15.   A   (p. 15-22)

16.   C   If a taxpayer acquires more than one house during the replacement period, gain
            is postponed from the first house to the third house. Any gain on the middle
            house is recognized. (p. 15-16)

17.   A   The transfer is nontaxable. (p. 15-24)

18.   B   Gain is recognized to the extent of boot received. (p. 15-5)

19.   D   (p. 15-17)

20.   A   (p. 15-4)

21.   B $50,000 - 15,000 = $35,000; See example 13. (p. 15-10)

22.   A   See IRC § 1032. (p. 15-23)

23.   D   Lesser of:
            $400,000 - 140,000 = $260,000 - 125,000 = $135,000; or
            $400,000 - 125,000 = $275,000 - 180,000 = $95,000   (p. 15-22)

24.   A $80,000 - 90,000 = ($10,000); Losses are not recognized under § 1031. (p. 15-5)

Problem

1. a. | | |
        |---|---|
        | Amount Realized | $63,900 |
        | Less: Adjusted Basis | -42,000 |
        | Realized Gain | $21,900 |

    b. | | |
        |---|---|
        | Adjusted Sales Price | $61,900 |
        | Less: Cost of New Residence | -72,000 |
        | Recognized Gain | $ 0 |

    c. | | |
        |---|---|
        | Cost of New Residence | $72,000 |
        | Less: Unrecognized Gain | -21,900 |
        | Basis of New Residence | $50,100 |

    (p. 15-18)

Code Section Recognition

1. § 1031

2. § 1033

3. § 1034

4. § 121

CHAPTER

16

PROPERTY TRANSACTIONS: CAPITAL GAINS AND LOSSES

CHAPTER HIGHLIGHTS

This chapter discusses the tax treatment of capital assets, including the special reporting requirements applicable to capital gains and losses. Historically, except for the years 1988 through 1990, long-term capital gains have received favorable tax treatment. Even in 1988 through 1990 when long-term capital gains were not granted favorable tax treatment, gains and losses from capital assets were required to be separately reported. The separate reporting of capital gains and losses is also necessary to apply certain limitations applicable to the deduction of capital losses.

I.   GENERAL CONSIDERATIONS

    A.   Capital gain or loss reporting arises from the sale or exchange of a capital asset. Since capital gains and losses are subject to special tax treatment, they must be separated from other gains and losses. The reason for the separate reporting requirement is that taxable income may vary significantly when both ordinary and capital gains and losses are present. For example, after reducing capital losses by capital gains, any remaining capital losses of noncorporate taxpayers may be deducted only to the extent of $3,000 annually.

    B.   General Scheme of Taxation. Gains and losses that are recognized must be properly classified. The following three characteristics determine proper classification:

        •   Tax status of the property (capital asset, § 1231 asset, or ordinary asset)

- Manner of the property's disposition (sale, exchange, casualty, theft, or condemnation)

- Holding period of the property (short term or long term).

II. CAPITAL ASSETS

A. Definition of a Capital Asset.

§ 1221 defines what is *not* a capital asset. A capital asset is all property held by the taxpayer (whether or not connected with his or her trade or business) other than:

- inventory or property held primarily for sale to customers in the ordinary course of business

- accounts and notes receivable

- depreciable property or real estate used in a business

- certain copyrights, literary, musical, or artistic compositions, letters or memoranda

- certain U.S. Government publications

The most common capital assets held by an individual are items such as a personal residence, automobile, or investment property (land, stock, bonds, etc.). Since losses on the sale or exchange of personal use property are not recognized, the taxpayer need only be concerned with the capital gain treatment of such property.

B. Effect of Judicial Action. The courts have held that motive must be determined to distinguish a capital from an ordinary asset. Capital asset determination by the courts hinges on whether the asset is held for investment purposes (capital asset) or business purposes (ordinary asset).

C. Statutory Expansions. There are several provisions in the Code which expand the definition of capital assets found in § 1221.

Dealers in securities must identify which securities are held for investment purposes; otherwise the securities are presumed to be inventory. To receive capital gain treatment on a sale, securities held for investment must be identified as such on the date of acquisition. Losses are considered capital losses if at any time the securities have been identified as being held for investment.

Under § 1237, if certain rules are met, real estate investors with limited development activity can avoid dealer status; thereby having any gain treated as capital gain rather than ordinary gain. See text for requirements and limitations.

Lump-sum distributions of an employee's pension or profit sharing plan are taxed in the current year. Under certain circumstances part of the gain may be taxed as a capital gain. See Chapter 19.

Nonbusiness bad debts are always treated as short-term capital losses.

III. SALE OR EXCHANGE

A. The recognition of a capital gain or loss requires a sale or exchange of a capital asset. The term "sale or exchange" is used in the Code but is not defined. A sale usually involves the receipt of money or the assumption of liabilities for property, and an exchange involves the transfer of property for other property.

B. Worthless securities which are capital assets are deemed to have become worthless on the last day of the taxable year.

C. Special Rule: Retirement of Corporate Obligations. As a general rule, collection of a debt does not constitute a sale or exchange, so it does not qualify for capital gain treatment for tax purposes. However, under § 1271, the retirement of corporate and certain governmental obligations is considered to be an exchange and therefore usually qualifies for capital gain or loss treatment.

D. Original Issue Discount. Bonds that are issued at less than maturity value may have an "original issue discount" (OID). If OID exists, it must generally be amortized over the life of the bond. As the OID is amortized, the basis of the bond to which the OID relates is increased by the amount of the amortization. Once the OID is fully amortized, the bond holder's basis in the bond will be its face value, thus there will be no gain on the redemption of the bond by the issuer.

E.   Options. The sale or exchange of an option to buy or sell property will generally produce capital gain or loss if the property is (or would be) a capital asset in the hands of the option holder.

If an option holder fails to exercise an option, the lapse is considered a sale or exchange on the option expiration date. If the option is exercised, the amount paid for the option is added to the purchase price of the property. The grantee then has a larger basis and the grantor has a larger gain.

F.   Patents. Under § 1235, inventors are given long-term capital gain treatment on patents. To qualify for this provision, a holder must transfer all substantial rights to a patent. A holder is the creator, inventor, or anyone who purchases the patent rights from the creator, except the creator's employer and certain related parties. To constitute all "substantial rights", the patent rights must not be limited geographically or in duration.

G.   Franchises, Trademarks, and Trade Names. Under § 1253, the transfer of a franchise, trademark, or trade name is not considered a sale or exchange of a capital asset if the transferor retains any significant power, right, or continuing interest concerning the subject matter of the franchise, trade-mark, or trade name.

- A noncontingent lump-sum payment of up to $100,000 is capitalized and may be amortized by the franchisee over the shorter of the franchise period or 10 years. Noncontingent lump-sum payments over $100,000 must be capitalized any may be amortized over 25 years. Both types are subject to § 1245 recapture.

- Contingent payments are ordinary income for the franchisor and a ordinary deduction for the franchisee.

This section does not apply to professional sports franchises.

H.   Lease Cancellation Payments. Payments received by a lessee for cancellation of a lease are treated as capital gains if the lease is a capital or § 1231 asset. Generally, a lease would be a capital asset if the property is used for personal use and an ordinary asset if the property is used in a trade or business. Payments received by a lessor for lease cancellation are always ordinary income because they are deemed to be in lieu of rental payments.

IV.   HOLDING PERIOD

A.   Property must be held more than one year to be long-term property.

B.   Review of Special Holding Period Rules.

The holding period of property received in a nontaxable exchange includes the holding period of the asset exchanged if such property is a capital or § 1231 asset.

The holding period of an asset received in a nontaxable transaction (e.g. a gift) where the basis carries over will generally include the holding period of the former owner. The holding period for inherited property is treated as long-term no matter how long the property is actually held. Taxpayers who acquire property in a disallowed loss transaction do not carry over the holding period or the basis.

C.   Short Sales.

A short sale is a form of speculation where a taxpayer sells borrowed property (usually stock) and later repays the lender with substantially identical property.

For short sales, the holding period of the property (except substantially identical property) sold is determined by the length of time the seller held the property used to repay the lender when closing the short sale.

V.   CAPITAL GAINS AND LOSSES OF NONCORPORATE TAXPAYERS

A.   Treatment of Capital Gains.

The first step in computing net capital gain is to net all long-term capital gains and losses and all short-term capital gains and losses. Next, taxpayers combine their net long-term gain or loss and their net short-term gain or loss. Any excess of net long-term capital gain over net short-term capital loss is a "net capital gain". This net capital gain is subject to a 28 percent maximum tax rate. If the net short-term capital gain exceeds the net long-term capital loss, the amount receives no special tax treatment and is included with other ordinary income.

B.   Treatment of Capital Losses.

If a taxpayer has a net capital loss for the year (either net long-term capital loss in excess of net short-term capital gain or net short-term capital loss in excess of net long-term capital gain) that loss could be limited. An individual taxpayer's maximum deduction against ordinary income is $3,000 per year. Any unused losses of an individual taxpayer are carried forward and keep their original character as long-term or short-term. These losses can be carried forward indefinitely.

C.   Capital gains and losses are reported on Schedule D of Form 1040.

VI.   CAPITAL GAINS AND LOSSES OF CORPORATE TAXPAYERS

The treatment of capital gains and losses for corporations differs from that of individuals in the following areas.

A.   An alternative tax rate of 34 percent is allowed in computing the tax on capital gains. Since the maximum corporate rate is 34 percent for ordinary income, there is nothing to be gained from the alternative capital gain tax rate.

B.   Capital losses offset capital gains only. Capital losses may not be deducted against ordinary income.

C.   There is a five year carryover and a three year carryback period for net capital losses. Corporate carryovers and carrybacks are always short-term, regardless of their original nature.

TEST FOR SELF-EVALUATION

True or False

Indicate which of the following statements are true or false by circling the correct answer.

(T)   F   1.   Inventory or stock used in a trade or business is not a capital asset as defined in § 1221.

(T)   F   2.   A depreciable building used in a taxpayer's trade or business is not a capital asset.

(T)   F   3.   Accounts and notes receivable acquired in the ordinary course of a trade or business or from the sale of inventory are not capital assets.

(T) F 4. The taxpayer's use of property is important in determining whether the property is an ordinary or capital asset.

T (F) 5. Dealers in securities will always have ordinary gains and losses on the sale of securities.

(T) F 6. Under § 1237, investors in real estate who engage in limited development activities may be allowed capital gain treatment.

(T) F 7. Taxable lump-sum distributions from qualified pension and profit-sharing plans are generally ordinary income (subject to certain transition rules).

T (F) 8. Nonbusiness bad debts are treated as long-term capital losses. *s. Term*

T (F) 9. The term "sale or exchange" is defined in the Internal Revenue Code.

(T) F 10. Losses on worthless securities which are capital assets are treated as arising from the sale or exchange of a capital asset on the last day of the taxable year.

(T) F 11. The retirement of a corporate bond is considered an exchange and therefore is usually subject to capital gain or loss treatment.

T F 12. If an option lapses, it is considered to be a sale or exchange on the last day of the taxable year.

T F 13. If an option is exercised, the amount paid for the option is added to the basis of the property subject to the option.

(T) F 14. The holder of a patent is entitled to long-term capital gain treatment if he or she transfers all substantial rights to the patent.

T (F) 15. The sale of a franchise always generates long-term capital gain under § 1253.

(T) F 16. Lease cancellation payments received by a lessee are capital gains if the lease is a capital or § 1231 asset.

T (F) 17. Lease cancellation payments received by a lessor are always long-term capital gains.

(T)   F   18.   Unused capital losses of noncorporate taxpayers can be carried forward indefinitely.

T   (F)   19.   Capital losses for corporate taxpayers are deductible against ordinary income, subject to the annual limitation.

(T)   F   20.   For 1992, an individual taxpayer's maximum deduction against ordinary income for a capital loss is $3,000.

T   (F)   21.   A truck used in a taxpayer's trade or business is a capital asset.

(T)   F   22.   The long-term holding period is more than one year.

T   F   23.   The holding period of property "sold short" is determined by the length of time the seller held the property used to close the short sale.

(T)   F   24.   Corporate capital losses carry back three years and forward five years and all carryovers are treated as short-term, regardless of the original nature of the loss.

(T)   F   25.   Contingent franchise payments are ordinary income to the franchisor and an ordinary deduction to the franchisee.

T   F   26.   A mode of operation, a widely recognized brand name, and a widely known business symbol are commonly call patents.

T   F   27.   A noncontingent lump-sum franchise fee of $120,000 could be amortized over 15 years.

Fill-in-the-Blanks

Complete the following statements with the appropriate word(s) or amount(s).

1.   The required holding period for a gain to be a long-term capital gain is more than ____one____ year.

2.   The holding period of property received in a nontaxable exchange generally __include__ the holding period of the former asset.

3.   In a short sale, the holding period of the property sold short is determined by the length of time the seller held the property used to _____ the lender when

closing the short sale.

4. Net gains from short-term capital transactions are taxed as ordinary _income_

5. The maximum capital loss that can be deducted against other income by a noncorp-
    orate taxpayer is ___3000___.

6. Unused capital losses of individuals can be carried forward for an _indefinite_ time
    period.

Multiple Choice

Choose the best answer for each of the following questions.

_____ 1. In 1992 T incurs a short-term capital loss of $5,000. T's gross income for 1992
           (not including the loss) is $20,000. If T is single, her adjusted gross income for
           1992 is:
           a. $20,000
           b. $19,000
           c. $18,000
           d. $17,000
           e. Some other amount

_____ 2. Assuming the same situation as in Question 1, what is T's short-term capital
           loss carryover for 1993?
           a. $1,000
           b. $2,000
           c. $3,000
           d. $4,000
           e. Some other amount

_____ 3. Tasty Taco sells franchises to independent operators. In 1992 it sold a
           franchise with an 8-year life to Pen Wilson for $70,000 plus 3 percent of sales.
           Tasty Taco retains significant rights to control management. If Pen's 1992
           sales amounted to $100,000, Tasty Taco would include in its computation of
           1992 taxable income:
           a. Long-term capital gain of $73,000
           b. Long-term capital gain of $70,000, ordinary income of $3,000
           c. Ordinary income of $73,000
           d. Ordinary income of $70,000, long-term capital gain of $3,000

e. Some other amount

_____ 4. Which of the following is a capital asset?
   a. Inventory
   b. Texaco stock owned by an investor
   c. Accounts receivable
   d. Land used in a trade or business
   e. None of the above

_____ 5. T owns a tract of land and subdivides it for sale. In 1992 she sells five lots for $10,000 each with a basis of $6,000 in each lot. Her total selling expenses are $2,000 and she meets the requirements of § 1237. T should report for 1992:
   a. Capital gain of $18,000
   b. Capital gain of $500, ordinary income of $17,500
   c. Capital gain of $17,500, ordinary income of $500
   d. Ordinary income of $18,000
   e. Some other amount

_____ 6. T invents a machine which he patents. The patent is assigned to a manufacturer in 1992 for $100,000, plus a $5 per machine royalty. During 1992 1,000 machines are sold. Assuming T transferred all substantial rights and has a zero basis in the patent, he should report for 1992:
   a. Long-term capital gain of $105,000
   b. Long-term capital gain of $100,000, ordinary income of $5,000
   c. Long-term capital gain of $5,000, ordinary income of $100,000
   d. Ordinary income of $105,000
   e. Some other amount

_____ 7. To receive long-term capital gain treatment an asset acquired must be held:
   a. One year or more
   b. Nine months or more
   c. More than one year
   d. More than six months
   e. None of the above

_____ 8. During 1992, T has net long-term capital gains of $12,000 and a net short-term capital loss carryover of $8,000. On his 1992 tax return, T should report:
   a. $12,000 net capital gain
   b. $9,000 net capital gain
   c. $8,000 net capital gain
   d. $4,000 net capital gain
   e. None of the above

9. During 1992 T, an individual, sells his personal automobile for $2,000. He purchased the automobile six years ago for $14,000. In addition, T has a $7,000 long-term capital gain from the sale of stock which he held as an investment. What amount should T report on his 1992 individual income tax return related to these transactions?
   a. $7,000 net capital gain
   b. $4,000 net capital gain
   c. $3,000 net capital loss
   d. $5,000 net capital loss
   e. Some other amount

10. S purchased stock on November 30, 1991 for $5,000. Due to a series of unfortunate events, S is notified on July 1, 1992 that the stock is totally worthless. Assuming S has no other capital transactions, what amount of loss should S report on her tax return for 1992?
    a. $5,000 long-term capital loss
    b. $5,000 short-term capital loss
    c. $3,000 long-term capital loss
    d. $3,000 short-term capital loss
    e. Some other amount

11. For 1992 T has net long-term capital gains of $20,000 and net short-term capital losses of $8,000. What is T's "net capital gain?"
    a. $20,000
    b. $17,000
    c. $12,000
    d. $8,000
    e. Some other amount

12. In December 1992, T receives a lump-sum distribution of $52,000 from a qualified pension plan. T contributed $12,000 to the plan and the employer contributed the rest. If T was a participant in the plan for a total of 8 years, he should report:
    a. Long-term capital gain of $24,000, ordinary income of $16,000
    b. Long-term capital gain of $10,000, ordinary income of $30,000
    c. Long-term capital gain of $40,000
    d. Ordinary income of $40,000
    e. Some other amount

13. T Corporation issues bonds at 95 percent of the face amount. The bonds are due in ten years. Which of the following is true?
    a. The bonds are not issued with original issue discount

(b.) The bonds are issued with original issue discount
c. These bonds are capital assets to T Corporation
d. The bond holders can only be individuals
e. None of the above

_____ 14. T buys an option on vacant land. He pays $4,000 for a three-year option to purchase land for $100,000. After six months T sells the option for $9,000. From this transaction, T would recognize:
a. LTCG of $5,000
b. STCG of $5,000
c. STCG of $9,000
d. STCG of $109,000
e. Some other amount.

_____ 15. Same as number 14, except T fails to exercise the option after the three year period. What is T's recognized gain or loss?
a. LTCG of $4,000
b. STCG of $4,000
c. LTCL of $4,000
d. STCL of $4,000
e. Some other amount

_____ 16. Y had the following items of income, gains, losses, and deductions in 1992.

Salary	$30,000
Nonbusiness bad debt	-2,500
Gain on stock held 8 months	5,000
Loss on stock held 3 years	-2,000
Home mortgage interest	12,000

What is Y's AGI for the year?
a. $30,500
b. $32,500
c. $33,000
d. $37,500
e. Some other amount

_____ 17. ZZZ Corporation has ordinary income from operations of $60,000, net long-term capital gain of $20,000, and net short-term capital loss of $30,000. What is ZZZ Corporation's taxable income for 1992?
a. $50,000
b. $60,000

c. $80,000

d. $90,000

e. Some other amount

18. Q, a cash basis individual taxpayer, executed a sale of stock on December 29, 1991. The sale was settled on January 4, 1992. The stock has a basis to Q of $20,000 and was acquired on December 27, 1989. The stock was sold for $25,000. What is Q's tax result from the sale?
   a. LTCG of $5,000 in 1992
   b. STCG of $5,000 in 1991
   c. LTCG of $5,000 in 1991
   d. STCG of $5,000 in 1991
   e. None of the above

19. When a taxpayer has a short sale of a capital asset it may be treated as:
   a. Ordinary income or short-term capital gain
   b. Long-term capital gain or short-term capital gain
   c. Short-term capital gain or ordinary income
   d. Short-term capital gain only
   e. None of the above

20. Corporations may carry unused capital losses to what other tax years?
   a. Forward indefinitely
   b. Back three and forward fifteen years
   c. Back three and forward five years
   d. Back three and forward seven years
   e. None of the above

21. T buys an expensive painting, "St. Sheila," for $20,000. The painting is used to decorate T's office and is of *investment quality*. The painting is 7 year class property (14.29% in the first year). How does T treat the painting for tax purposes?
   a. $20,000 is deducted in the first year.
   b. $2,858 is deducted in the first year.
   c. The cost of the painting cannot be deducted.
   d. The § 179 election applies to the painting.
   e. None of the above.

22. For 1992, T, a single taxpayer, has taxable income of $75,000 including net capital gain of $40,000. His regular tax calculation for 1992 is $18,905 [(15% x $21,450) + 28% ($51,900 - $21,450) + 31% ($75,000 - $51,900)]. What is T's tax using the alternative tax on net capital gains?

   a. $18,212
   b. $7,012
   c. $11,200
   d. $18,905
   e. Some other amount

Problem

1. During 1992 Pat Felde had the following stock transactions:

Description	Acquired	Sold	Sales Price	Basis	
100 shs Exxon	2/01/88	11/05/92	$6,000	$2,500	3500 LT
100 shs ATT	6/11/92	10/03/92	$4,000	$4,500	−500 ST
100 shs IBM	3/12/92	08/22/92	$6,000	$5,200	+800 ST
100 shs GM	5/12/84	09/15/92	$8,000	$5,000	+3000 LT
100 shs Ford	9/15/81	12/01/92	$6,000	$7,000	−1000 LT

Calculate the following amounts to arrive at Pat's net amount included in or deducted from gross income for 1992.

Net short-term capital gain or loss   +300

Net long-term capital gain or loss   5500

Net capital position   5800

Amount included in income   5800

Code Section Recognition

Indicate, by number, the appropriate Code Section where each of the following items are found.

_____ 1. Definition of a capital asset.

_____ 2. Limited sales of real property.

_____ 3. Worthless securities.

_____ 4. Options.

_____ 5. Patents.

_____ 6. Short sales.

SOLUTIONS TO CHAPTER 16

True or False

1. True (p. 16-3)

2. True (p. 16-3)

3. True (p. 16-3)

4. True (p. 16-5)

5. False Dealers may designate securities as held for investment. (p. 16-5)

6. True (p. 16-6)

7. True (p. 16-7)

8. False Nonbusiness bad debts are treated as short-term capital losses. (p. 16-7)

9. False The term is not defined in the Code. (p. 16-7)

10. True (p. 16-7)

11. True (p. 16-8)

12. False It is a sale or exchange on the day it lapses. (p. 16-9)

13.   True   (p. 16-9)

14.   True   (p. 16-11)

15.   False   Franchises usually produce ordinary income on their sale. (p. 16-12)

16.   True   (p. 16-13)

17.   False   Lease cancellation payments received by a lessor are ordinary income. (p. 16-13)

18.   True   (p. 16-20)

19.   False   Corporations are not permitted to deduct capital losses against ordinary income. (p. 16-24)

20.   True   (p. 16-20)

21.   False   Depreciable assets used in a trade or business are excluded from the definition of a capital asset. (p. 16-3)

22.   True   (p. 16-14)

23.   True   (p. 16-16)

24.   True   (p. 16-24)

25.   True   (p. 16-12)

26.   False   They are called franchises. (p. 16-12)

27.   False   The fee has to amortized over 25 years. (p. 16-12)

Fill-in-the-Blanks

1.   one (p. 16-14)

2.   includes (p. 16-15)

3.   repay (p. 16-16)

4.   income (p. 16-19)

5. $3,000 (p. 16-20)

6.   indefinite (p. 16-20)

Multiple Choice

1.   D $20,000 - 3,000 (maximum) = $17,000. (p. 16-20)

2.   B $5,000 - 3,000 = $2,000. (p. 16-20)

3.   C $70,000 + 3% (100,000) = $73,000 ordinary income. (p. 16-12)

4.   B   (p. 16-3)

5.   A   5 x $10,000 = $50,000 - 2,000 - (5 x $6,000) = $18,000. (p. 16-6)

6.   A $100,000 + ($5 x 1,000) = $105,000. (p. 16-11)

7.   C   (p. 16-14)

8.   D   (p. 16-20)

9.   A   The loss on the sale of the personal automobile is not deductible. (p. 16-15, 18)

10.   C   (p. 16-8, 20)

11.   C $20,000 - 8,000 = $12,000. (p. 16-18)

12.   D $52,000 - 12,000 = $40,000 ordinary income. (p. 16-7)

13.   B $\frac{1}{4}$% x 10 Years = $2\frac{1}{2}$%, the maximum discount is exceeded. (p. 16-8)

14.   B $9,000 - 4,000 = $5,000 STCG. (p. 16-9)

15.   C   (p. 16-9)

16.   A   Salary $30,000
          Short-term capital gain $5,000
          Short-term capital loss   -2,500
          Net short-term capital gain $2,500

          Long-term capital loss   -2,000

          Excess of NSTCG over NLTCL   500
          Adjusted gross income $30,500   (pp. 16-18, 20)

17.   B   Net STCL are not allowed for corporations. (p. 16-24)

18.   C   The date of sale is the date of execution. (p. 16-26)

19.   B   (p. 16-16)

20.   C   (p. 16-24)

21.   C   (p. 16-5)

22.   A   Regular tax: (15% x $21,450) + 28%($35,000 - $21,450) = $7,012
          Alternative tax on NCG: 28% ($40,000) = $11,200
          Total $18,212
          (p. 16-19)

Problem

1.   Net short-term capital gain:

          IBM $800
          ATT   -500 $300

      Net long-term capital gain:

          Exxon $3,500
          GM   3,000
          Ford   -1,000 $5,500

      Net capital position $5,800

      Amount included in income $5,800

Code Section Recognition

1.   § 1221

2.   § 1237

3.   § 165

4.   § 1234

5.   § 1235

6.   § 1233

CHAPTER

17

PROPERTY TRANSACTIONS: SECTION 1231 AND RECAPTURE PROVISIONS

CHAPTER HIGHLIGHTS

This chapter summarizes Code § 1231 which grants favorable long-term capital gain treatment on the sale or exchange of business properties or involuntary conversions. Also covered are recapture provisions which provide that certain gains which would otherwise qualify for capital gain treatment are to be treated as ordinary income. The impact of the passive activity provisions on gains and losses is also discussed.

I. § 1231 ASSETS

   A. Relationship to Capital Assets.

      § 1231 assets are not capital assets because they are excluded under § 1221(2). The concept of § 1231 assets was enacted by Congress in 1942 to ease the burden of taxation on the sale of business assets and to help the war effort.

      § 1231 provides that a net gain on § 1231 property is treated as a long-term capital gain, and a net loss is treated as an ordinary loss.

   B. Property Included. § 1231 property includes the following:

      • Depreciable or real property used in a business or for the production of income

      • Timber, coal, or domestic iron ore to which § 631 applies

- Livestock held for draft, breeding, dairy, or sporting purposes

- Unharvested crops on land used in a business

- Certain nonpersonal use capital assets

C.   Property Excluded. The following property is not § 1231 property:

- Property held less than the long-term holding period (the long-term holding period is greater than one year)

- Property where casualty losses exceed casualty gains for the taxable year

- Inventory and property held primarily for sale to customers

- Copyrights; literary, musical, or artistic compositions; certain U.S. government publications

- Intangible assets such as accounts and notes receivable

D.   Special Rules for Certain § 1231 Assets.

The difference between the basis of timber and the fair market value on the first day of the year during which the timber is cut may be treated as § 1231 gain, provided the timber is held for sale or use in a business and has been held for the required long-term holding period.

Coal or domestic iron ore royalties or other sale proceeds therefrom may be treated as § 1231 gain.

Special holding period rules apply to the classification of gains and losses on livestock as § 1231 gain or loss. Cattle and horses must be held for at least 24 months while other livestock must be held for at least 12 months. Poultry is excluded from § 1231 treatment.

The sale of unharvested crops, held for the long-term holding period, may be treated as the sale of a § 1231 asset provided the crop production costs have been capitalized.

Certain business and investment properties may be subject to § 1231 treatment if the gain or loss is the result of a casualty or theft.

E. General Procedure for § 1231 Computation. The general procedure for calculating § 1231 gains and losses is as follows:

Net all long-term casualty gains and losses from nonpersonal use property.

- If the casualty gains exceed the casualty losses, combine the excess with other § 1231 gains.

- If the casualty losses exceed casualty gains, exclude all losses and gains from further § 1231 computations. All casualty gains are then considered ordinary income and casualty losses are deductible for AGI if business related and from AGI (subject to the 2 percent of adjusted gross income limitation), if not.

Net all § 1231 gains (including any net casualty gains) and losses.

- If the gains exceed the losses, net § 1231 gains are offset by non-recaptured § 1231 losses for the previous five years; the excess is treated as long-term capital gain. Any offset amount is ordinary income.

- If the losses exceed the gains, all gains are ordinary income and business losses are fully deductible. Other casualty losses (arising from income-producing property) are deductions from adjusted gross income.

II.   § 1245 RECAPTURE

A. Congress enacted § 1245 to prevent taxpayers from receiving the dual benefits of depreciation deductions which offset ordinary income and § 1231 long-term capital gain treatment when the property is sold. Under § 1245, gain on the disposition is treated as ordinary income to the extent of depreciation taken. Any excess gain is either § 1231 gain or casualty gain if the property was disposed of in a casualty event. § 1245 does not apply where the taxpayer has a realized loss on the disposition of an asset.

B. § 1245 property includes all depreciable personal property, including livestock. Nonresidential buildings acquired after 1980 and before 1987 are subject to § 1245 if accelerated cost recovery (ACRS) is used. The following special property is subject to § 1245 treatment:

- Amortizable personal property such as patents, copyrights, leaseholds, and professional sports contracts

- Amortization of reforestation expenditures and costs to remove handicap barriers

- Amounts expensed under § 179

- Elevators and escalators acquired before January 1, 1987

- Certain depreciable tangible real property

- Amortization taken on pollution control facilities, railroad grading and tunnel boring equipment, on-the-job training, and child care facilities

- Agricultural and horticultural structures and petroleum storage facilities

- Nonresidential realty placed in service after 1980 and before 1987 (15-year, 18-year, or 19-year property) on which ACRS was taken.

III.   § 1250 RECAPTURE

A.   § 1250 property includes depreciable real property which is not subject to § 1245.   § 1250 is similar to § 1245, but under § 1250 only "additional depreciation" is subject to recapture. This additional amount is the accelerated depreciation taken in excess of straight-line depreciation that would have been allowed. Unless property is disposed of during the first year, § 1250 does not apply to real property placed in service after 1986 because the straight-line method of depreciation is required.

B.   Computing Recapture on Nonresidential Real Property. For § 1250 property, other than residential rental property, the following general rules apply:

- Post-1969 amount recaptured is depreciation taken in excess of straight-line after 1969.

- If property is held one year or less, all depreciation taken is recaptured.

- Special rules apply to dispositions of substantially improved § 1250 property.

C. Computing Recapture on Residential Rental Housing. Recapture on residential rental housing is computed in the same manner as other § 1250 property except that only additional depreciation attributable to periods after 1975 is recaptured in full. Depreciation prior to 1976 and after 1969 may be partially recaptured depending on the taxpayer's holding period.

D. For tax years after 1980 and before 1987 (ACRS property).

Nonresidential property (office buildings etc.) is subject to § 1245 recapture if the ACRS statutory method is used (i.e. all the depreciation is recaptured).

Residential real property (apartments etc.). The recaptured amount is the depreciation claimed over the depreciation that would have been allowed if straight-line depreciation were used.

For real property acquired after 1986 only straight-line depreciation can be used; therefore, there is no § 1250 recapture (except for property held less than one year).

E. § 1250 Recapture Situations. § 1250 applies to the following property for which accelerated deprecation was used:

- Residential real estate acquired before 1987

- Nonresidential real estate acquired before 1981

- Real property used outside the United States

- Certain government-financed or low-income housing

IV. CONSIDERATIONS COMMON TO § 1245 AND § 1250.

A. Recapture under § 1245 and § 1250 does not apply in the following situations:

- For a gift of property, the recapture potential carries over to the donee.

- If property is transferred by death the recapture does not carry to the heir.

- For a charitable transfer, the recapture potential reduces the amount of the charitable deduction under § 170.

- For tax-free transactions in which the adjusted basis of the property carries over to the transferee, recapture potential also carries over. § 351 tax-free incorporations fall into this category.

- Gains recognized under the like-kind exchange or involuntary conversion provision are subject to recapture as ordinary income under §§ 1245 and 1250.

B. Other Applications. Special rules apply in the following situations:

- For installment sales, recapture gain is recognized in full in the year of sale. Furthermore, all gain is ordinary income until recapture potential is fully absorbed.

- For a distribution of property subject to recapture, gain must be recognized by the distributing corporation to the extent of the recapture.

V. SPECIAL RECAPTURE PROVISIONS

A. Special Recapture for Corporations. Corporations selling depreciable realty will be subject to an "ordinary gain adjustment." This adjustment is equal to 20 percent of the excess of the § 1245 potential recapture over the actual § 1250 recapture. § 1231 gain is converted to ordinary income to the extent of this adjustment.

B. Recapture of Investment Tax Credit Basis Reduction. The basis of property eligible for the investment tax credit before 1986 sometimes was reduced by an amount equal to one-half the investment tax credit claimed. This reduction is subject to § 1245 recapture. However, if part of the investment credit taken is recaptured, one-half of the recapture is added back to the property's basis before computing gain or loss.

C. Gain from Sale of Depreciable Property Between Certain Related Parties. In a sale or exchange of depreciable property between an individual and a controlled corporation or partnership or between certain other related parties, any gain recognized is ordinary income. Depreciable means subject to depreciation in the hands of the transferee. Recapture under §§ 1245 and

1250 is applied before recapture under the related party provisions.

D.   Rehabilitation Expenditures for Low-Income Rental Housing. § 1250 recaptures a portion of the low-income housing rapid amortization under § 167(k).

E.   Intangible Drilling Costs and Depletion. Intangible drilling and development costs are recaptured on the sale or disposition of such property, if such costs were expensed instead of capitalized. The gain on disposition of the property is subject to recapture as follows:

- For property acquired before 1987, the IDC expensed after 1975 in excess of what cost depletion would have been had the IDC been capitalized.

- For properties acquired after 1986, the IDC expensed.

VI.   PASSIVE ACTIVITY LOSSES

When a passive activity is disposed of, any suspended losses and current year losses of the activity are fully deductible. Any gain from the disposition is offset by the current and suspended losses of the activity sold. Any remaining gain is then available to allow current and/or suspended losses of other passive activities to be deducted. The recognized gain still receives normal treatment under the property disposition rules.

VII.   REPORTING PROCEDURES

Form 4797 is used to report noncapital gains and losses, including § 1231 gains and losses, and §§ 1245 and 1250 gains. Form 4684, which is used for reporting casualties and thefts, should be completed first since a resulting net gain will impact the computation of § 1231 gains and losses.

TEST FOR SELF-EVALUATION

True or False

Indicate which of the following statements are true or false by circling the correct answer.

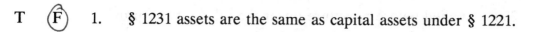

T (F) 1. § 1231 assets are the same as capital assets under § 1221.

(T) F 2. A contract to cut timber owned more than one year is a § 1231 asset.

T (F) 3. The primary tax advantage of a § 1231 asset is that gains are ordinary income and losses are capital losses.

T (F) 4. All livestock must be held for at least 24 months to qualify as a § 1231 asset.

(T) F 5. Inventory is not a § 1231 asset.

(T) F 6. Net gains from other than personal use property disposed of by casualty or theft are § 1231 gains.

(T) F 7. § 1245 applies to depreciable personalty and requires that all depreciation be recaptured if the gain realized exceeds the potential recapture amount.

(T) F 8. Depreciation on elevators and escalators acquired before 1987 is recaptured under § 1245.

T (F) 9. Professional baseball and football players contracts are not § 1245 property.

T (F) 10. All depreciation on pre-1987 residential § 1250 property is recaptured to the extent of gain on disposition.

(T) F 11. Any net gain from the disposal of § 1245 property that is not recaptured is either § 1231 gain or casualty gain.

T (F) 12. For gifts of property subject to depreciation recapture, the donor must recapture the depreciation, not the donee.

(T) F 13. For a charitable transfer, the recapture potential reduces the amount of the charitable contribution deduction under § 170.

(T) F 14. Generally, if the adjusted basis in a transaction carries over to the transferee, the recapture potential also carries over.

T (F) 15. In an installment sale, capital gain treatment applies first, then recapture under § 1245 or 1250.

T   F   16.   Intangible drilling costs that are expensed on property acquired after 1986 are recaptured to the extent of the lesser of the gain realized or the IDC expensed.

T   (F)   17.   The net § 1231 gain is offset by nonrecaptured § 1231 losses from the previous 6 years.

T   (F)   18.   All depreciation on post-1986 nonresidential rental property is recaptured.

T   (F)   19.   A gift transaction triggers recapture under § 1245, but not under § 1250.

T   (F)   20.   Chickens that are held for 12 months are § 1231 assets.

(T)   F   21.   For real property acquired after 1986 there usually will be no § 1250 recapture because depreciation is limited to straight-line.

(T)   F   22.   In determining the amount of passive losses allowed as a result of gain arising from the disposition of a passive activity, gain from the disposition of the activity is first offset by current and suspended passive losses of that activity.

T   (F)   23.   § 1245 recapture is often referred to as partial recapture while § 1250 recapture is referred to as full recapture.

(T)   F   24.   For § 1245 recapture it does not matter which method of depreciation is used.

(T)   F   25.   The § 1245 recapture rules apply before there is any casualty gain

Fill-in-the-Blanks

Complete the following statements with the appropriate word(s) or amount(s).

1.   § 1245 and 1250 recapture rules normally ___override___ all other Code sections.

2.   § 1239 imposes restrictions on sales or exchanges between an individual and his or her ___controlled___ corporation.

3.   To meet the definition of "control" under § 1239, the taxpayer must own more than ___50___ percent of the corporation's outstanding stock.

4.   Intangible drilling and development costs that are paid or incurred are recaptured if such costs were ___expensed___ instead of capitalized.

Multiple Choice

Choose the best answer for each of the following questions.

_____   1.   Which of the following is not a § 1231 asset?
         a. A delivery truck owned 5 months
         b. Timber owned two years
         c. An apartment owned five years
         d. Unharvested crops used on land in a trade or business
         e. All of the above are § 1231 assets

_____   2.   To qualify as a § 1231 asset, cattle and horses must be held at least:
         a. 6 months
         b. 12 months
         c. 18 months
         d. 24 months
         e. None of the above

_____   3.   Mr. I.C. Ewe sold Exxon stock (owned 10 years) for a $25,000 gain in 1992. In addition, he had a loss of $10,000 on the sale of one acre of land used in his business. The land was purchased five years ago. Mr. Ewe's net gain from the sale or exchange of capital assets for 1992 will be:
         a. -0-
         b. $5,000
         c. $10,000
         d. $25,000
         e. Some other amount

_____   4.   On January 6, 1992, Isadora Xena sold § 1245 business equipment. She had purchased this equipment for $5,000 three years ago and had claimed straight-line ACRS depreciation of $2,500 on it. If the selling price was $4,000, Ms. Xena should recognize:
         a. § 1231 gain of $1,500
         b. § 1245 gain of $1,500
         c. § 1231 loss of $500
         d. § 1245 loss of $500
         e. Some other amount

_____ 5. Assume the same situation as in Question 4, except that the selling price was $2,000. Ms. Xena should recognize:
   a. § 1245 loss of $500
   ⓑ § 1231 loss of $500
   c. § 1245 loss of $2,000
   d. § 1231 loss of $2,000
   e. Some other amount

_____ 6. Assume the same situation as in Question 4, except that the selling price was $5,500. Ms. Xena should report:
   a. § 1245 gain of $3,000
   b. § 1231 gain of $3,000
   ⓒ § 1245 gain of $2,500, § 1231 gain of $500
   d. § 1245 gain of $500, § 1231 gain of $2,500
   e. Some other amount

_____ 7. Becky Smith acquired residential rental property on January 1, 1986 at a cost of $200,000. She used the accelerated method of cost recovery under ACRS. The asset is sold on January 1, 1992 for $250,000. Total cost recovery allowed during the period the asset was held by Becky Smith was $64,000. Straight-line depreciation would have yielded a $42,000 total. What is Becky's recapture under § 1250?
   a. -0-
   ⓑ $22,000
   c. $42,000
   d. $64,000
   e. Some other amount

_____ 8. T owns 100 percent of T Corporation. In 1992 T sells a truck (basis of $6,000) to T Corporation for $7,500. T Corporation will use the truck in its business. T should report:
   a. A capital gain of $1,500
   b. A capital loss of $1,500
   ⓒ Ordinary income of $1,500
   d. No gain or loss
   e. Some other amount

_____ 9. In the current year, T donates to Goodwill Industries § 1245 property acquired three years ago, The property has a fair market value of $20,000 and an adjusted basis of $12,000. If the property is subject to $4,000 of § 1245 recapture potential, what is T's charitable contribution deduction?
   a. $20,000

b. $12,000
c. $8,000
d. $16,000
e. Some other amount

_____ 10. T Corporation distributes as a dividend property subject to recapture potential. If the recapture potential is $500 and the property's fair market value exceeds the adjusted basis by $800, T Corporation should recognize:
a. $500 ordinary income, $300 § 1231 gain
b. $800 ordinary income
c. $300 ordinary income, $500 § 1231 gain
d. No recognized gain or loss
e. Some other amount

_____ 11. In 1992, Jim Dox has a § 1231 gain of $12,000 on property that he sold. During 1989, Jim reported a § 1231 loss of $7,000, which has not been recaptured. Jim did not have any other § 1231 gains or losses during the past five years. What is Jim's ordinary income for 1992 as a result of the above transactions?
a. $-0-
b. $12,000
c. $7,000
d. $5,000
e. Some other amount

_____ 12. In 1992, Z Corporation has potential § 1245 recapture of $100,000 and § 1250 recapture of $40,000 on the sale of § 1250 property. The § 291 ordinary gain adjustment would be:
a. -0-
b. $12,000
c. $6,000
d. $15,000
e. Some other amount.

_____ 13. Jim Waugh acquired nonresidential realty in 1985 for $200,000. His total ACRS deductions claimed on the realty (assuming a straight-line election was not made), totaled $90,000, which gives him an adjusted basis of $110,000. In 1992, Jim sells the property for $230,000, for a gain of $120,000. Jim should report:
a. $120,000 § 1231 gain.
b. $120,000 ordinary income.
c. $30,000 § 1231 gain and $90,000 ordinary income.

    d. $30,000 ordinary income and $90,000 § 1231 gain.

    e. Some other amount.

14. Jerry Canning has a passive activity with a suspended loss of $10,000. In the current year he disposes of the activity for a net long-term capital gain of $23,000. In the current year he has a profit of $3,000 from the activity. Assuming Jerry has no other gains or losses from passive activities during the current year, what is Jerry's reportable long-term gain from this disposition?
    a. $-0-
    b. $13,000
    c. $20,000
    d. $23,000
    e. Some other amount

15. Several years ago, Herb Mutter purchased a tract of land with timber on it. The land cost $50,000 and the timber cost $100,000. On the first day of 1992, the timber was appraised at $175,000. In September 1992, the timber was cut and sold for $195,000. If Herb elects § 1231 what is his § 1231 gain on the sale of the timber?
    a. $-0-
    b. $20,000
    c. $75,000
    d. $95,000
    e. Some other amount

16. On January 1, 1992, Geneva Gwen sells nineteen-year nonresidential realty with accumulated depreciation of $200,000. The property was depreciated under an accelerated method. Straight-line depreciation would have been $110,000. The property was sold on January 1, 1992 with a recognized gain of $245,000. What is the depreciation recapture on this realty?
    a. $-0-
    b. $200,000
    c. $90,000
    d. $45,000
    e. Some other amount

17. G Corporation sold equipment for $37,000 on December 31, 1992. The equipment had been purchased on January 4, 1989 for $40,000 and the equipment had an adjusted basis of $32,000 on the date of sale. From this transaction G should report?
    a. No gain or loss
    b. $8,000 ordinary income

c. $5,000 ordinary income
d. $5,000 § 1231 gain
e. $3,000 § 1231 loss

_____ 18. During 1992, H recognized § 1231 gains of $15,000 and § 1231 losses of $11,000. H's AGI before § 1231 gains and losses is $50,000. After accounting for § 1231 transaction, what is H's AGI?
a. $50,000
b. $65,000
c. $39,000
d. $54,000
e. Some other amount

_____ 19. § 1231 property includes all of the following except:
a. Stock held for investment
b. Timber, coal, and domestic iron ore
c. Real property used in a trade or business
d. Livestock (other than poultry) held for breeding purposes
e. Depreciable property used in a trade or business

_____ 20. During 1992, M has a net § 1231 gain of $50,000. Last year, M had a net § 1231 loss of $15,000. In 1992, M should report:
a. $50,000 long-term capital gain
b. $50,000 ordinary income
c. $15,000 ordinary income and $35,000 long-term capital gain
d. $15,000 long-term capital gain and $35,000 ordinary gain
e. None of the above

Problem

1.   Sid Tekel owns a § 1245 asset that was acquired two years ago at a cost of $8,500, on which he has claimed ACRS depreciation of $1,700. In 1992 Sid sells this asset for $10,250. Besides the § 1245 asset, he disposes of a residential § 1250 asset for $102,500 in 1992. This asset originally cost $80,000 and he has claimed accelerated depreciation of $13,500 since 1979. Straight-line depreciation would have been $8,750 on this asset. Sid did not have any § 1231 loss in prior years. Using the following table, calculate Sid's gain or loss and ordinary income recapture (if any).

	Sec. 1245 Asset	Sec. 1250 Asset
Sales price	10,250	102 500
Adjusted basis	-6 800	66 500
Gain realized	3450	36 000
Recapture potential	1700	4750
Ordinary income	1700	4750
§ 1231 gain	1750	31 250

Code Section Recognition

Indicate, by number, the appropriate Code Section where the following items are found.

_____ 1. Depreciable assets used in a trade or business.

_____ 2. Recapture on depreciable real estate.

_____ 3. Recapture on depreciable personalty.

_____ 4. Gain on the sale of depreciable property between "related" parties.

SOLUTIONS TO CHAPTER 17

True or False

1. False   Capital assets and § 1231 assets are not the same. (p. 17-2)

2. True   (p. 17-4)

3. False   Gains are capital gains and losses are ordinary. (p. 17-2)

4. False   Livestock other than cattle and horses only has to be held 12 months or more. (p. 17-5)

5.   True   (p. 17-4)

6.   True   (p. 17-5)

7.   True   (p. 17-11)

8.   True   (p. 17-12)

9.   False   Player contracts are § 1245 property. (p. 17-12)

10.   False   Only the excess over straight-line is recaptured. (p. 17-16)

11.   True   (p. 17-11)

12.   False   Recapture potential passes to the donee. (p. 17-17)

13.   True   (p. 17-18)

14.   True   (p. 17-18)

15.   False   In an installment sale, recapture gain is recognized in full in the year of sale. (p. 17-19)

16.   True   (p. 17-22)

17.   False   The previous 5 years, not 6 years (p. 17-7)

18.   False   There is no recapture because only straight-line depreciation can be used (unless the property is disposed of within the first year. (p. 17-14)

19.   False   A transfer of property by gift does not cause recapture under § 1250 or 1245. (p. 17-17)

20.   False   Poultry is excluded from the definition of § 1231 assets. (p. 17-5)

21.   True   (p. 17-14)

22.   True   (p. 17-23)

23.   False   § 1245 recapture is referred to as full recapture, while § 1250 recapture is referred to as partial recapture. (pp. 17-11, 14)

24.   True   (p. 17-11)

25.   True   (p. 17-11)

Fill-in-the-Blanks

1.   override (p. 17-19)

2.   controlled (p. 17-21)

3.   50 (p. 17-21)

4.   expensed (p. 17-22)

Multiple Choice

1.   A   (p. 17-4)

2.   D   (p. 17-5)

3.   D   (p. 17-2)

4.   B $5,000 - 2,500 = $2,500 adjusted basis. $4,000 - 2,500 = $1,500 gain realized, which is less than the depreciation recapture potential. Therefore, the realized gain is all § 1245 gain. (p. 17-11)

5.   B $2,000 - 2,500 = ($500) § 1231 loss. (p. 17-11)

6.   C $5,500 - 2,500 = $3,000 gain realized, of which $2,500 is § 1245 gain and $500 is § 1231 gain. (p. 17-11)

7.   B $250,000 - 136,000 (basis) = $114,000 gain realized
            $64,000 - 42,000 = $22,000 recapture. (p. 17-14)

8.   C $7,500 - 6,000 = $1,500 ordinary income because of § 1239. (p. 17-21)

9.   D $20,000 - 4,000 = $16,000. (p. 17-18)

10.   A   (p. 17-20)

11.   C   (p. 17-7)

12.   B   20% x ($100,000 - 40,000) = $12,000. (p. 17-20)

13.   C   All of the depreciation claimed is recaptured for ACRS nonresidential real property depreciated under the accelerated method. (p. 17-14)

14.   D   The recognized gain is treated in the same manner as other normal property dispositions. (p. 17-23)

15.   C $175,000 - 100,000 = $75,000. (p. 17-4)

16.   B   The recapture is under § 1245, therefore all the deprecation is recaptured as ordinary income. (p. 17-12)

17.   C $37,000 - 32,000 = $5,000 ordinary income. (p. 17-11)

18.   D $50,000 + ($15,000 - 11,000) = $54,000. (p. 17-7)

19.   A   (p. 17-3)

20.   C   § 1231 "lookback" treats $15,000 as ordinary income, with the balance being a long-term capital gain. (p. 17-7)

Problem

1.

	Section 1245 Asset	Section 1250 Asset	
Sales price	$10,250	$102,500	
Adjusted basis	-6,800	-66,500	
Gain realized	$ 3,450	$ 36,000	
Recapture potential	$1,700	$4,750	Note (1)
Ordinary income	$1,700	$4,750	
§ 1231 Gain	$1,750	$31,250	

Note (1) $13,500 - 8,750 = $4,750

Code Section Recognition

1. § 1231

2. § 1250

3. § 1245

4. § 1239

CHAPTER

18

ACCOUNTING PERIODS AND METHODS

CHAPTER HIGHLIGHTS

This chapter discusses some of the options available to taxpayers in choosing accounting methods and periods. The cash, accrual, and hybrid accounting methods are covered along with the special accounting methods available for long-term construction contracts, installment sales, and inventory valuation.

I.   ACCOUNTING PERIODS

    A.   Taxpayers may be entitled to use a calendar year or a fiscal year in filing a tax return. Most individual taxpayers use a calendar year. However, certain other taxpayers may be eligible to use a fiscal year ending on the last day of any month. If certain conditions are met, taxpayers may use a 52-53 week year so that their year always ends on the same day of the week.

           The tax year of a partnership is dependent on the tax year of the majority partners. If the majority partners do not have the same tax year, the tax year of the principal partners must be adopted. If the principal partners do not have the same tax year, the tax year which results in the least deferral of income must be used.

           S Corporations generally must use a calendar year.

           Partnerships and S corporations can elect an otherwise impermissible tax year if any one of the following conditions are met:

- A business purpose for the tax year can be demonstrated.

- The deferral period is not more than three months and the entity agrees to make "required tax payments."

- The entity retains the same tax year it had for its fiscal year ending in 1987 and agrees to make "required tax payments."

The required tax payments are computed by applying the highest individual tax rate plus one percent to an estimate of the deferral period income.

Personal Service Corporations (PSCs) must generally use the calendar year. A fiscal year may be retained or used if one of the following applies:

- A business purpose can be demonstrated,

- The deferral period is not more than three months and a proportionate part of the annual salaries of shareholder-employees is paid to the shareholders during the deferral period, or

- The same fiscal year is retained that was used for its fiscal year ending in 1987 and the required minimum salary payments are made.

See the text for the calculation of the required minimum salary payments for a personal service corporation (PSC).

B. Changes in the Accounting Period. To change an accounting period a taxpayer must have the consent of the IRS. The IRS will not usually grant a change unless the taxpayer can establish a substantial business purpose for the change. If the taxpayer has an NOL for the short period, the IRS may require that the loss be carried forward for six years.

C. Taxable Periods of Less Than One Year. A short year is a period of less than 12 months. A taxpayer may have a short year for the first tax reporting period, the final income tax return, or as a result of a change in the tax year. Due to the progressive tax rate structure, the short period tax must be "annualized" if the short year is due to a change in the tax year. Special calculations are required for the annualization of an individual taxpayer's taxable income.

The tax is computed on the amount of the annualized income and then converted to a short period tax. The conversion is made using the following formula:

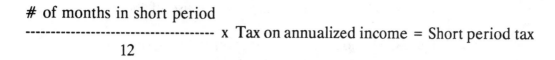

# of months in short period
-------------------------------------- x Tax on annualized income = Short period tax
12

D. Mitigation of the Annual Accounting Period Concept.

There are several provisions in the tax law designed to give taxpayers relief from the bunching of income because of arbitrary accounting periods. An example of such relief is the net operating loss carryover provision.

Under the "claim of right" doctrine an amount is includible in income on actual or constructive receipt if the taxpayer has an unrestricted claim to the amount, even if the taxpayer's right to the income is disputed. If the taxpayer is later required to repay such income, a deduction is allowed in the year of repayment, or in the case of amounts exceeding $3,000, the year in which the income was included if the tax benefit is greater.

II. ACCOUNTING METHODS

A. Permissible Methods.

The Code requires taxpayers to report taxable income under the method of accounting regularly used by the taxpayer in keeping his or her books, provided the method is consistently employed and clearly reflects income. The tax law recognizes three methods: (1) cash receipts and disbursements, (2) accrual, and (3) hybrid (a combination of cash and accrual).

Taxpayers for whom inventories are a significant income producing factor must use the accrual method in computing sales and cost of goods sold. Special accounting methods, which are discussed later in this chapter, are permitted for installment sales and long-term contracts.

B. Cash Receipts and Disbursements Method - Cash Basis. Under the cash method, income is recognized when the taxpayer actually or constructively receives cash and deductions are taken in the year of payment. There are exceptions to these rules for cash basis taxpayers. For example, capital expenditures and prepaid items such as interest cannot be deducted in the current period. Certain taxpayers cannot use the cash method. These include corporations other than S Corporations, partnerships with a corporate partner, and tax shelters. Farming businesses, qualified personal service corporations and certain entities with $5,000,000 or less of average gross receipts are excepted from the prohibition of the use of the cash method.

C.   Accrual Method. The accrual method of accounting requires that income be recognized when: (1) all events have occurred which fix the right to receive such income, and (2) the amount can be determined with reasonable accuracy. An accrual basis taxpayer who receives prepaid income (e.g. rent) in advance must usually recognize the income on a cash basis. An expense is deductible for the year in which all events have occurred which determine the fact of liability, and the amount of the liability can be determined with reasonable accuracy, and then only if "economic performance" has occurred. In the case of services or property to be provided, economic performance occurs in the year the services or property are actually provided. Certain liabilities, such as for taxes and worker's compensation, are not deductible until paid. There are several exceptions to the economic performance test such as for bad debt reserves of small banks, etc. See text for details.

D.   Hybrid Method. A hybrid method involves the use of both cash and accrual accounting concepts. It is common for a taxpayer to report sales and cost of goods sold on the accrual method and other items of income and deductions on the cash method.

E.   Change of Method.

Taxpayers make an election to use an accounting method when they file an initial tax return and use a particular method. Taxpayers who later want to change a method of accounting must obtain the permission of the IRS.

A correction of errors such as incorrect postings, omissions of income or deductions, or an incorrect calculation of tax liability does not constitute a change in accounting method. An error may be corrected by filing an amended return.

Permission from the IRS is necessary to change an erroneous method of accounting to a correct method.

If the IRS requires a taxpayer to change accounting methods to clearly reflect income and the amount of a required positive adjustment exceeds $3,000, certain averaging techniques are available to prevent the bunching of income.

To voluntarily change accounting methods, the taxpayer must file a request for a change within the first 180 days after the beginning of the taxable year of the desired change. An adjustment due to a change in method initiated by the taxpayer is required to be spread over future periods.

III. SPECIAL ACCOUNTING METHODS

A. Installment Method. The installment method applies to gains but not losses. Under the installment method, gains are recognized from the sale of property when installments are collected.

The installment method may not be used for any of the following:

- Gains on property held in the ordinary course of business.

- Depreciation recapture under § 1245 or 1250.

- Gains on stocks or securities traded on an established market.

Exceptions to the first item generally include the following:

- Timeshare units

- Residential lots

- Any property used or produced by a farming business

As a general rule, those sales that are eligible must be reported using the installment method. Conditions for electing out of the installment method are discussed later.

The recognized gain for installment sales is computed by using the following formula:

$$\frac{\text{Total gain}}{\text{Contact price}} \times \text{Collections} = \text{Recognized gain}$$

Total gain is the selling price reduced by selling expenses and the adjusted basis of the property. The selling price is the amount received by the seller, including receivables from the buyer and liabilities assumed by the buyer. Contract price is generally the amount the seller will receive, other than interest, from the buyer (selling price less the seller's liabilities assumed by the purchaser). Collections are payments received in the tax year less any interest income.

If the installment sale contract does not provide for interest of an amount at least equal to the Federal rate, then interest will be imputed at the Federal rate. The Federal rate is the rate the Federal government pays to borrow money and is published monthly by the IRS. The imputed interest reduces the selling price and as a result, increases the percentage relationship of the payment in the year of sale to the total selling price.

Sales between related parties may be subject to the special provisions of § 453(e) of the Code. This provision separates transactions regarding related parties into a "first" and "second" disposition. If the second disposition takes place within two years of the first disposition, then the gain on the first disposition may be recognized. See text for example.

The Code prohibits use of the installment method for sales of depreciable property between certain related taxpayers.

B.   Disposition of Installment Obligations. If installment notes are disposed of, gain which was previously deferred, must be recognized. The gain recognized is equal to the difference between the amount realized or the fair market value of the obligation and the basis of the obligation. Exceptions to this rule include transfers to controlled corporations, contributions to partnerships, and transfers due to the death of the taxpayer. Borrowing against installment notes causes recognition of the gain in most cases. In some cases taxpayers may be required to make interest payments on amounts of taxes deferred by using the installment method. See text for rules.

C.   Repossessions of Property. Generally on repossessions of property, taxpayers have a recognized gain on the transaction. The gain or loss is equal to the FMV of the property received (reduced by repossession expenses) less the unrecovered basis. However, on the repossession of real property, the gain recognized from the repossession cannot exceed the total cash collected (other than interest) by the seller less the gain previously recognized from collections. In addition, the seller's gain cannot exceed the original gain less the sum of the previously recognized gain and the expenses of repossession.

D.   Electing Out of the Installment Method.

An election not to use the installment method is made by reporting the gain under the taxpayer's usual accounting method on a timely filed return. A cash basis taxpayer cannot realize less than the value of the property sold. This allows a cash basis taxpayer to report gain or loss as an accrual basis taxpayer.

If the taxpayer elects out of the installment method, permission from the IRS is required to revoke the election.

E.   Long-Term Contracts.

Generally a taxpayer must accumulate all of the direct and indirect costs incurred under a contract. Mixed service costs must be allocated to production. For example, fringe benefit costs would be allocated as follows:

$$\frac{\text{Labor on the contract}}{\text{Total salaries and labor}} \times \text{Total cost of fringe benefits}$$

Taxpayers use one of the following two methods of accounting for long-term contracts:

- The completed contract method

- The percentage of completion method

The completed contract method can be used only on certain real estate construction contracts (see text). All other contractors must use the percentage of completion method.

Under the completed contract method revenue and expenses relating to the contract are recognized when the contract is completed. Under the percentage of completion method, a portion of the gross contract revenue, based on the ratio of the contract costs incurred for the period to the estimated total costs under the contract, is included in income each period.

IV.   INVENTORIES

A.   Determining Inventory Cost.

The cost of inventory is the invoice price less any discounts, plus freight and other handling costs. The cost of goods manufactured must be determined using the uniform capitalization rules. Inventory may be valued at the lower of cost or market except for LIFO inventories. Taxpayers using the LIFO method must value inventory at cost.

Taxpayers may use specific identification, FIFO, LIFO, or average cost methods of inventory valuation for tax purposes. A taxpayer may use any of these methods, but the method selected must be used consistently from year to year.

    B.   The LIFO Election.

A taxpayer may adopt LIFO by using the method in the tax return for the year of change and attaching to the tax return the proper form for the change. Once the election is made, it cannot be revoked unless the IRS gives permission. The change will usually be granted if the request is filed timely.

TEST FOR SELF-EVALUATION

True or False

Indicate which of the following statements are true or false by circling the correct answer.

T   F   1.   If certain conditions are met, a taxpayer may adopt a 52-53 week fiscal year.

T   F   2.   For an accrual basis taxpayer to take a deduction, the "all events test" including economic performance must be met.

T   F   3.   If taxpayers do not keep adequate books and records, they are required to use a calendar tax year.

T   F   4.   The Internal Revenue Service will automatically grant requests for changes to fiscal years from calendar years.

T   F   5.   All short years must have the tax calculated on an annualized basis.

T   F   6.   The standard deduction will be allowed in calculating short-period income of an individual taxpayer.

T   F   7.   The Code requires that taxable income be computed under the method of accounting regularly used by a taxpayer in keeping books, provided the method clearly reflects income.

T   F   8. Taxpayers who have more than one trade or business must use the same method of accounting for each trade or business.

T   F   9. A cash basis taxpayer must include in income all amounts actually or constructively received as cash or its equivalent.

T   F   10. Expenses for a cash basis taxpayer must usually be paid before they are allowed as a deduction for tax purposes.

T   F   11. All cash expenses of a cash basis taxpayer are deductible when paid.

T   F   12. An accrual basis taxpayer recognizes income when it is earned.

T   F   13. As a general rule, reserves for expenses of an accrual basis taxpayer are allowed as a deduction.

T   F   14. A hybrid accounting method uses elements of both cash and accrual methods.

T   F   15. The correction of an error in a tax return is usually considered a change in accounting method.

T   F   16. A taxpayer may file a request for a change in accounting method at any time during the tax year.

T   F   17. A transfer at death causes deferred gain on installment notes to be recognized in full.

T   F   18. Income from long-term contracts must always be recognized under the percentage of completion method.

T   F   19. A taxpayer who has average annual gross receipts for the three prior years of $25,000,000 may use the completed contract method of accounting for long-term contracts.

T   F   20. The installment method of reporting is not allowed for depreciation recapture under § 1245 or 1250.

T   F   21. Sales of real property must have a selling price of more than $1,000 to qualify for the installment method.

T   F   22.   Internal Revenue Service permission is required to adopt the LIFO inventory method for tax purposes.

T   F   23.   In periods of inflation, the use of the LIFO inventory method produces a lower tax liability than the use of the FIFO inventory method.

T   F   24.   Lower of cost or market inventory cannot be used for tax purposes.

T   F   25.   Direct costing is an acceptable method for calculating taxable income.

T   F   26.   The contract price in an installment sale is generally the total amount (except interest) the seller will collect from the purchaser.

T   F   27.   Partnerships, S corporations, and Personal Service Corporations can never elect a fiscal year for tax years after 1986.

T   F   28.   The S corporation required tax payment is due by April 15th (or later as prescribed by the IRS) of each tax year.

T   F   29.   The IRS applies an objective gross receipts test to determine if an entity has a natural business year. Under this test, 25% of the gross receipts must be realized in the final two months of the tax year for the prior three consecutive years.

T   F   30.   Taxpayers may be required to pay interest on deferred taxes from an installment sale if outstanding obligations exceed $5,000,000 at the close of the year.

T   F   31.   Generally, the gain recognized from the repossession of real property cannot exceed the total cash collected (other than interest) by the seller less the gain previously recognized from collections.

T   F   32.   §§ 483 and 1274 provide that if a deferred payment contract for the sale of property with a selling price greater than $2,000 does not contain a reasonable interest rate, a reasonable rate is imputed.

Fill-in-the-Blanks

Complete the following statements with the appropriate word(s) or amount(s).

1.   The IRS may require an NOL from a "short year" arising from a change in accounting

period to be carried forward _____ years.

2.   The contract price in an installment sale is generally the total amount (excluding interest) the seller will ultimately _____ from the purchaser.

3.   If an installment contract has a stated interest rate of less than _____ percent of the Federal rate, the IRS will impute interest at the Federal rate.

4.   The cost of goods produced or manufactured by the taxpayer must be determined by using the uniform _____ rules of inventory costing.

5.   Inventories may be valued at the lower of cost or market except for _____ inventories.

6.   Taxpayers using LIFO must value inventory at _____.

7.   During a period of rising prices, LIFO will generally produce a lower ending inventory and a _____ cost of goods sold.

8.   Once a LIFO election is made, it _____ be revoked without the permission of the IRS.

Multiple Choice

Choose the best answer for each of the following questions.

_____ 1.   X Corporation, a calendar-year taxpayer, would like to switch to a fiscal year ending June 30, 1992. The last day that X can file the election (Form 1128) is:
a. July 15, 1992
b. August 15, 1992
c. September 15, 1992
d. October 15, 1992
e. None of the above

_____ 2.   G Corporation obtained permission to change from a calendar year to a fiscal year ending March 31. For the short period (January 1 to March 31), the corporation had taxable income of $24,000. The annualized income for 1992 would be:
a. $96,000
b. $6,000

    c. $48,000
    d. -0-
    e. Some other amount

_____ 3. In 1992 T Corporation, an accrual basis taxpayer, declared a $9,000 bonus payable in 1992 to X, its sole shareholder. The bonus was reasonable in amount and the corporation had sufficient cash to pay the bonus in December, although the bonus was actually paid in January 1993. From these transactions, X should report:
    a. $9,000 ordinary income in 1993
    b. $9,000 long-term capital gain in 1993
    c. $9,000 ordinary income in 1992
    d. No income in 1992
    e. Some other amount

_____ 4. Imputed interest will not be calculated in which of the following examples:
    a. A deferred contract on real estate
    b. If the interest rate is less than the Federal rate
    c. A deferred contract with a selling price of $2,500
    d. Installment sales of personalty
    e. None of the above

_____ 5. The California Limited Publishing Company invests $60,000 in printing 20,000 copies of a book. Twelve thousand copies were sold in the first two years of operation, and none have been sold over the last four years. Regardless, the company expects the books will sell in the future and thus it leaves the price the same ($20 per copy). How much may the taxpayer write off (expense) in the current year?
    a. -0-
    b. $120,000
    c. $240,000
    d. $360,000
    e. Some other amount

_____ 6. T is a small building contractor who agrees to construct a building for $200,000. In 1992 she incurs costs of $90,000 and in 1993 costs of $70,000. An architect estimates the building is 60 percent complete in 1992 and the building is completed in 1993. If T uses the *completed contract method* for 1992, she should report income of:
    a. -0-
    b. $30,000
    c. $10,000

    d. $40,000

    e. Some other amount

7. In January 1992, a husband sells stock to his wife for $100,000, its fair market value. The husband's basis in the stock was $45,000. Under terms of the sale, his wife pays $25,000 down and issues notes for the balance, payable over ten years plus interest at 10 percent. Four months later the wife sells the stock for $105,000. If the husband elects installment sale treatment, how much gain should the husband report in 1992?

    a. -0-

    b. $13,750

    c. $14,250

    d. $55,000

    e. Some other amount

8. T sells a parcel of real estate (basis of $40,000) for $100,000, receiving $20,000 as a down payment and the buyer's note for the balance, payable over a period of five years at the Federal rate of interest. The first payment on the note is due next year. If T uses the installment method under § 453, how much gain should be reported in the year of sale?

    a. $60,000

    b. $40,000

    c. $12,000

    d. -0-

    e. Some other amount

9. Assume the same situation as in Question 8. How much gain (excluding interest) should T report in each of the next five years?

    a. $9,600

    b. $16,000

    c. $80,000

    d. $48,000

    e. Some other amount

10. T sold land (basis of $12,000) to X for $20,000 receiving a down payment of $5,000 and notes for $5,000 per year for the next three years, plus interest at the Federal rate. After making one payment, when the balance due is $10,000, X defaults. At the time of repossession, the land is worth $30,000. T's expenses of repossession amount to $2,000. What is T's recognized gain on the repossession?

    a. $2,000

    b. $4,000

    c. $6,000
    d. $10,000
    e. Some other amount

_____ 11. In 1992 T uses the lower of cost or market and FIFO inventory method. The FIFO cost of the ending inventory was $40,000 and its market value was $34,000. Therefore, the ending inventory for 1992 was $34,000. In 1993 T switched to the LIFO inventory method. How much income, if any, must T recognize for 1993?

    a. -0-
    b. $2,000 ordinary income
    c. $2,000 long-term capital gain
    d. $2,000 long-term capital loss
    e. Some other amount

_____ 12. Carol Venable's corporation (a personal service corporation) paid her a salary of $132,000 during the fiscal year ended October 31, 1992. The corporation can continue to use its fiscal year, provided Carol receives a salary of how much during the period November 1 to December 31?

    a. $-0-
    b. $33,000
    c. $22,000
    d. $11,000
    e. Some other amount

_____ 13. The ABCD Partnership is owned by A Corporation, B Corporation, C Corporation, and individual D. The partners have the following tax years.

    A (30%) September 30
    B (25%) September 30
    C (25%) June 30
    D (20%) December 31

On what date must the partnership's tax year must end?
    a. June 30
    b. September 30
    c. December 31
    d. Any date the partnership chooses
    e. Some other date

_____ 14. In 1991 H Corporation, an accrual basis taxpayer, sold defective merchandise that caused injury to the purchaser. H admitted liability in 1992 and paid the

customers claim in January 1993. What year is the purchaser's tort claim deductible?
a. 1991
b. 1992
c. 1993
d. The tort is not deductible

_____ 15. X Corporation, an accrual basis corporation, files its 1992 California state income tax return in April 1993. When the return was filed X had to pay an additional tax of $6,000. Due to an error in the original tax return, the corporation filed an amended California tax return in November 1993 and paid an additional $10,000 in tax. How much of the state taxes paid is deductible in 1992?
a. $-0-
b. $6,000
c. $10,000
d. $16,000
e. Some other amount

_____ 16. Ms. J owns a small coin shop. She values her inventory using the lower of cost or market method. What is J's ending inventory for 1992 based on the following information?

	Cost	Market
Gold coins	$10,000	$ 8,000
Silver coins	12,000	14,000
Rare silver dollars	4,000	9,000
Rare dimes	2,000	1,000
Total	$28,000	$32,000

a. $25,000
b. $28,000
c. $31,000
d. $32,000
e. Some other amount

_____ 17. B Corporation was to switch from the FIFO to the LIFO inventory method for tax purposes. In order to make this change B Corporation
a. Must spread the adjustment over six years
b. Request permission from the IRS within 90 days of the change
c. Must have a "business purpose" for making the change
d. Must file a tax return using the LIFO method

e. None of the above

_____ 18. In 1992, Acme Contractors, Inc. entered into a contract to build a building for a local university for $12,000,000. The estimated time to complete the building was two years and the estimated cost is $10,000,000. At the end of 1992 the accumulated costs on the project are $4,000,000. Acme uses the percentage of completion method on the contract. At the end of 1992, the chief engineer estimates the building is 50 percent complete. Acme must recognize what amount of profit from this contract for 1992?
a. $-0-
b. $800,000
c. $1,000,000
d. $1,200,000
e. Some other amount

_____ 19. M corporation, an accrual basis taxpayer, sold defective merchandise that injured a customer. M was held liable for $100,000 in 1992. After an appeal, M corporation pays the customer $75,000 in 1993. How does M corporation treat this liability for tax purposes?
a. Nothing is deductible because economic performance has not occurred.
b. M can deduct $100,000 in 1992.
c. M can deduct $75,000 in 1992.
d. M deducts $100,000 in 1992 and then reports $25,000 as income in 1993.
e. None of the above.

_____ 20. In 1991, S sold land held as an investment for $400,000 (basis of $100,000). S received cash of $50,000 and a note for $350,000 due in five years. In 1992, S borrowed $200,000 using the note as security. How much is S's recognized gain in 1992?
a. $-0-
b. $175,000
c. $200,000
d. $350,000
e. Some other amount

Problems

1. Jill Richards acquired a duplex in 19X5 which she held as rental property. The original cost of the property was $80,000. During 19X5 Jill spent $14,500 for capital improvements on the property. For tax years 19X5 and 19X6, a total of $5,300 of depreciation was claimed on the property under the straight-line method. In the cur-

rent year, 19X7, Jill sold the property for $120,000, receiving $20,000 on March 1st as a cash down payment and the buyer's note for $100,000 at the Federal rate of interest. The note is payable at $10,000 per year for ten years, with each payment due on December 1st, beginning in 19X7. Her selling expenses were $6,800. If Jill uses the § 453 installment sale treatment on this transaction, calculate the amount of taxable gain that must be reported during 19X7. Use the following worksheet.

a. Gross sales price   _____

    Selling expenses   _____

    Adjusted basis   _____

    Net profit   _____

b. Gross profit percentage   _____

c. 19X7 taxable gain   _____

2. Tecate Limited, a partnership, has a fiscal year ending on October 31. For the prior fiscal year ended October 31, 1993 Tecate Limited had taxable income of $96,000. What is Tecate's required tax payment that is due in 1994 (assuming there were no required tax payments in the prior year).

                                                    $_____

Code Section Recognition

Indicate, by number, the appropriate Code Section where the following items are found.

_____ 1. General rules for methods of accounting.

_____ 2. Changes in accounting periods.

_____ 3. Installment method.

_____ 4. Imputed interest.

_____ 5. General rules for inventories.

SOLUTIONS TO CHAPTER 18

True or False

1.   True   (p. 18-2)

2.   True   (p. 18-12)

3.   True   (p. 18-2)

4.   False   The IRS will grant requests where there is a substantial business purpose for the change. (p. 18-6)

5.   False   The tax for the first and last years does not have to be annualized. (p. 18-7)

6.   False   The standard deduction is not allowed. (p. 18-8)

7.   True   (p. 18-9)

8.   False   A different method of accounting may be used for each trade or business. (p. 18-10)

9.   True   (p. 18-10)

10.   True   (p. 18-10)

11.   False   Certain prepaid expenses must be capitalized and amortized. (p. 18-10)

12.   True   (p. 18-11)

13.   False   Reserves are usually not allowed as a deduction. (p. 18-14)

14.   True   (p. 18-14)

15.   False   A correction of an error is not a change in accounting method. (p. 18-14)

16.   False   The request must be made within the first 180 days of the year. (p. 18-14)

17.   False   A transfer due to a taxpayer's death does not cause deferred gain to be recognized. (p. 18-24)

18.   False   In certain cases, the completed contract method may be used for long-term contracts. (p. 18-30)

19.   False   The maximum is an average of $10,000,000. (p. 18-28)

20.   True   (p. 18-17)

21.   False   There is no minimum amount required for the selling price. (p. 18-17)

22.   False   IRS permission is not needed. (p. 18-34)

23.   True   (p. 18-33)

24.   False   Lower of cost or market can be used for tax purposes except where the LIFO method is used. (p. 18-33)

25.   False   Direct costing is not allowed for valuing inventories. (p. 18-31)

26.   True   (p. 18-18)

27.   False   They can elect a fiscal year if certain tests are met. (p. 18-4)

28.   True   (p. 18-4)

29.   True   (p. 18-6)

30.   True   (p. 18-24)

31.   True   (p. 18-25)

32.   False   The price has to greater than $3,000. (p. 18-20)

Fill-in-the-Blanks

1.   six (p. 18-7)

2.   collect (p. 18-18)

3.   100 (p. 18-20)

4.   capitalization (p. 18-32)

5.   LIFO (p. 18-33)

6.   cost (p. 18-34)

7.   larger (p. 18-33)

8.   cannot (p. 18-34)

Multiple Choice

1.   B   (p. 18-6)

2.   A $24,000 x (12÷3) = $96,000. (p. 18-7)

3.   C   (p. 18-11)

4.   C   (p. 18-20)

5.   A   (p. 18-33)

6.   A   (p. 18-29)

7.   D $100,000 - 45,000 = $55,000 realized. Because the wife sold the stock four months later, the entire $55,000 realized gain must be recognized by the husband. (p. 18-22)

8.   C   [($100,000 - 40,000)÷$100,000] x $20,000 = $12,000. (p. 18-18)

9.   A   [($100,000 - 40,000)÷$100,000] x $16,000 = $9,600. (p. 18-18)

10.   A $8,000 (original gain) - $4,000 (gain previously recognized) - $2,000 (repossession costs) = $2,000. The special limitation applies. (p. 18-28)

11.   B   ($40,000 - 34,000)÷3 years = $2,000 ordinary income. (p. 18-34)

12.   C   (2÷12) x $132,000 = $22,000. (p. 18-5)

13.   B   The year end must be the same as the majority interest partners. (p. 18-3)

14.   C   The tort is deductible in the year paid. (p. 18-13)

15.   B   Recurring payments within 8.5 months meet the economic performance test. (p. 18-13)

16.   A $8,000 + 12,000 + 4,000 + 1,000 = $25,000. (p. 18-33)

17.   D   Approval to change is not needed. (p. 18-34)

18.   B   ($4,000,000÷$10,000,000) x ($12,000,000 - 10,000,000) = $800,000. (p.18-30)

19.   C   (p. 18-12)

20.   B   [($400,000 - $50,000) ÷ $400,000] x $200,000 = $175,000. (p. 18-24)

Problems

1.   a.   Gross sales price $120,000

           Selling expenses   -6,800

           Adjusted basis:
              Original cost $80,000
              Capital improvements   14,500
              Depreciation   -5,300
                                                                       -89,200

           Net Profit $24,000

      b.   Gross profit percentage: $24,000÷$120,000 = 20 percent

      c.   Taxable gain:

              Amount received in 19X7:
                 Down payment $20,000
                 12/1/X7 payment   10,000

                 Total received $30,000
                 Gross profit %   20%

               Taxable gain   <u>$6,000</u>   (p. 18-18)

2. $96,000 x (2÷12) x 32% = $5,120. (p. 18-4)

Code Section Recognition

1.   § 446

2.   § 442

3.   § 453

4.   § 483

5.   § 471

CHAPTER

19

DEFERRED COMPENSATION

CHAPTER HIGHLIGHTS

This chapter covers various deferred compensation plans which are available to employees and self-employed taxpayers. Deferred compensation means that an employee receives compensation after the services are performed. Contributions to such plans and income on the contributions are generally not taxed to employees until the funds are actually received. Such favorable tax treatment is meant to encourage deferred compensation plans which supplement the Social Security system.

I.   QUALIFIED PENSION, PROFIT SHARING, AND STOCK BONUS PLANS

A.   Types of Plans. The tax law provides substantial benefits for retirement plans that meet certain qualifications. Three types of plans qualify under the law: (1) pension, (2) profit sharing, and (3) stock bonus.

A pension plan is a deferred compensation arrangement which provides for systematic payments of retirement benefits to employees who meet the requirements set forth in the plan. There are two basic types of pension plans, defined benefit plans and defined contribution plans.

A profit sharing plan is an arrangement established and maintained by an employer to provide for employee participation in the company's profits, either current or accumulated profits.

A stock bonus plan is a plan established and maintained by an employer to provide contributions of the employer's stock to the plan. There is no requirement that contributions be dependent on profits.

An employee stock ownership plan (ESOP) is a stock bonus plan that qualifies as a tax-exempt employee trust under § 401(a).

B.   Qualification Requirements.

To be "qualified," a plan must meet the following requirements:

- Exclusive benefit requirement

- Nondiscriminatory rules

- Participation and coverage requirements

- Vesting requirements

- Distribution requirements

The plan must be created by an employer for the exclusive benefit of the employees or their beneficiaries. To meet the exclusive benefit requirement, the investment must be of the type that a "prudent person" would make.

The plan must not discriminate in favor of employees who are highly compensated. A plan is not considered discriminatory if contributions and benefits uniformly relate to compensation.

At a minimum, the plan must provide that all employees in the covered group who are 21 years of age are eligible to participate after completing one year of service. Furthermore, the plan must cover a reasonable percentage of the company's employees.

The plan must meet certain vesting requirements for both the employer and employee contributions. The employee must, from the date of contribution, have a nonforfeitable right to the accrued benefits from his own contributions. Benefits from employer contributions must be nonforfeitable in accordance with one of two minimum vesting schedules.

Uniform minimum distribution rules exist for all qualified plans, IRAs, unfunded deferred compensation plans of state and local governments and tax-exempt employers, and tax sheltered custodial accounts and annuities.

Distributions must begin no later than April 1 of the calendar year following the calendar year in which the participant attains the age of 70½. This date is not affected by the actual date of retirement or termination. Various penalties exist if the required distribution is not made.

Early distributions are subject to an additional 10 percent tax. Excess distributions are subject to a 15 percent excise tax.

C.   Tax Consequences to the Employee and Employer.

The primary tax benefit of a qualified plan to the employee is that the employer contributions to the plan are not subject to income taxation until such amounts are made available or distributed to the employee. In addition, earnings on the contributions are not taxable until withdrawn.

Employee contributions have been previously subject to taxation, therefore part of the payments from the plan are excluded from the employee's income under the annuity rules of § 72.

An employee who receives a lump-sum distribution from a qualified plan is subject to various special rules on the distribution. See text for rules.

D.   Limitations on Contributions to and Benefits from Qualified Plans.

Under a defined contribution plan, the annual addition to an employee's account cannot exceed the smaller of $30,000 or 25 percent of the employee's compensation. If the plan is a defined benefit plan, the annual benefit payable to an employee is limited to the smaller of $112,221 (in 1992) or 100 percent of the employee's average compensation for the highest three years of employment. For collectively bargained plans with at least 100 participants, different annual limitations apply (see text).

The employer's contribution is deductible when paid into the pension trust. An employer's deduction for contributions to profit-sharing and stock bonus plans is limited to 15 percent of the compensation of the plan participants. If there are two or more plans, the percentage limitation is increased to 25 percent. Any unused contributions can be used in later years as a carryover deduction, subject to certain limitations.

E.   Top-Heavy Plans.

A top-heavy plan is generally one which provides more than 60% of the cumulative benefits to an employer's key employees. Key employees include officers, the ten employees owning the largest interest in an employer, a greater-than-five percent owner of an employer, or an employee who has annual compensation greater than $150,000 and who owns more than one percent of the employer.

F.   Cash or Deferred Arrangement Plans.

A § 401(k) plan allows participants to elect either to receive up to $8,728 (in 1992) in cash or to have a contribution made on their behalf to a profit sharing or stock bonus plan. The plan may also be a salary reduction agreement. Any pretax amount elected as a contribution is not includible in the employee's gross income and is 100% vested. The employer contributions and earnings on the contributions are tax deferred.

II.   RETIREMENT PLANS FOR SELF-EMPLOYED INDIVIDUALS

Self-employed individuals and their employees are allowed to receive qualified retirement benefits under H.R. 10 (Keogh) plans.

A.   Coverage Requirements. Contributions and benefits of a self-employed individual are subject to the general percentage, ratio, and average benefits tests applied to other qualified plans.

B.   Contribution Limitations. The maximum annual contribution that may be made to a defined contribution Keogh plan is the smaller of $30,000 or 25 percent of earned income. Earned income is reduced by the Keogh contribution which means that the contribution is limited to 20 percent of income before the contribution. There is a 15 percent (instead of 25 percent) limit on contributions to profit sharing Keogh plans. Under a defined benefit Keogh plan, the annual benefit payable to an employee is limited to the smaller of $112,221 (in 1992) or 100 percent of the employee's average compensation for the highest three years of employment.

III.   INDIVIDUAL RETIREMENT ACCOUNTS (IRAs)

A.   General Rules.

All taxpayers may have an individual retirement account. The maximum contribution is the smaller of $2,000 ($2,250 for a spousal account) or 100 percent of compensation. If the taxpayer is not covered by another plan, or if the taxpayer's AGI is not more than $25,000 for single taxpayers, $40,000 for married taxpayers, filing jointly, and $0 for married taxpayer's, filing separately, the IRA contribution is fully deductible. If the taxpayer is covered by another qualified retirement plan, the deduction is phased out 20 cents on the dollar until it is no longer available once AGI reaches $35,000 for single taxpayers, $50,000 for married taxpayers, filing jointly, and $10,000 for married taxpayers, filing separately.

Simplified employee pension (SEPs) plans are available to employers as an alternative to regular qualified plans. The employer may contribute to an IRA covering an employee the lesser of 15 percent of the employee's earned income or $30,000.

If both spouses have earned income, each may establish a separate IRA. When only one spouse is employed, a spousal IRA may be established for the unemployed spouse provided the employed spouse is eligible to establish an IRA.

A taxpayer may make a contribution to an IRA at any time before the original due date (April 15th) of his or her tax return and still claim the amount as a deduction for the year.

B. Penalty Taxes for Excess Contributions. There is a cumulative nondeductible 6 percent excise penalty tax imposed on the smaller of any excess contributions or the market value of the plan assets determined at the close of the tax year.

C. Taxation of Benefits. A participant has a zero basis in his or her deductible contributions to an IRA, and once retirement payments are received, they are included in ordinary income. Payments made to a participant before age 59½ are subject to a nondeductible 10 percent penalty tax on such actual or constructive payments.

IV. NONQUALIFIED DEFERRED COMPENSATION PLANS

A. Underlying Rational for Tax Treatment. Nonqualified deferred compensation plans allow individuals to defer income taxes on income payments until they are possibly in a lower tax bracket. Unlike qualified plans, most deferred compensation plans do not have to meet the discrimination, funding, coverage and other requirements.

B.   Tax Treatment to the Employer and Employee. In an unfunded NQDC plan, the employee relies upon the company's promise to make the compensation payment in the future. In this case, the employee is taxed when the compensation is paid or made available and the employer is allowed a deduction when the employee recognizes income.

V.   RESTRICTED PROPERTY PLANS

A.   General Provisions. A restricted property plan is an arrangement whereby an employer transfers property to an employee at no cost or at a bargain price. The fair market value of the transferred property is included in gross income of the employee the earlier of when the property is no longer subject to substantial risk of forfeiture or when the employee has the right to transfer property free of the substantial risk of forfeiture.

B.   Substantial Risk of Forfeiture. A substantial risk of forfeiture exists if a person's rights to full enjoyment of such property are conditioned on the future performance, or refraining from the performance, of substantial services by the employee. An employee may elect within 30 days after the receipt of restricted property, to recognize immediately, as ordinary income the excess of fair market value over the amount paid for the property. Any future appreciation is considered capital gain instead of ordinary income.

C.   Employer Deductions. An employer is allowed a tax deduction for restricted property for the same amount and at the same time that the employee is required to include the compensation in income.

VI.   STOCK OPTIONS

A.   In General. A stock option gives an individual the right to purchase a stated number of shares of stock from a corporation at a certain price within a specified period of time.

B.   Incentive Stock Options.

Incentive stock options (ISO) are designed to help corporations attract management. To qualify for incentive stock option treatment the option holder must be an employee of the corporation from the date the option is granted until three months before the date of exercise. Under this plan there are no tax consequences when an option is granted or exercised. Once the option is exercised and the stock is sold, any gain is long-term capital gain to the employee provided the employee holds the stock for a certain period of time.

The excess of the fair market value of the stock at the date of exercise over the option price is a tax preference item for the alternative minimum tax.

C.   Nonqualified Stock Options.

The fair market value of nonqualified stock options must be included in the employee's income at the date the stock options are granted.

If the fair market value is not ascertainable, then the difference between the fair market value of the stock at the exercise date and the option price is ordinary income in the year of exercise.

The corporation will receive a deduction at the same time and in the same amount as the income recognized by the employee.

TEST FOR SELF-EVALUATION

True or False

Indicate which of the following statements are true or false by circling the correct answer.

T   F   1.   The three basic types of qualified plans are pension plans, profit sharing plans, and stock bonus plans.

T   F   2.   Profit sharing plans maintain separate accounts for each participant in the plan.

T   F   3.   A stock bonus plan is a deferred compensation arrangement established to provide contributions to the plan of stock other than the employer's stock.

T   F   4.   The two types of qualified pension plans are defined contribution plans and defined benefit plans.

T   F   5.   A defined contribution plan provides a formula which defines the benefits employees are to receive.

T   F   6.   An ESOP is a defined contribution plan that is either a qualified stock bonus plan or a stock bonus plan and a money purchase plan, each of which qualify under § 401(a).

T   F   7.   A qualified plan does not have to be for the exclusive benefit of employees or their beneficiaries.

T   F   8.   The contributions or benefits of a qualified plan may discriminate in favor of employees who are officers, stockholders, or highly compensated.

T   F   9.   In all qualified plans, employer contributions must vest immediately.

T   F   10.   Employer contributions to qualified plans are not subject to taxation until such amounts are made available or distributed to the employees.

T   F   11.   It is possible for a taxpayer to be covered by a qualified retirement plan and also have a Keogh plan to which contributions are made in the current year.

T   F   12.   All lump-sum distributions qualify for the special ten-year averaging rule.

T   F   13.   For 1992, the maximum contribution to a defined contribution plan is the smaller of $30,000 or 25 percent of the employee's compensation.

T   F   14.   For _all_ defined benefit plans, the maximum contribution for 1992 is the smaller of $112,221 or 100 percent of the employee's average compensation for the three highest paid years of employment.

T   F   15.   The maximum deduction permitted each year for contributions to profit sharing and stock bonus plans is 15 percent of the compensation paid or accrued with respect to the participants in the plan.

T   F   16.   All employees of a company must be covered under its Keogh plan in order for the plan to be qualified.

T   F   17.   All individual taxpayers with earned income can qualify for an individual retirement account.

T   F   18.   The maximum deductible IRA contribution for an unmarried taxpayer with AGI of $25,000 or less is $2,000, regardless of how many accounts the taxpayer has.

T   F   19.   Employee benefits under a qualified plan must vest under one of two alternative schedules.

T   F   20.   Unless special circumstances apply, the earliest age to withdraw funds without penalty from an deductible IRA is 59½ years old.

T   F   21.   All IRA contributions of an individual are deductible.

Fill-in-the-Blanks

Complete the following statements with the appropriate word(s) or amount(s).

1.   The deduction for an IRA is limited to the smaller of _____ or the individual's taxable compensation from personal services.

2.   In an IRA, a participant has a _____ basis in his or her deductible contributions.

3.   The doctrine of _____ receipt is an important concept relating to the taxability of nonqualified deferred compensation.

4.   In a restricted property plan, if an employee performs services and receives property, the fair market value of the property in excess of any amount paid is _____ in the gross income of the employee.

5.   If a person's rights to full enjoyment of property are conditioned on future performance, or the refraining from the performance of substantial services there is said to be a substantial _____ of forfeiture.

6.   An employee may elect within _____ days after the receipt of restricted property to recognize immediately as ordinary income the excess of fair market value over the amount paid for the property.

7.   In a restricted property plan, the employer is allowed a deduction for the same amount and at the same time the employee is required to _____ the compensation in income.

8.   If a nonqualified stock option has a readily ascertainable fair market value, the value of the option must be included in the employee's _____ at the date of the grant.

9. If a nonqualified stock option does not have a readily ascertainable price, the employee's recognized income in the year of _____ is the amount equal to the difference between the fair market value of the stock at the exercise date and the option price.

Multiple Choice

Choose the best answer for each of the following questions.

_____ 1. The qualified pension plan of Grossmont Corporation calls for both the employer and employee to contribute 6% of the employee's compensation to the plan. This plan is a:
   a. Defined benefit plan
   b. Defined contribution plan
   c. Profit sharing plan
   d. Stock bonus plan
   e. None of the above

_____ 2. Brian Shay, age 66, has accumulated $920,000 in a defined contribution plan, $120,000 of which represents his own after-tax contributions. What is the excise tax due, if Brian takes a lump-sum distribution?
   a.   -0-
   b. $7,500
   c. $15,525
   d. $12,575
   e. Some other amount

_____ 3. Dee Walsh has completed 6 years of service with her employer. If her pension plan uses "graded vesting," what is Dee's nonforfeitable percentage?
   a. 10%
   b. 40%
   c. 60%
   d. 80%
   e. Some other amount

_____ 4. Assume the same situation as in Question 3. If the plan vests under "cliff vesting," what percentage of the employer's contributions must be vested?
   a. 100%
   b. 55%
   c. 50%
   d. 45%

e. Some other amount

5. Karen Hreha, receives a $500,000 payment under a golden parachute agreement entered into in 1992. Karen's statutory base amount is $360,000. What amount of this payment is not deductible to the corporation under § 280G?
   a. -0-
   b. $120,000
   c. $360,000
   d. $140,000
   e. Some other amount

6. I.M. Sweet is single and self-employed. During the current year, her adjusted gross income was $14,000, including interest of $12,500 and salary of $1,500. The maximum amount that could be contributed to an IRA and deducted by Sweet is:
   a. -0-
   b. $1,500
   c. $2,000
   d. $2,100
   e. Some other amount

7. Assume the same situation as in Question 6, except that Sweet's adjusted gross income is all from salary. The maximum amount that could be contributed by Sweet to an IRA is:
   a. -0-
   b. $1,500
   c. $1,200
   d. $2,000
   e. Some other amount

8. I. Shade, C.P.A., is self-employed and has established a Keogh (H.R. 10) plan (not a profit sharing plan). The plan states that he will contribute the maximum percentage of earned income to the plan. His self-employment income before any Keogh deduction for 1992 is $190,000. Shade's deduction for this plan is:
   a. $47,500
   b. $38,000
   c. $30,000
   d. $90,000
   e. Some other amount

9. Currently, the basic required minimum coverage for a qualified plan for all

employees is:

a. 25 years old and 3 years of service
b. 21 years old and 1 year of service
c. 18 years old and 3 years of service
d. 21 years old and 3 years of service

_____ 10. T was employed by Z Corporation at a salary of $70,000. Z Corporation contributes to a retirement plan for T that allows extra voluntary § 401(k) contributions. For 1992, what is the maximum additional amount that T may contribute to this plan?

a. -0-
b. $8,728
c. $10,728
d. $2,000
e. Some other amount

_____ 11. T Corporation and T, a cash basis employee, enter into an employment agreement which provides for an annual salary of $140,000. Of this amount, $120,000 is to be paid currently and $20,000 is to be paid in 10 installments on T's retirement. How much would be taxable to T in the current year?

a. -0-
b. $100,000
c. $120,000
d. $140,000
e. Some other amount

_____ 12. In the current year, T is granted a nonqualified stock option to purchase 200 shares of stock from his employer at $9 per share. On the date the options are issued, the stock was selling on the New York Stock Exchange for $14 per share. For the current year T should report:

a. $1,000 long-term capital gain
b. $1,000 ordinary income
c. $1,800 ordinary income
d. $1,800 long-term capital gain
e. Some other amount

_____ 13. On March 1, 1991, T is granted a nonqualified stock option for 100 shares of common stock at $12 per share. On that date, there is no readily ascertainable fair market value for the stock. T exercised the option on May 1, 1992, when the stock is selling for $20 per share. The stock is sold for $30 in 1995. For 1992, T should recognize:

a. No gain or loss

b. $800 ordinary income
c. $800 long-term capital gain
d. $1,200 ordinary income
e. Some other amount

14. T is a sole proprietor with six employees. She has offered her employees a SEP IRA, which all six have elected to participate in. W, an employee, has a salary of $18,000 for the current year. In 1992, how much of a contribution may T make to W's IRA if W is married with a nonworking spouse?
    a. -0-
    b. $2,000
    c. $2,250
    d. $2,700
    e. Some other amount

15. On March 1, 1991, T is given a nonqualified option on 100 shares of his employer's stock. The option price and FMV are $75 per share on the date the option is granted. T exercises the option on April 1, 1992 when the price of the stock is $125 per share. He sells the stock on October 15, 1992 for $200 per share. What is T's reported gain in 1992?
    a. -0-
    b. $12,500 long-term capital gain
    c. $12,500 ordinary income
    d. $5,000 long-term capital gain
    e. Some other amount

16. T has $15,000 in a deductible IRA and $5,000 in a nondeductible IRA. In the current year, T withdraws $1,000 from the nondeductible IRA. What portion of the withdrawal is included in T's income?
    a. $-0-
    b. $250
    c. $750
    d. $1,000
    e. Some other amount

17. In the current year, Nancy Bailey is over 70½ years old. As of December 31 of last year, her IRA account had a balance in it of $157,300. Her life expectancy multiple is 14.3 and she has taken out a total of $22,000 from the IRA in prior years. Her required minimum distribution from this IRA is:
    a. $-0-
    b. $11,000
    c. $9,462

    d. $135,300

    e. $157,300

_____ 18. Mr. and Mrs. D had compensation of $22,000 and $25,000 respectively. Their AGI for 1992 was $47,000 and Mr. D was an active participant in a qualified plan. What is the maximum amount that they each may deduct for contributions to an IRA?

    a. $-0-

    b. $600

    c. $1,400

    d. $2,000

    e. None of the above

_____ 19. Z is a new employee in a qualified retirement plan in 1992. Z would be considered a highly compensated employee if

    a. he owns 4.1 percent of the stock of the company.

    b. he not an officer or member of the top-paid group in the company and his salary is $85,000.

    c. he is an officer in the company and his salary is $60,000.

    d. he is a union steward and his salary is $52,000.

    e. None of the above

_____ 20. In order to be considered a "qualified" plan, a retirement plan must meet all these requirements except:

    a. Certain vesting rules

    b. Nondiscrimination rules

    c. Exclusive benefit requirement

    d. The *res judicata* requirement

    e. All of the above must be met

_____ 21. In which type of qualified plan does an employer's contribution to the employee's plan have to vest immediately?

    a. Simplified employee pension (SEP) plan

    b. Defined benefit plan

    c. Profit sharing plan

    d. Defined contribution plan

    e. All of the above must vest immediately

Code Section Recognition

Indicate, by number, the appropriate Code Section where the following items are found.

_____ 1. Qualified pension, profit-sharing, and stock bonus plans.

_____ 2. Individual retirement accounts.

_____ 3. Top-heavy plans.

_____ 4. Individual retirement account deductions.

_____ 5. Restricted property plans.

_____ 6. Incentive stock options.

SOLUTIONS TO CHAPTER 19

True or False

1.   True   (p. 19-2)

2.   True   (p. 19-3)

3.   False   A stock bonus plan uses the employer's stock. (p. 19-4)

4.   True   (p. 19-3)

5.   False   A defined contribution plan does not define benefits. (p. 19-3)

6.   True   (p. 19-4)

7.   False   The plan must be for the exclusive benefit of employees. (p. 19-6)

8.   False   Plans cannot discriminate. (p. 19-6)

9.   False   Vesting of employer contributions may occur over a period of time as prescribed by law. (p. 19-8)

10.   True   (p. 19-11)

11.   True   (p. 19-19)

12.   False   Ten-year averaging has been replaced with a 5-year forward averaging rule,

to which certain limitations apply. (p. 19-12)

13.   True   (p. 19-14)

14.   False   For certain collectively bargained plans, lower limits may apply. (p. 19-15)

15.   True   (p. 19-16)

16.   False   Employee coverage must follow the corporate coverage rules. (p. 19-19)

17.   True   (p. 19-20)

18.   True   (p. 19-20)

19.   True   (p. 19-8)

20.   True   (p. 19-23)

21.   False   There are AGI limitations for taxpayers covered under other qualified plan(s). (p. 19-20)

Fill-in-the-Blanks

1. $2,000 (p. 19-20)

2.   zero (p. 19-23)

3.   constructive (p. 19-24)

4.   includible (p. 19-27)

5.   risk (p. 19-27)

6.   thirty (p. 19-28)

7.   include (p. 19-29)

8.   income (p. 19-32)

9.   exercise (p. 19-32)

Multiple Choice

1. B   (p. 19-3)

2. B   ($920,000 - 120,000 - 750,000) x 15% = $7,500. (p. 19-10)

3. D   See table in text. (p. 19-8)

4. A   After 5 years the benefits are 100% vested. (p. 19-8)

5. D $500,000 - 360,000 = $140,000. (p. 19-26)

6. B   Lesser of $2,000 or $1,500. (p. 19-20)

7. D   Lesser of $2,000 or $14,000. (p. 19-20)

8. C   20% x $190,000 = $38,000 = = > max of $30,000. (p. 19-19)

9. B   (p. 19-6)

10. B   (p. 19-18)

11. C   (p. 19-24)

12. B   ($14 - $9) x $200 = $1,000. (p. 19-32)

13. B   ($20 - $12) x $100 = $800. (p. 19-32)

14. D $18,000 x 15% = $2,700. (p. 19-21)

15. B   ($200 - $75) x $100 = $12,500 LTCG. (p. 19-32)

16. C   ($15,000÷$20,000) x $1,000 = $750. (p. 19-24)

17. B $157,300÷14.3 = $11,000. (p. 19-9)

18. B $2,000 - [($7,000÷$10,000) x $2,000] = $600. (p. 19-20)

19. C   Z is an officer and has salary over $45,000 (150% x $30,000). (p. 19-8)

20. D   (p. 19-6)

21.   A   (p. 19-21)

Code Section Recognition

1.   § 401

2.   § 408

3.   § 416

4.   § 219

5.   § 83

6.   § 422

CHAPTER

20

CORPORATIONS AND PARTNERSHIPS

CHAPTER HIGHLIGHTS

This chapter provides a brief overview of the tax provisions applicable to the formation and operation of corporations, S corporations, and partnerships, as well as the tax consequences of corporate liquidations.

I.   **WHAT IS A CORPORATION?**

     A.   **Compliance with State Law.** Although important, compliance with state law is not the only requirement to qualify for corporate tax status. The degree of business activity at the corporate level is the key consideration for corporate tax status.

     B.   **The Association Approach.** Under the association approach, it is possible for an organization to be taxed as a corporation although it is not a legal corporation under state law. If an association has more corporate than noncorporate characteristics, then it will be taxed as a corporation. The corporate characteristics are:

         •   Associates

         •   Objective to carry on a business and divide the gains therefrom

         •   Continuity of life

- Centralized management

- Limited liability

- Free transferability of interests

According to the Regulations, if an organization has the first two characteristics and three of the last four, it is an association (corporation) for tax purposes.

II.   INCOME TAX CONSIDERATIONS

A.   General Tax Consequences of Different Forms of Business Entities. A business may be conducted as a sole proprietorship, partnership, or corporation. Sole proprietorships and partnerships are not separate taxable entities, so all transactions are reported on the tax returns of the owners or partners. On the other hand, corporations (other than S corporations) are recognized under the tax law as separate taxpaying entities. S corporations are treated in a manner similar to partnerships.

Individuals and Corporations Compared. Individual and corporate tax rules vary in several situations. These situations include:

- Capital gains and losses; carryback and carryover provisions

- Charitable contribution limitations

- Net operating losses

- Special deductions for corporations

Net capital gains of corporate taxpayers are included in ordinary income. Capital losses of corporations are deductible only against capital gains. Corporate capital losses carry back three years and forward five years. All capital loss carrybacks or carryovers become short-term capital losses.

Corporate charitable contributions are limited to ten percent of taxable income, computed without regard to the charitable contribution deduction, net operating loss carryback or capital loss carryback, and the dividends received deduction. Excess contributions are carried over to the succeeding five years.

The net operating loss deduction for a corporation is usually equal to taxable income including any dividends received deduction. The NOL is carried back three years and forward fifteen years. An election may be made to forgo the carryback period.

B.   Deductions Available Only to Corporations.

A corporate taxpayer is allowed a deduction for dividends received from other corporations. The amount of the deduction depends on the amount of stock owned in the dividend paying corporation. If the ownership percentage is less than 20%, then the deduction is 70%; if the ownership percentage is 20% or more and less than 80%, then the deduction is 80%; and if the ownership percentage is 80% or more, then the deduction is 100%. The deduction is limited to the appropriate percentage of taxable income computed without regard to any net operating loss deduction, the dividends received deduction, and any capital loss carryback. However, there is no taxable income limit if a net operating loss results from the dividends received deduction.

Corporations are entitled to amortize organizational expenses over a period of 60 months or more. Organizational expenses include legal and accounting services incident to organization, expenses of temporary directors, expenses of organizational meetings, and fees paid to the state of incorporation.

C.   Determination of Tax Liability.

The current corporate tax rates are:

Taxable Income	Tax Rate
0 - $50,000	15%
$50,001 - $75,000	25%
Over $75,000	34%

Corporations pay an additional tax on taxable income over $100,000. The additional tax is five percent of taxable income over $100,000 up to a maximum of $11,750 (the tax savings because of the lower rates applicable to the first $75,000 of taxable income).

Qualified personal service corporations (PSCs) are taxed at a flat 34 percent rate on all taxable income. They do not get any benefit from the graduated rate schedule.

Corporations are subject to an alternative minimum tax similar to individual taxpayers. See Chapter 12.

D. Filing Requirements.

Generally, corporations file tax returns on Form 1120, however, certain small corporations may file the corporate short Form 1120A. S Corporations use Form 1120S. The corporate income tax return must be filed by the fifteenth day of the third month following the close of the tax year. Corporations must file a tax return even when they do not have taxable income. Estimated payments must be made on a quarterly basis if the tax liability is expected to be $500 or more.

E. Reconciliation of Taxable Income and Accounting Income. Corporate taxpayers must reconcile taxable income to financial statement income since these amounts are rarely the same. The reconciliation is done on Schedule M-1 of Form 1120.

III. FORMING THE CORPORATION

A. Capital Contributions.

The receipt of money or property in exchange for capital stock or as a capital contribution is not income to the corporation. Contributions by other than shareholders are not income to the corporation and a corporation has a zero basis in such contributions.

Debt financing is often more advantageous to a corporation than equity financing since interest payments are deductible and dividend payments are not. In certain instances, such as when a corporation issues debt with features similar to capital stock, the IRS may contend that the debt is really a form of stock and disallow the interest deduction.

B. Transfers to Controlled Corporations. If property is exchanged for stock in a corporation and the shareholders are in "control" of the corporation after the transfer, pursuant to § 351, gain on the transfer is not recognized. Gain or loss is postponed by adjusting the basis of the stock and property. The basis of the stock received by the shareholder in a § 351 transaction is equal to the basis of the property transferred plus any gain recognized by the shareholder, less the fair market value of any boot received by the shareholder. The basis of property received by the corporation is equal to the basis in the hands of the transferor plus any gain recognized to the transferor shareholder. Realized gain is recognized to the extent that the shareholder receives boot.

IV. OPERATING THE CORPORATION

A. **Dividend Distributions.** Corporate distributions of cash or property to shareholders are dividends to the extent the corporation has accumulated or current earnings and profits (E&P). Any distribution in excess of E&P is a nontaxable return of capital and reduces the basis of the stock held by the shareholder. If there is a distribution in excess of E&P and in excess of the shareholder's stock basis, the excess amount is treated as a capital gain assuming the stock is a capital asset. While E&P is similar to retained earnings, numerous differences may arise in its calculation. For example, nontaxable stock dividends do not affect E&P.

Distributions of property are valued at fair market value. The shareholder's basis in the property received is also the fair market value. The corporation must recognize gain on the distribution of appreciated property to the shareholder.

In closely-held corporations the IRS may contend that certain economic flows to a shareholder are constructive dividends; and, therefore, the corporation and shareholder may lose certain tax benefits. Constructive dividends include:

- Unreasonable compensation
- Excessive rent paid to shareholders
- Interest on certain debt to shareholders
- Advances to shareholders
- Interest-free or below-market loans
- Certain shareholder use of corporate property
- Absorption of personal expenses by the corporation
- Bargain purchase of corporate property by shareholders

B. **Stock Redemptions.** Redemptions of stock in a corporation are treated as dividends under § 301 unless the redemption can qualify as a sale or exchange under § 302 or 303.

V.   **LIQUIDATING THE CORPORATION**

    A.   General Rule of § 331 and Exceptions. Under § 331, shareholders recognize gain or loss (usually capital) in a corporate liquidation. If the liquidating corporation is a subsidiary, then under § 332 no gain or loss is recognized by the parent corporation on the liquidation.

    B.   Basis Determination. The shareholder's basis in property received in a liquidation is usually its fair market value. The basis of property received from a subsidiary under § 332 is the basis of the property to the subsidiary unless the basis rules of § 338 apply. In such a case, the basis of the property to the parent is the parent's basis in the subsidiary's stock.

    C.   Effect of the Liquidation on the Corporation. Under the general rule of § 336, the liquidating corporation recognizes any gain or loss, except in certain parent-subsidiary situations.

VI.   **THE S CORPORATION ELECTION**

    A.   Justification for the Election. The S Corporation election allows qualified small corporations to elect not to pay the corporate income tax and to pass the income through to its shareholders. To qualify, a corporation must have the following characteristics:

- Be a domestic corporation

- Not be a member of an affiliated group

- Have 35 or fewer shareholders

- Have as its shareholders only individuals, estates, and certain trusts

- Not have a nonresident alien shareholder

- Have only one class of stock outstanding

    B.   Operational Rules.

The S Corporation is a tax-reporting entity, not a taxpaying entity. Taxable income and losses are reported by the shareholders.

Certain items pass through to the shareholders of a S Corporation "as is." Examples of items that are passed from the S Corporation to its shareholders without changing identity are:

- Tax-exempt income
- Capital gains and losses
- § 1231 gains and losses
- Charitable contributions
- Foreign tax credits
- Depletion
- Nonbusiness income and losses under § 212
- Intangible drilling costs.
- Investment interest and expenses under § 163(d)
- Certain portfolio income
- Passive gains, losses, and credits under § 469
- Tax preference items and alternative minimum tax adjustments

Taxable income of the S Corporation is equal to the net of all items which are not passed through "as is" to the shareholders. The dividends received deduction and net operating loss deduction are not allowed to the S Corporation.

Taxable income and separately stated items are passed through to the shareholders as of the last day of the S Corporation's tax year, allocated on a per share and per day of stock ownership basis.

The shareholder's basis in the S Corporation's stock will be increased or decreased by the pass through of income or loss (including the separately stated items). Distributions will decrease the basis of the stock. Losses in excess of the basis are applied against the basis of loans that the shareholders may have made to the corporation, and any remaining loss is carried forward until there is basis against which to deduct the loss.

VII. PARTNERSHIPS

A. Nature of Partnership Taxation. Partnerships are not separate taxable entities. Instead partnership income is passed through to the partners. A partnership tax return is an information return only. It provides the necessary information to determine a partner's income and expenses.

B. Partnership Formation. Under § 721 no gain or loss is recognized to a partnership or any of its partners on the transfer of property to a partnership in exchange for a capital interest in the partnership. If the partner receives money, an interest for services, or transfers property with a liability more than basis, gain may be recognized on the transfer.

The partner's basis in his or her partnership interest is the sum of money contributed plus the adjusted basis of other property transferred. A partner's basis is determined without regard to any amount on the partnership books such as the capital or equity account. The partner's basis will be increased or decreased by gains, losses, contributions, withdrawals, and changes in partnership liabilities.

The basis of property contributed to a partnership by a partner is equal to the adjusted basis of the property to the partner.

C.   Partnership Operation.

The reporting of partnership income requires that certain transactions be segregated and reported separately. Such items as charitable contributions, capital gains and losses, dividends, etc., must be allocated separately to the partners. Otherwise the taxable income of a partnership is calculated like that of an individual without the following deductions:

- Exemptions
- Deduction for foreign taxes paid
- Net operating losses
- Itemized deductions

Partnership losses pass through to partners and are deductible to the extent of the partner's basis in the partnership interest at the end of the tax year. Losses in excess of the basis, carry forward and can be used against future income in a manner similar to S corporation losses.

A partner engaging in a transaction with a partnership is regarded as a nonpartner. If the partner's direct or indirect interest is more than 50 percent, or the transaction is between two partnerships in which the same persons own more than 50 percent, losses from the sale or exchange of property will be disallowed.

Payments made by a partnership to one of its partners for services rendered or for the use of capital, to the extent they are determined without regard to the partnership income, are called guaranteed payments. Such payments are generally deductible by the partnership and must be reported as income by the partner.

TEST FOR SELF-EVALUATION

True or False

Indicate which of the following statements are true or false by circling the correct answer.

T F 1. All legal corporations will be taxed as corporations for Federal tax purposes.

T F 2. It is possible for an organization that is not a legal corporation under state law to be taxed as a corporation for Federal tax purposes.

T F 3. Sole proprietorships and partnerships are not separate taxable entities.

T F 4. A regular corporation is recognized as a taxable entity.

T F 5. A partner engaging in a transaction with his partnership is generally regarded as a nonpartner or as an outsider. However a loss on a sale or exchange between a partnership and a 60 percent partner would be disallowed.

T F 6. Net capital losses of a corporation are deductible against ordinary income.

T F 7. When carried back or forward, a corporate long-term capital loss becomes a short-term capital loss.

T F 8. Corporate charitable contributions are limited to 10 percent of taxable income computed without regard to the charitable contribution deduction, NOL carrybacks or capital loss carrybacks, and the dividends received deduction.

T F 9. A net operating loss deduction is carried back three years and forward five years.

T F 10. The dividends received deduction is always equal to 80 percent of dividends received.

T F 11. The purpose of the dividends received deduction is to prevent triple taxation.

T   F   12.   Currently, the maximum corporate tax rate is 34 percent (disregarding the 5% surtax); and the rate applies to taxable income over $75,000.

T   F   13.   Qualified organizational expenditures under § 248 may be written off over 50 months or more.

T   F   14.   Expenses incident to the printing and sale of stock certificates will not qualify as § 248 expenses.

T   F   15.   Each partner must include in income his or her share of partnership income and any guaranteed payments from the partnership whose tax year ends with or within the partner's tax year.

T   F   16.   A corporate tax return is due on the fifteenth day of the third month following the close of the tax year.

T   F   17.   The purpose of Schedule M-1 of Form 1120 is to reconcile retained earnings at the end of the year to the retained earnings at the beginning of the tax year.

T   F   18.   The receipt of money or property in exchange for stock produces recognized gain to the recipient corporation.

T   F   19.   If a corporation has excessive debt in its capital structure and a substantial portion of the debt is held by shareholders, the corporation may have thin capitalization problems.

T   F   20.   Control for purposes of nonrecognition of gain or loss under § 351 means stock ownership of at least 80 percent of the total combined voting power of all classes of stock entitled to vote and at least 80 percent of the total number of shares of all other classes of stock.

T   F   21.   Gain will never be recognized on a § 351 transfer to a controlled corporation.

T   F   22.   The term "earnings and profits" is defined in the Code.

T   F   23.   Earnings and profits and retained earnings will always be the same amount.

T   F   24.   Partnership losses reduce a partner's basis in his partnership interest, but not below zero and any excess is lost to the partner.

T F 25. Since a partnership is not a taxable entity, it does not have to file any type of tax return.

T F 26. A corporation with gross sales of $625,000 can file a Form 1120A (corporate short form) since its gross receipts are less than $1,000,000.

Fill-in-the-Blanks

Complete the following statements with the appropriate word(s) or amount(s).

1. A distribution of property to a shareholder is measured by the _____ of the property on the date of distribution.

2. The additional tax paid by corporations is five percent of taxable income over $100,000 up to a maximum of $_____.

3. Under the general rule of § 331, gain or loss is recognized to the shareholder in a corporate _____.

4. Under the general rule of § 334, the basis of property received by shareholders in a liquidation is _____.

5. The maximum number of shareholders in an S Corporation is _____.

6. Unlike corporations, partnerships are not considered separate taxable _____.

7. A partner's basis in his partnership interest is _____ by additional capital contributions.

8. Partnership taxable income and distributions are reported on Form _____.

9. Taxable income of a partnership is computed (with exceptions) in the same manner as the taxable income of an _____.

10. A partner's deductions for partnership losses may not exceed the partner's adjusted _____ of his or her partnership interest at the end of the partnership year in which the losses were incurred.

11. Payments made to partners for services or use of capital, computed without regard to partnership income, are called _____ payments.

Multiple Choice

Choose the best answer for each of the following questions.

_____ 1. Samuelson Corporation's taxable income for 1992 was $120,000, all from regular operations. Samuelson's tax liability before credits would be:
a. $57,600
b. $44,100
c. $30,050
d. $26,400
e. Some other amount

_____ 2. Which of the following items do not pass through separately from an S Corporation to its shareholders?
a. Long-term capital gains
b. Tax-exempt interest
c. Wages of employees
d. Short-term capital gains
e. § 1231 losses.

_____ 3. Which of the following could not be a shareholder in an S Corporation?
a. Corporation
b. Individual
c. Certain trusts
d. Estate

_____ 4. In 1992 Lamden Corporation had gross income of $80,000, including $50,000 of dividends received from domestic corporations of which it owned less than 20 percent of the stock. Lamden had business expenses of $33,000. What is the 1992 dividends received deduction?
a. -0-
b. $35,000
c. $50,000
d. $32,900
e. Some other amount

_____ 5. In 1992 T Corporation had a net long-term capital loss. If this loss is carried over to T's 1993 income tax return, it will be treated as a:

a. Ordinary loss
b. § 1231 loss
c. Long-term capital loss
d. Short-term capital loss
e. None of the above

_____ 6. Xeno Corporation is a closely-held corporation. Its sole shareholder is Philo Xeno. The corporation currently pays Philo a salary of $600,000 per year. A reasonable salary for a person in Philo's position would be $200,000 per year. During an IRS audit, the government will probably contend that there is a constructive dividend of:
a. $-0-
b. $200,000
c. $400,000
d. $600,000
e. Some other amount

_____ 7. Porter Corporation had taxable income of $100,000 for 1992 before considering charitable contributions. If during the year the corporation gave $12,000 in cash to a qualified charitable organization, how much of the $12,000 contribution may the company deduct for the current year?
a. -0-
b. $12,000
c. $10,000
d. $9,500
e. Some other amount

_____ 8. Sharon Lightner contributes property with a basis of $15,000 and a fair market value of $18,000 to a partnership in exchange for a 25 percent interest therein. Her basis in the partnership interest is:
a. -0-
b. $15,000
c. $18,000
d. $33,000
e. Some other amount

_____ 9. Assume the same situation as in Question 8. What is the basis of the property to the partnership if Sharon recognized no gain on the transfer of the property to the partnership?
a. -0-
b. $15,000
c. $18,000

d. $33,000
e. Some other amount

_____ 10. Toole Corporation, a calendar year S Corporation, has taxable income for 1992 of $25,000. If there is one shareholder and she receives a cash distribution from Toole of $40,000 on July 1, 1992, how much ordinary income should she report on her 1992 individual income tax return, assuming her basis is sufficient to cover any dividend?
a. $100,000
b. $60,000
c. $25,000
d. $40,000
e. Some other amount

_____ 11. T Corporation, an accrual basis calendar year taxpayer, was formed and became operational on July 1, 1992. The following expenses were incurred during its first year of operation:

Expenses of organizational meetings	$600
Fee for state charter	$300
Expenses for sale of stock	$300

What is T Corporation's maximum organization expense deduction under § 248 for 1992?
a. $180
b. $240
c. $90
d. $120
e. Some other amount

_____ 12. A and B form AB Corporation. A contributes cash of $50,000 and B contributes property with a basis of $20,000 and a fair market value of $50,000. If A and B own all the stock in AB Corporation immediately after the transfer, what is B's recognized gain on the transfer?
a. $-0-
b. $30,000
c. $20,000
d. $50,000
e. Some other amount

_____ 13. Assume the same situation as in Question 12. What is B's basis in the stock he receives from AB Corporation?

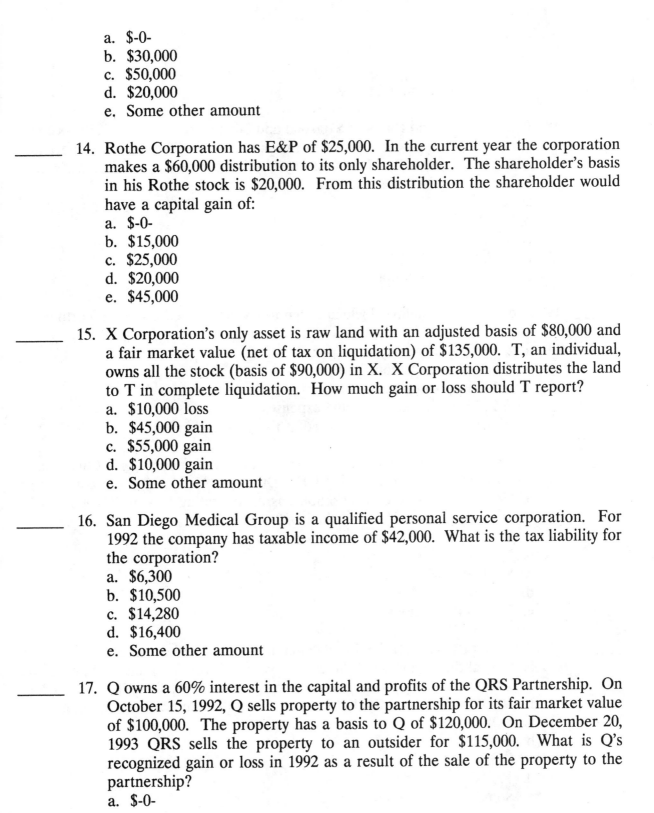

a. $-0-
b. $30,000
c. $50,000
d. $20,000
e. Some other amount

14. Rothe Corporation has E&P of $25,000. In the current year the corporation makes a $60,000 distribution to its only shareholder. The shareholder's basis in his Rothe stock is $20,000. From this distribution the shareholder would have a capital gain of:
    a. $-0-
    b. $15,000
    c. $25,000
    d. $20,000
    e. $45,000

15. X Corporation's only asset is raw land with an adjusted basis of $80,000 and a fair market value (net of tax on liquidation) of $135,000. T, an individual, owns all the stock (basis of $90,000) in X. X Corporation distributes the land to T in complete liquidation. How much gain or loss should T report?
    a. $10,000 loss
    b. $45,000 gain
    c. $55,000 gain
    d. $10,000 gain
    e. Some other amount

16. San Diego Medical Group is a qualified personal service corporation. For 1992 the company has taxable income of $42,000. What is the tax liability for the corporation?
    a. $6,300
    b. $10,500
    c. $14,280
    d. $16,400
    e. Some other amount

17. Q owns a 60% interest in the capital and profits of the QRS Partnership. On October 15, 1992, Q sells property to the partnership for its fair market value of $100,000. The property has a basis to Q of $120,000. On December 20, 1993 QRS sells the property to an outsider for $115,000. What is Q's recognized gain or loss in 1992 as a result of the sale of the property to the partnership?
    a. $-0-

b. ($20,000)
c. $5,000
d. ($12,000)
e. Some other amount

_____ 18. P contributes land (basis of $100,000 and fair market value of $150,000) to a partnership for a 40% interest in the partnership. The land is subject to a mortgage of $80,000 which is assumed by the partnership. What is P's basis in her partnership interest?
  a. $-0-
  b. $100,000
  c. $52,000
  d. $48,000
  e. Some other amount

_____ 19. A partnership is allowed which of the following deductions at the partnership level?
  a. § 162 trade or business expenses
  b. § 170 charitable contributions
  c. § 172 net operating losses from prior years
  d. § 212 production of income expenses
  e. None of the above are allowed at the partnership level

_____ 20. Y is a 40% shareholder in an S Corporation. On January 1, 1992 his basis in the S Corporation stock is $25,000. During 1992, Y loans the corporation $5,000. For 1992, the corporation has an operating loss of $90,000. What amount of loss may Y deduct in 1992?
  a. $-0-
  b. $25,000
  c. $30,000
  d. $36,000
  e. Some other amount

_____ 21. A regular (C) corporation has a deficit in accumulated earnings and profits of $20,000 at the beginning of the current year. Current earnings and profits are $7,000. During the year the corporation distributes $10,000 to its shareholders. How much of the distribution is taxable as a dividend to the shareholders?
  a. $-0-
  b. $3,000
  c. $10,000
  d. $7,000
  e. Some other amount

_____ 22. In the current year, B Inc. (a retail furniture store) donates unsold furniture to the Goodwill Army (a qualified charity for the care of the needy). The furniture is inventory and has a basis to B of $20,000 and a fair market value of $26,000. What is B's charitable contribution deduction for this gift?
a. $-0-
b. $20,000
c. $23,000
d. $26,000
e. Some other amount

Problems

1. Three individuals (A, B, and C) form a closely-held corporation with the following investments:

		Basis to Transferor	FMV	Number of Shares
From A:	Cash	$20,000	$20,000	
	Equipment	$75,000	$80,000	100
From B:	Equipment	$10,000	$15,000	5
From C:	Land	$60,000	$50,000	50

In addition to the five shares of stock, B receives $10,000 in cash. The value of the stock is $1,000 per share. Based on the above information, complete the answers to the following questions.

	A	B	C
Realized gain (or loss)	_____	_____	_____
Recognized gain (or loss)	_____	_____	_____
Basis of the property to the corporation (excluding cash)	_____	_____	_____
Stock basis to shareholder	_____	_____	_____

2.   Crown Corporation was formed and began operations on January 2, 1992. The adjusted trial balance as of December 31, 1992, is as follows:

Account	Debit	Credit
Cash	$35,000	
Accounts receivable		8,000
Land	15,000	
Building	50,000	
Accumulated depreciation-building		3,000
Accounts payable		18,000
Common stock		10,000
Revenue		275,000
Interest on certificate of deposit		10,000
Cost of goods sold	95,000	
Compensation of officers	70,000	
Salaries and wages	25,000	
Repairs	6,000	
Depreciation expense	3,000	
State taxes	9,000	
Total	$316,000	$316,000

Based on the above information, calculate Crown Corporation's taxable income.

Revenue _____

Cost of goods sold _____

Gross profit _____

Other income _____

Total income _____

Expenses _____

Taxable income _____

3.   Bhrionn Corporation reported taxable income, before special items, of $600,000. Selected information available from the corporate records is as follows:

Federal income tax expense $204,000
Book depreciation   140,000
Tax depreciation   85,000
Life insurance proceeds on death of an officer   100,000

What is Bhrionn's net income per books?

Net income per books   _____

Adjustments: _____

                                        _____

                                        _____

Taxable income   _____

Code Section Recognition

Indicate, by number, the appropriate Code Section where the following items are found.

_____ 1. The dividends received deduction.

_____ 2. Organizational expense deduction.

_____ 3. Transfers to controlled corporations.

_____ 4. Corporate distributions.

_____ 5. Stock redemptions.

_____ 6. General rules for corporate liquidations - effect on shareholders.

_____ 7. Definition of an S Corporation.

_____ 8. Gain or loss on contributions of property to partnerships.

_____ 9. Partner/partnership transactions.

SOLUTIONS TO CHAPTER 20

True or False

1. False   Some corporations may not be recognized as separate entities for tax purposes.(p. 20-2)

2. True   (p. 20-3)

3. True   (p. 20-4)

4. True   (p. 20-4)

5. True   (p. 20-30)

6. False   Corporate capital losses can only offset capital gains. (p. 20-6)

7. True   (p. 20-6)

8. True   (p. 20-6)

9. False   NOLs are carried back three years and forward 15 years. (p. 20-7)

10. False   The dividends received deduction is equal to either 70%, 80%, or 100% of dividends received and may be subject to limitations based on taxable income. (p. 20-8)

11. True   (p. 20-8)

12. True   (p. 20-10)

13. False   § 248 expenses may be written off over 60 months or more. (p. 20-10)

14. True   (p. 20-10)

15. True   (p. 20-31)

16. True   (p. 20-12)

17. False   Schedule M-1 reconciles financial net income to taxable income. (p. 20-12)

18. False   A corporation does not recognize a gain on the receipt of money or property

in exchange for its stock. (p. 20-15)

19. True   (p. 20-15)

20. True   (p. 20-16)

21. False   Realized gain is recognized to the extent of boot received. (p. 20-16)

22. False   E&P is not defined in the Code. (p. 20-18)

23. False   The calculation is not the same. (p. 20-18)

24. False   The excess losses carry forward for each partner. (p. 20-30)

25. False   Partnerships file an information return, the Form 1065. (p. 20-27)

26. False   Gross sales have to be under $500,000. (p. 20-11)

Fill-in-the-Blanks

1. fair market value (p. 20-18)

2. $11,750 (p. 20-10)

3. liquidation (p. 20-20)

4. fair market value (p. 20-21)

5. 35 (p. 20-22)

6. entities (p. 20-27)

7. increased (p. 20-27)

8. 1065 (p. 20-27)

9. individual (p. 20-29)

10. basis (p. 20-30)

11. guaranteed (p. 20-31)

Multiple Choice

1. C   15% ($50,000) + 25% ($25,000) + 34% ($45,000) + 5% ($20,000) = $30,050. (p. 20-10)

2. C   (p. 20-24)

3. A   (p. 20-22)

4. D   70% x $50,000 = $35,000 general rule;   70% x $47,000 = $32,900 limitation (p. 20-9)

5. D   (p. 20-6)

6. C $600,000 less $200,000. (p. 20-19)

7. C   10% x $100,000 = $10,000 maximum. (p. 20-6)

8. B   (p. 20-27)

9. B   (p. 20-29)

10. C   (pp. 20-24)

11. C   [($600 + 300)÷60 months] x 6 months = $90. (p. 20-10)

12. A   (p. 20-15)

13. D   (p. 20-16)

14. B
Distribution	$60,000
Dividend	-25,000
Return of Capital	-20,000
Capital gain	$15,000

(p. 20-17)

15. B $135,000 - 90,000 = $45,000. (p. 20-20)

16. C   34% x $42,000 = $14,280. (p. 20-11)

17. A   Q is a related party, therefore the loss is not recognized. (p. 20-31)

18.   C $100,000 - ($80,000 x 60%) = $52,000. (p. 20-28)

19.   A   (p. 20-30)

20.   C   40% x $90,000 = $36,000; however, the loss is limited to the basis in the S corporation stock plus the loan of $5,000, $30,000. (p. 20-26)

21.   D   The distribution is taxable to the extent of current E&P. (p. 20-17)

22.   C $20,000 + 50%($26,000 - $20,000) = $23,000. (p. 20-7)

Problems

1.

	A	B	C
Realized gain (or loss)	$5,000	$5,000	-$10,000
Recognized gain (or loss)	-0-	5,000	-0-
Basis of the property to the corp. (ex. cash)	75,000	15,000	60,000
Stock basis (p. 20-16)	95,000	5,000	60,000

2.

Revenue	$275,000
Cost of goods sold	-95,000
Gross profit	$180,000
Other income	10,000
Total income	$190,000
Expenses	-113,000
Taxable income	$ 77,000

3. Net income per books $441,000

    Federal income tax   204,000

    Depreciation ($140,000 - $85,000)   55,000

    Life insurance proceeds   -100,000

    Taxable income $600,000
    (p. 20-12)

Code Section Recognition

1. § 243

2. § 248

3. § 351

4. § 301

5. § 302

6. § 331

7. § 1361

8. § 721

9. § 707